Irish Minstrelsy, Or, Bardic Remains Of Ireland

You are holding a reproduction of an original work that is in the public domain in the United States of America, and possibly other countries. You may freely copy and distribute this work as no entity (individual or corporate) has a copyright on the body of the work. This book may contain prior copyright references, and library stamps (as most of these works were scanned from library copies). These have been scanned and retained as part of the historical artifact.

This book may have occasional imperfections such as missing or blurred pages, poor pictures, errant marks, etc. that were either part of the original artifact, or were introduced by the scanning process. We believe this work is culturally important, and despite the imperfections, have elected to bring it back into print as part of our continuing commitment to the preservation of printed works worldwide. We appreciate your understanding of the imperfections in the preservation process, and hope you enjoy this valuable book.

CAROLAN.

The Celebrated Irish Bard.

ISH MINSTRELSY.

BARDIC ...

ENGLISH POETICAL TRANSLATIONS

BY JAMES HARDIMAN

VOL. I.

1831.

IRISH MINSTRELSY,

OR

BARDIC REMAINS OF IRELAND;

WITH

ENGLISH POETICAL TRANSLATIONS.

COLLECTED AND EDITED,

WITH NOTES AND ILLUSTRATIONS,

BY JAMES HARDIMAN, M. R. I. A.

"Bíonn gnáδh agam ap δhántaigh ir ap cheolταigh."

"I will give thee a book—it containeth the Songs of the bards of Erin, of the bards of the days that are gone." JOHN PHILPOT CURRAN.

VOL I.

LONDON:

JOSEPH ROBINS, BRIDE COURT, BRIDGE STREET.

1831.

TO THE RIGHT HONORABLE

THOMAS SPRING RICE,

REPRESENTATIVE IN PARLIAMENT FOR THE CITY OF

LIMERICK,

A STEADY FRIEND TO THE BEST INTERESTS OF IRELAND,

THIS WORK,

UNDERTAKEN WITH A VIEW TO PRESERVE AND ILLUSTRATE

A PORTION OF ANCIENT IRISH LITERATURE,

IS RESPECTFULLY INSCRIBED,

BY HIS OBEDIENT SERVANT,

JAMES HARDIMAN.

Dublin, September 1*st,* 1831.

891.68
H26

CONTENTS OF VOL. I.

	PAGE
Introduction	i
Memoir of Carolan	xli
Memoir of Thomas Furlong	lxix

PART I.—REMAINS OF CAROLAN.

Fáilte do Cheárbhalláin	Welcome to Carolan	5
Máire Maguidhir	Mary Maguire	9
Fanní Biadhtach	Fanny Betagh	13
Brighitt Crús	Bridget Cruise	15
Leighiór gach galar an t-uircíbhe	Whiskey is the potion	19
Plaingstígh an Stafardaich, nó Ol-pé Cheárbhalláin	Planxty Stafford, or Carolan's Receipt	23
Eadbhart O'Corcráin	Edward O'Corcoran	27
Seón Hart	Doctor Harte	29

CONTENTS.

Inghín uí Mhórdha, no reach-bhac bheal-áith-seannaigh	O'More's Fair Daughter, or the Hawk of Ballyshannon .	33
Feidhlim ua Néill . . .	Phelim O'Neill . . .	39
Plainxtíbhe Péaton . . .	Planxty Peyton . .	43
Madam Crofton	Madam Crofton . .	45
Mairgharíad n-i Chorcráin	Peggy Corcoran . .	49
Seón Jónes	John Jones	53
Gráser Nuinsun	Gracey Nugent . .	57
Máible shéimh n-í Cheallaigh	Mild Mable Kelly . .	61
Cupán uí h-Eaghra . . .	The Cup of O'Hara .	65
Mairgharíad Brún . . .	Peggy Browne . . .	67
Seóirse Brabron	George Brabazon . .	71
Brighitt n-ic uí Mháile .	Bridget O'Malley . .	75
Seághan Glas	Shane Glas	79
Séamas Pluincéadt . . .	James Plunkett . .	83
Nansíbh Cooper	Nancy Cooper . . .	87
Márbhna air bhás a mhná	Carolan's Monody on the death of his Wife	91
Usill-chúmhaíbh os cionn uaigh mheic Uib . . .	Lament for Mc. Cabe	95
Márbhna Cheárbhallán .	Elegy on Carolan . .	97
Flainn	Epigrams, 110—113—117 —118—124—132	

CONTENTS.

ADDENDA.

A h-uircíbhe chroíbhe na n-anmann	Why, Liquor of Life	141
'S í mo chreach! bean dheannaighe na féile	Ode to Drunkenness	147
Magaidh Laidir	Maggy Laidir	155
Oid do'n t-rаoi Coinbeаlbhán	Ode to a Minstrel	180
*bloghadh	A Fragment	185
Rann	Epigram	189
*Ol-dán	Bacchanalian	192
*Móta ghrámne óig	Moatagrenoge	194
*Carаdh an t-rúgain	Twisting of the Rope	195

PART II.—SENTIMENTAL SONG.

Brighdín Pádruic	Bridget Fergus	205
⁎ Eibhlín a Rúin	Eileen a Roon	211
Páirtín Fionn	Paistheen Fion	217
Síle bheag n-i Chomhdealbhain	Little Celia Connellan	221
Stuairín na m-bachall m-breagh, réidh	The Lass of fair flowing tresses	225

Those thus marked * are not translated.

CONTENTS.

Tigheapna Mhaigheó	Lord Mayo	229
Droighnean donn	The Brown Thorn	235
Cairiol Múmhan	Cashel of Munster, or the "Clar Bog Deal"	239
Máire Chuirle	Molly a Store	243
Caitilín Tirrall	Catherine Tyrrell	247
An Chúil-fhionn	The Coolin	251
Roirín dubh	Roisin Dubh	255
Uileacán dubh O!	Uileacan Dubh O!	259
Ceann dubh dílear	Cean Dubh Deelish	263
Eibhlín a rúin	Old Eileen a Roon	265
Eadhmonn an Chnoic	Emon a Knock	269
Ann ra m-baile ro	In this calm sheltered villa	275
béile n-i Chiaraḃháin	Eleanor O'Kirwan	279
Fiadhaidhe bhéara	The Hunter of Bearhaven	283
Tá ráigheada agur cnead	Wounded by Cupid's burning dart	287
Deirdre bheagh-ghnúireach	Blooming Deirdre	291
Máire rúin	Mary a Roon	297
Honor an chúil ómraich	Honor of the Amber Locks	301
Airling an óig-fhir	The Young Man's Dream	305
A ghrádh agur a rúin bhil	Mary of Meelick	311

CONTENTS.

*beul-áth-shámhnáis	Ballyhaunis	326
*bloghádh	A Fragment	330
*An Sréic Seóigheach	The Humours of Joyce Country	331
Cormac óg	Young Cormac	333
*bínsín luachra	The Bunch of Rushes	334
*Condae Mhaigheó	County Mayo	337
*bloghádh	A Fragment	341
*Ód	An Ode	343
bloghádh	A Fragment	344
*Eóchaill	Youghal Harbour	348
*Muirnín na gruaige báine	My fair-haired Darling	354
bloghádh	A Fragment	365

INTRODUCTION.

REMAINS OF ANCIENT IRISH LITERATURE.—IMPORTANCE OF OUR OLD DOCUMENTS.—EARLY FILEAS.—IRISH MUSIC.—PRINCIPAL BARDS FROM THE ERA OF CHRISTIANITY TO THE CONVERSION OF THE IRISH, AND THENCE TO THE LAST CENTURY.—THEIR EDUCATION, CHARACTER, AND PRODUCTIONS.—IRISH LANGUAGE.—WELL ADAPTED FOR LYRICAL COMPOSITION.—METRE AND VERSIFICATION.—TITLE OF THE PRESENT WORK.—ITS ORIGIN AND PROGRESS.—CONCLUSION.

AFTER ages of neglect and decay, the ancient literature of Ireland seems destined to emerge from obscurity. Those memorials which have hitherto lain so long unexplored, now appear to awaken the attention of the learned and the curiosity of the public; and thus, the literary remains of a people once so distinguished in the annals of learning, may be rescued from the oblivion to which they have been so undeservedly consigned. That the ancient Irish possessed ample stores in their native language, capable of captivating the fancy, enlarging the understanding, and improving the heart, is well known to those acquainted with the mouldering membranes which have survived to our times. The historical importance of our annals has been acknowledged by the most learned men of Europe for the last three centuries. They are written in the language of the first inhabitants of Europe; and, with a simplicity of detail which truth only can confer, they record the primæval state of this island, the origin of its early inhabitants, their history, religion, and laws, and the arts known amongst them for several generations. Former writers have brought discredit on our history by injudiciously blending with it the fictions of romance; and succeeding authors, unable or unwilling to separate the truth from the fable, became contented copyists, and thus encreased the evil which they pretended to remedy. Eager for temporary applause, which they mistook for permanent fame, they forced on the world their crude essays, which were remarkable only for distortion of fact and boldness of conjecture. The original documents, which would have guided them to truth, were wholly neglected, or but partially explored. Hence, the imperfect state of our early history, and the erroneous opinions entertained of it by many, even of the learned, at the present day. The difficulty of procuring the documents alluded to, and the still greater difficulty of deciphering them when procured, may be alleged as an excuse for the indolence, or ignorance, of which our countrymen have reason to complain in the generality of their historical writers. But this is a plea that cannot be admitted. Those chroniclers of error ought to have rendered themselves competent, or have remained for ever silent. What is true of the past will apply equally to the future. Until the difficulties alluded to shall be overcome, all attempts to illustrate, with certainty or authority, the earlier parts of our history must prove abortive. —Having judged it necessary to make the few foregoing observations on the most important use to be made of those neglected muniments, it now remains to ascertain what information they afford on the subject at present under consideration—the ancient poetry of Ireland.

That this country, from an early period, was famous for the cultivation of the kindred arts of poetry and music, stands universally admitted. The works of the prejudiced Cambrensis, and the annals of Wales and Scotland, might be adduced in evidence of the fact; but we require not the aid of foreign proof, our domestic records supply abundant information on the subject. Although most of the records of the days of paganism were destroyed by the zeal of the first Christian Missionaries, and much of what then escaped, with many of later times, met with a similar fate from the barbarity of the Danes, and the destructive policy of the English, yet sufficient remains to enable us to trace those arts to a remote period in Ireland. The early settlers, afterwards distinguished by the name of Milesians, derived their origin from that part of the earth, where poetry and music appear coeval with the formation of society. Accordingly we find the poet and musician numbered in the train of these celebrated invaders. The bards AMERGIN, the son of their leader, and LUGAD, the son of ITH, are particularly named. The latter is called, in old writings, " The first poet of Ireland," Ceb Kib h-Ep., and there still remain, after a lapse of nearly three thousand years, fragments of these ancient bards, some of which will be found included in the following pages, with proofs of their authenticity *. After these, but anterior to the Christian era, flourished ROYNE FILE, or the poetic,

---

* *Vol. II. p.* 347, *et seq.* These ancient fragments are preserved in the old historical Record, entitled *Leabhar Ghabhaltus,* or the " Book of Invasions;" a copy of which, *transcribed* in the twelfth century, and now in the Duke of Buckingham's library at Stowe, is particularly described in the late DOCTOR O'CONOR's invaluable Catalogue of the MSS. there preserved. This learned man observes, " that we should refer this species of poetry to a very remote age, no one who has read *Strabo* will wonder. The HIBERNI derive their origin from the IBERI; and Strabo mentions a people of *Iberia* and *Bætica,* who could produce poems nearly 6000 years old. (*Lib.* 3rd). Let, however, the specimens of Irish poetry still remaining speak for themselves. The oldest Saxon poetry extant is King Alfred's."—*Cat. Stowe, I.* 23.—

and FERCEIRTNE, a bard and herald; some of whose remains will also be found with the foregoing. LUGAR and CONGAL lived about the birth of Our Redeemer, and many of their verses, particularly those of the latter, are still extant*. The subjects and language of these insular poems afford internal evidence of an antiquity transcending that of any literary monument in the modern languages of Europe.

In that remote period the cultivation of music kept pace with the progress of poetry. The *Dinn Seanchas*†, compiled by AMERGIN MAC AMALGAID, A. D. 544, relates that in the time of GEIDE, monarch of Ireland, A. M. 3143, " the people deemed each others voices sweeter than the warblings of a melodious harp, such peace and concord reigned among them, that no music could delight them more than the sound of each others voice: *Temur (Tarah)*

---

* In numerous old vellum MSS.—To these may be added ADHNA, and NEIDE his son, who flourished about the same time, fragments of whose writings, in the *Bearla Feine*, or *Phœnician dialect* of the Irish, are extant in the MSS. of Trinity College, Dublin.

† Or " History of noted places in Ireland." This curious piece of ancient topography is preserved in the Books of *Lecan* and *Ballimote;* two celebrated MSS. volumes, in folio vellum, containing transcripts of numerous miscellaneous tracts and poems of antiquity. The former of these was carried to France by James II. and after his death, lodged in the Irish college at Paris, where it remained until the year 1787, when it was

vi INTRODUCTION.

was so called from its celebrity for melody, above the palaces of the world. *Tea,* or *Te,* signifying melody or sweet music, and *mur,* a wall. *Te-mur,* the wall of music*." In the same ancient tract, music is again alluded to, in the relation of a youthful dream or vision of Cahiremore, monarch of Ireland, which, amongst other things, describes, " a delightful hill, surpassing all others in height, whereon stood hosts; and there grew a most beautiful and stately tree, like gold, whose variegated and luxuriant foliage, when moved by the wind, yielded the most melodious music ever heard, and on it grew delicious fruit, pleasing to every one's taste †."

---

restored to this country by Doctor O'Kelly, superior of that college, and deposited in the library of the Royal Irish Academy, Dublin. The *Book of Ballimote,* also said to have been brought from Paris, was presented to the same library. By an entry at fo. 180, of the latter, it appears that it was purchased in 1522, by Hugh O'Donnell, from Mc Donogh of Corran, for 140 milch cows. None of the contents of these volumes have been published. The *Dinn Seanchas* contains poems of Finin Mac Luchna, a bard of the second century, Fionn Mac Cubhail and Fergus Fionnbell, who, with the celebrated Oisin, (Ossian,) lived in the third century, and others.

* *Book of Ballimote.*—Temup ſin ol Amaiŋʒen, &c.— *See fo.* 188, *a. col.* 1.

† " Cnoc oebinð oyа ciñð biblinðаibh аiрbe ʒаc tulаiʒ co ſloʒаib аnð bili eðpocc аmаil oн iүin cnuc cormаð comulu арa аiрði ʒаc ceol inа buillib brec tаiү аcoipti m tаlаm in tаn nа mbenаð ʒаot poʒа copаið do ʒаc аen."— *Id. fo.* 198, *col.* b.

The royal druid Bree, thus interpreted the dream : " You are the tree who shall rise high to the sovereignty, over all the nation; the wind blowing on the leaves, and producing harmony, is the sweetness of your words in giving laws and ordinances to the people ; and the fruit you saw, are the many blessings that shall come on your subjects in your reign." The first of these extracts contains the earliest allusion to the harp* which I have met

---

* Mr. Gunn, in his interesting inquiry respecting the performance of the harp in the Highlands of Scotland, until it was discontinued about 1734, 4to, Edinburgh, 1807, says—" I have been favored with a copy of an ancient *Gaelic* poem, together with the music to which it is still sung in the Highlands, in which the poet personifies and addresses a very old harp, by asking what had become of its former lustre ? The harp replies, that it had belonged to a *King of Ireland*, and had been present at many a royal banquet; that it had afterwards been successively in the possession of Dargo, son of the druid of Baal—of Gaul—of Filan—of Oscar—of O'Duivne—of Diarmid—of a Physician—of a Bard—and lastly, of a Priest, who in a secluded corner was meditating on a white book."—This, like every other research connected with the natives of the Highlands, leads to their Irish origin. It has faded from the recollection of most of our countrymen, that until a late period, Ireland was the school of the Highland Scotch. " The gentlemen of note *probably were, partly at least,*" (these words in italics the lawyers would call guarded or unwilling evidence,) " educated in Ireland, to which country *all* who adopted either *poetry* or *music* as a profession, were *uniformly* sent to finish their education, *till within the memory of persons still living*."—JAMIESON'S *Introduction to Letters from the North of Scotland*,

INTRODUCTION.

with, though it is frequently mentioned in Irish poems ascribed to Columba, and others of the sixth century*. It is considered needless to multiply extracts, to shew the early knowledge and progress of music in Ireland. Proved to have existed as far back as the most ancient annals extend, its origin, like that of our round towers, must be sought for in the East†.

London, 1822. This writer further adds, "Till within the memory of persons still living, *the School for Highland poetry and music was Ireland*, and thither professional men were sent to be accomplished in those arts. The *cruit, clarsach*, or harp, was the proper instrument of the Celts. The bagpipe was introduced by the Goths, from Scandinavia."—*Same work, Vol. II.* 65.—These are unpalatable truths for the advocates of Scotland's pretensions to *Ossian*.

* Quoted by the Irish annalists TIGERNACH and the FOUR MASTERS.—See Doctor O'Conor's splendid edition of the principal Irish annals to the time of the English Invasion, printed at the expence of his Grace the Duke of Buckingham and Chandos, 4 *vols. quarto*, 1813—26.

† The native strains of several oriental nations have been observed to bear a close affinity to Irish music. Many have been found in *Persia*, and the mountainous parts of *India*. Marsden, in his *History of Sumatra*, says, "The Sumatran tunes much resemble to my ear those of the native Irish, and have usually like them a flat third." Our countryman, Sir William Ousely, observes, that several of the *Hindoo* melodies possess the native simplicity of the Scotch and Irish.—*Oriental Collections, Vol. I. p.* 74.—Many of the Siamese melodies, remarkable for softness, sweetness, and simplicity, resemble the Scotch and Irish.—*Crawford*.—Mr. Thompson in his preface to the select melodies of Scotland, (in which, by the way, he has

The music of Ireland is better known to the world, at the present day, than its poetry. In the sweet-

embodied many Irish airs,) observes that, "Melodies of the Scottish cast have been remarked among the Moors in Barbary, and the natives of North America." He might have added the West India islands, for thither did Oliver Cromwell and his myrmidons,---they to whom Ireland was parcelled out under the memorable Act of *Settlement*,—cause thousands of the native Irish to be transported and sold as slaves. These unfortunate people brought with them their language and music, of which vestiges remain to the present day.

Ireland gave its music to Scotland, and thence it may be traced in the modern history of the art, imparting its beauties and sweetness to Italy. According to the poet Tassoni, the ancient music of the Scotch or Irish, and particularly the compositions of the first James of Scotland, was imitated by GESUALDUS, the chief of the Italian composers, and greatest musical improver of the sixteenth century. The celebrated GEMINIANI frequently declared that the works of Gesualdus were his first and principal study. Hence probably his acknowledged partiality for Irish music, and his well known admiration of the bard, CAROLAN. Our countryman, GOLDSMITH, alludes to the opinion of Geminiani "that we have in the dominions of Great Britain no original music except the Irish." —*See British Mag.* 1760.—It is amusing to see how our Scottish neighbours invariably treat this subject. Among others, Mr. Tytler in his dissertation on Scottish music, (*Trans. Soc. Antiq. of Scotland, Vol. I.* 475.) after noticing the imitations of James I. by Gesualdus, exclaims, "How perfectly characteristic this of the pathetic strains of the old *Scottish* Songs! what an illustrious testimony to their excellency!" But, quoting the following passage from Major, " In Cithara *Hibernenses aut Silvestres Scoti*, qui in illa arte præcipui sunt," he says, " To these Sylvan ministrels, I *imagine* we are indebted for many

est strains of natural feeling, the former found its ready way to every heart, and became endenizened in every clime, while the latter, wrapped in an ancient and expressive but proscribed and insulated language, has been generally neglected, particularly since the spread of the English tongue amongst us, and the downfall of the Milesians. Men there were, no doubt, who, knowing and valuing its beauties, have protected and cherished it amidst every vicissitude, as a precious depository of the genius of former times. But these generations have passed away. The few who inherit their spirit are gradually disappearing, and thus Irish poetry, with all its charms, may be left to linger awhile, and then sink into oblivion, unless rescued by the timely interposition of those who still retain some respect for the ancient honour of their country.

The nature and value of this venerable deposit now remain for investigation. Some ancient bards, anterior to the Christian era, have been already noticed. Thence, to a recent period, a numerous host of the principal " sons of song," whose names may appear uncouth to our modern ears, will pass,

---

fine old songs which are more varied in their melody, and more regular in their compositions, as they approach nearer to modern times." Here the ingenious investigator suppressed the word *Hibernenses* altogether, because it pointed out but too clearly the origin of these old *Scottish* songs.

in tedious, perhaps, but necessary review, before the reader. These men's works are stamped with genius and learning, and are preserved in various records of the highest authority. In the second century CIOTHRUADH, the bard, addressed a poem to the monarch CON, which is preserved in the book of Munster*. FINGIN, in the same reign, produced a poem, on the approaches to Tarah, preserved in the Dinn Seanchas—*Lecan*, f. 239. Some fragments of LUACHNA, another bard of that period, and of FERGUS FIONNBELL, or the " Sweet-voiced," who lived in the third century, are found in the same record. The bard OISIN is here omitted, for although there appear some poems ascribed to him in many old manuscripts, yet strong doubts are entertained of their authenticity. In the fourth and fifth centuries flourished the nervous and poetic TORNA, one of whose poems is given in the following collection; and DUBTHACH, the son of LUGAR, a bard who embraced the Christian faith in the time of St. Patrick. Two curious poems of the latter, on the privileges and duties of his order, and of the royal rights and duties of the King of Tarah, as monarch of Ireland, are preserved in the *Leabhar na Cceart*†. A hymn

---

* In the library of the Royal Irish Academy.

† The "Book of Rights," containing an account of the rights and revenues of the Monarch of Ireland; and the revenues and subsidies of the provincial Kings. It was originally compiled by ST. BENIN, who died A. D. 468, and is contained

to the Redeemer, by Dubthach, after his conversion*, is found in the *Felire Anguis,* a poetical calendar, compiled about the end of the eighth century, and preserved in the *Leabhar Breac,* or " Speckled Book," a valuable miscellany, now in the library of the Royal Irish Academy. The foregoing are the most noted Pagan bards, whose poems and rhapsodies have descended to our times. The names and works of others have been handed down; and there can be no doubt but that more will be brought to light when the Irish MSS. scattered throughout these islands, and on the continent of Europe, as before alluded to, shall be recovered.

The introduction of Christianity gave a new and more exalted direction to the powers of poetry.

---

in the books of BALLIMOTE, fo. 147, and LECAN, fo. 184.—This tract shews, that the Ancient Irish were governed according to some of the best and safest principles of civil liberty. From Dubthach's poem on his own order, it appears, that, " The learned poets and antiquaries are free from tribute, as long as they follow their own profession. They shall be ready to direct the kings and nobles, according to the laws; preserve the records of the nation, and the genealogies of families; and instruct youth in the arts and sciences, known in the kingdom." Our princes, like the Arabians, always retained their bards, musicians, and story tellers. These were the historians and heralds of the kingdom.

* JOCELINE, in the twelfth century, says of Dubthach, " Carmina quæ quondam peregit in laudem falsorum deorum, jam in usum meliorem mutans et linguam, poemata clariora composuit in laudem omnipotentis.—Ch. 45.

Among the numerous bards, who dedicated their talents to the praises of the Deity, during the three succeeding centuries, the most distinguished are, FEICH, the bishop, whose poem, first published by the learned Colgan, is in the hands of every Irish scholar; AMERGIN, author of the *Dinn Seanchas;* the famous COLUMCILLE; DALLAN and SEANCHAN, some of whose minor poems are contained in this collection; CINFAELA, the learned, who revised the *Uraicepht,* or " Primer of the Bards," preserved in the book of Ballimote, and in the library of Trinity College, Dublin; the celebrated ADAMNAN; and ANGUS, the pious author of the Felire, or Hierology in verse, already mentioned. Most of these poems afford internal evidence that their construction is founded on the traditional rythmical songs of the Pagan bards. Their metre and their jingle are national. They follow a long established practice well known to the bards of former times[*]. After

---

[*] DOCTOR O'CONOR.—This learned antiquary refers to the chapter, " DE CRONANO POETA," in Adamnan's valuable life of Columba, who died A. D. 596, as decisive proof that poetry was studied according to rules, and professed *as an art*, at that period in Ireland.—*Cat. I.* 23.—The narrative is this: Columba sitting with some monks on the banks of *Logh Cei,* (in the present Co. Roscommon,) had some conversation with *the poet* Cronan, near the mouth of the river *Bos,* now *Boyle,* which flows into that lake. When the poet retired, the monks expressed their regret, that Columba had not asked him to sing

the death of ANGUS, about the year 800, the incursions of the Danes, for a time, silenced the Muses, yet some famous bards flourished between that period and the arrival of the English. In 884, died, according to the annals of the Four Masters, MAOLMURA (MILES) of Fathan, described, in the Book of Invasions, as " a skilful and truly learned poet," whose works are distinguished for loftiness of thought, and strength of expression. Three valuable historical poems, by Maolmura, are preserved in the Books of Invasions and Lecan. Contemporary with him was FLANN, the son of LONAN, a graceful and elegant writer, who is called, in the annals of the Four Masters, the " Virgil of Ireland." Within the next century, we find the bards CORMACAN and KENETH O'HARTIGAN, whose valuable poems, particularly those of the latter, are inserted in the Book of Invasions, and the Dinn Seanchas; MAC GIOLLA CAOIMH, a sweet poet, one of whose elegies will be found in this collection; and the learned EOCHY O'FLOINN, who died in 984, and whose invaluable historical poems are preserved in the Books of Lecan, Ballimote, and Invasions. About the beginning of the eleventh century lived MAC LIAG, (Secretary and Biographer of the patriotic Monarch BRIAN, killed at

---

some *Canticle* in *modulation*, according to the *Rules of his Art*. " Cur a nobis regrediente Cronano, aliquod, *ex more suæ Artis*, canticum non postulasti modulalibiliter decantari ?"—*L. I.* c. 32.

Clontarf, A. D. 1014,) whose pathetic poems, on the death of his royal master, are given in the present collection. The originals of these, and other pieces by this bard, are contained in the *Leabhar Oiris*. The learned historical poems of CUAN O'LOCHAN, FLAN of Bute, and GIOLLA KEVIN, (who flourished in this century,) preserved in the records so often mentioned, shew that the general gloom of ignorance, which at that time overspread the rest of Europe, had not reached this island. The poems of the latter bard have been published by Doctor O'Conor, in his *Rerum Hibernicarum Scriptores,* vol. I., with translations and notes, of great value to the Irish historian. In the early part of the twelfth century flourished O'MULCONRY, the annalist and poet, who sung of the aboriginal tribes of Ireland in sweetly flowing verse, preserved in the Book of Lecan; the learned O'CASSIDY, abbot of Ardbracken in Meath, whose well known historical poem, " Sacred Erin! Island of Saints," is printed in the work above alluded to; and O'DUN, chief bard to the Prince of Leinster, who died in 1160, and whose historical poems are preserved in the valuable volumes of *Lecan, Ballimote,* and other ancient MSS.—Such were the *principal* bards of Ireland down to the Anglo-Norman invasion. Not imaginary personages, like many, called into fabulous existence by the zeal of some neighbouring nations, in asserting claims to early civilization and literature, but men long celebrated in the annals of their country, and whose works, still extant, are pointed out with as much perspicuity as the limits of these pages would allow. The nature and character of these works are deserving of peculiar attention. They do not possess any of the wild barbarous fervor of the Scandinavian Scalds; nor yet the effeminate softness of the professors of the " gay science," the *Troubadours* and *lady-bards* of the period to which we are now arrived. The simplicity of expression, and dignity of thought, which characterize the Greek and Roman writers of the purest period, pervade the productions of our bards: and, at the present day, they are particularly valuable for the important aids which they furnish, towards elucidating the ancient state of this early peopled and interesting island *.

---

* The History of Ireland, even since the reign of HENRY II. is yet to be written, and it will so remain, until the Anglo-Norman, or legal records of Dublin, and the " State Papers" of London, shall be combined with our domestic annals. Such of the native writers as were versed in the latter, were denied all access to the records of the pale. The privileged English were unacquainted with the Irish accounts, and withal so prejudiced against the country, that they neither would, (their works are the proof,) nor could they, even if inclined, have related the whole truth. Another, and perhaps a more copious source of information than either, remains to be noticed. It is well known, that from the time of the dissolution of monasteries, to the end of the seventeenth century, numerous records were carried out of Ireland, by proscribed

For two centuries after the invasion of Henry II. the voice of the muse was but feebly heard in Ireland. The genius of the nation withered at the approach of slavery. The bards were few, but among them were some of considerable eminence. The pious and highly gifted DONOGH O'DALY, abbot of Boyle, in Roscommon, was called the Ovid of Ireland, from the sweetness of his verse. He died in 1244, leaving several excellent poems, chiefly on divine subjects,

---

Ecclesiastics and other Irish Exiles, to various parts of Europe. It might safely be concluded, even if there was not the best evidence on the point, that among those records were some of the most ancient and valuable, relating to the Country.— The writer, having represented these facts to the Right Honorable the late Commissioners of Records in Ireland, submitted the propriety of their causing inquiry to be made on the subject, by means of queries, through the office of the Secretary for foreign affairs, to the different courts of Europe, who might give directions to the proper authorities, heads of universities, colleges, monasteries, libraries, &c. to transmit catalogues of any such documents as might be found in their possession. The Commissioners approved of the suggestion, and having expressed their sense of its "great value if successful in any of its points," were pleased on 22nd April, 1822, to order that their Secretary should take the necessary measures to make the proposed inquiry.—13th Annual Report, 1823.—The writer, thereupon, drew up a statement with references to the several places in Europe, from Denmark to Spain, where research ought to be made; but, though the then time of general peace, was rather favorable, yet he regrets to state that nothing further was done on the subject. It is mentioned here with a hope that it may be resumed at some future period.

which, even to *the present day,* are familiarly repeated by the people in various parts of the country. CONWAY, a bard of the O'Donnells of Tyrconnell, about the same time, poured forth some noble effusions to celebrate the heroic actions of that powerful sept. One of the most distinguished writers of this period was JOHN O'DUGAN, (chief poet of O'Kelly, Prince of Imania, in Conaught,) who died in the year 1372, and whose name and works are still remembered and repeated by the people. His topographical poem, describing the principal Irish families of Conaught, Meath, and Ulster, at the time of the English invasion, is particularly valuable. Not a line of these bards has ever been printed. The limits here prescribed preclude the possibility of particularizing the poets of the two succeeding centuries. If they evinced less talent, let it be remembered that they were more oppressed than their predecessors*.

---

* The sharpest arrows of the settlers were always directed against the bards. Those whom they failed to subdue, they endeavoured to corrupt. Of this we have an instance on the patent roll, 49 Edward III. *Donald O'Moghane,* an *Irish Minstrel,* (Ministrallus Hibernicus) " for that he, not alone, was faithful to the king, but was also the cause of inflicting many evils on the Irish enemies," obtained license to dwell in the English quarters.--This recreant bard was one of the very few traitors of his Order, of which Patriotism was the motto and ruling principle. Like Alfred, the Irish bards went amongst the enemy, to learn their situation, strength, and intentions, which they never failed to report to their countrymen. By a similar roll of 13 Henry VI. we learn that the Irish *Mimi* (a species of

They fell with their country; and like the captive Israelites, hung their untuned harps on the willows. Well might they exclaim, with the royal psalmist:

>Now while our harpes were hanged soe,
>   The men, whose captives then we lay,
>Did on our griefs insulting goe,
>   And more to grieve us thus did say:
>You that of musique make such show,
>   Come sing us now a Sion lay;
>O no, we have nor voice nor hand,
>For such a song, in such a land.

But the spirit of patriotism at length aroused the bards from their slumbers, and during the cruel

---

comic actors,) *Clarsaghours* (harpers,) *Tympanours* (tabourers,) *Crowthores* (the earliest violin players,) *Kerraghers* (players at chess or tables,) *Rymours, Skelaghes,* (Raconteurs or taletellers,) *Bardes,* and others, contrary to the statute of Kilkenny, went amongst the English and exercised their arts and minstrelsies (minstrelsias et artes suas,) and that they afterwards proceeded to the Irish enemies, and led them upon the king's liege subjects.—*Rot-Pat.*—Here it may be observed that the Irish bards do not appear to have attempted regular dramatic composition. The mimic representation of human actions on the stage, was forgotten amid the tragic scenes of horror and devastation which were daily witnessed throughout the land. The Colonial theatre in Dublin, was *English,* and had no connexion or sympathy with the Irish people. The rude shows, however, exhibited in Hoggin Green, in that city, in 1528, before the appearance of the regular drama in England, were of mixed origin, partly imitated from ancient Irish customs.

reign of Elizabeth, many men of genius started up throughout Ireland, who devoted their talents to the vindication of their suffering country. Of these, the most considerable were MAOLIN OGE MAC BRODIN, the most eminent poet of his time; O'GNIVE of Claneboy, who distinguished himself by several compositions to excite the natives against the English, and whose spirited poem on the " Downfall of the Gael" is included in this collection; TEIGE DALL O'HIGGIN, brother to Maolmuire, archbishop of Tuam, whose genius was of a superior order, and whose poems are amongst the best in our language; O'MULCONRY, whose fine poem, in the Phœnician dialect of the Irish, addressed to the chieftain O'ROURKE of Briefny, is contained in this work; and the learned and philosophic MAC DAIRE of Thomond, and his gifted contemporary O'CLERY of Donegal, whose talents shine so conspicuously, as opposite leaders, in the *Iomarba,* or " *Contention of the Bards,*" about the year 1600. (See vol. ii. p. 345). Here I close the series of ancient bards, having arrived at the period which may now be considered as dividing our ancient and modern history. The estimation in which they were at all times held by their countrymen, may be learned from an English writer of the reign of Elizabeth, the accomplished Sir Philip Sydney, who, in his defence of poesy, tells us that " In Ireland their poets are held in devout reverence." A love of poetry has always distinguished our countrymen. No people have ever been more ready, according to the injunction of the sacred pensman, to honour such as by their skill found out musical tunes and published verses in writing: and if patriotism, genius, and learning, are entitled to regard amongst mankind, no men were ever more deserving of national honour than the ancient bards of Ireland*.

It now remains to consider their successors to recent times; and here it may be necessary to observe, that the only poets mentioned throughout this work, are such as wrote solely in their native language. An enumeration of the principal of these, for the two

---

* The Irish princes, like the Arabians, always retained a numerous band of bards, musicians, and story-tellers, in their train. The bards became the historians of their deeds, and the heralds of their families. Some of the public duties of their Order have been already noted, from the Book of Rights, p. xii, and the important nature of these duties prove the confidence and esteem in which their professors were held. Until the destruction of the Irish Monarchy, the inauguration poems were solemnly sung by the royal bards, attired in scarlet robes, a practice which was continued to a later period on the accession of the provincial kings. A similar custom was observed in Scotland. "The first coronation of the kings of Scotland, of which we have any particular account, is that of Alexander III. in 1249. On this occasion, a *Highland bard*, dressed in a scarlet tunic or robe, repeated on his knees, in the gaelic language, the genealogy of Alexander and his ancestors up to Fergus the first king of Scotland."—*Gunn's Treatise on the Harp.*

last centuries, is given in the margin*; and poems of many of them will be found in this collection. It

---

* "The art of poetry," says the venerable Charles O'Conor in his Dissertations, "declined as the nation itself declined, but still some eminent poets appeared, from time to time, but diverted *in most instances* from the ancient moral and political uses, to the barren subjects of personal panegyric." Though our author was generally right in his opinions on Irish subjects, yet the foregoing cannot be received without many qualifications. Of the eminent poets, however, alluded to, the following are particularly to be noticed, since the days of Elizabeth. —FERGAL and EOGAN MAC AN BHAIRD, *(Ward,)* two bards of Lecale, who sung of the great northern septs of *Magennis* of Down; *Mac Sweeny* of Donegal; *O'Donnel* of Tyrconnell; and *O'Neill* of Tyrone.—O'HUSSEY, a Franciscan friar, author of several divine poems and hymns, and some miscellaneous stanzas, which are remarkable for sweetness of versification.—JOHN MAC WALTER WALSH of the mountains, in the co. Kilkenny, an elegiac and pastoral poet of considerable merit.—ANGUS O'DALY, the "red bard" of Cork, a powerful satyrist.—O'HUSSEY of Orgial, (Louth) the bard of the *Maguires* of Fermanagh, a fine genius, of whom there remain several excellent miscellaneous poems.—O'BRUDAR of Limerick, who evinced a masterly skill in poetry, and whose muse pathetically described the political troubles of Ireland during the 17th century.—JAMES COURTNEY of Louth, author of several sweet elegiac and pastoral pieces, and many superior epigrams abounding with wit and agreeable raillery, who died early in the last century.—MAC GOURAN of Leitrim, a witty and humorous bard, whose poem entitled the "Revelry of O'Rourke," has been versified by Swift.—O'NEACHTAN of Meath, a learned and highly gifted poet, and miscellaneous writer.—EOGAN O'RAHELLY of Kerry, a man of learning and great natural powers, who has left many poems of superior merit.—PATRICK LINDEN of the Fews in Armagh, a sweet

has been so long fashionable to decry that persecuted body, that the writer regrets it has not fallen to others

---

lyric poet who lived in the early part of the last century, and whose productions display considerable genius.—The Rev. OWEN O'KEEFFE of Cork, author of many fine poems on moral and patriotic subjects.—TEIGE O'NEACHTAN of Dublin, a learned miscellaneous writer, author of a dictionary of his native tongue, and of several excellent poems on various subjects. He died about the year 1744.—COLLA MAC SHEAN, or JOHNSON, of Mourne in Downe, a lyric poet, and musician, author of some popular songs.—DONOGH MACNAMARA of Waterford, an original genius, who wrote a mock Eneid in an elegant and lively strain, and other poems of acknowledged merit.—HUGH MAC CURTIN of Clare, an Irish Lexicographer, and author of several odes and elegies.—JOHN MAC DONALD surnamed CLARAGH, of Charleville, co. Cork, an eminent bard, and a man of extensive learning, whose poems are among the best in our language.—JOHN TOOMEY of Limerick, a miscellaneous poet, died 1775.—ART MAC COVEY of the Fews, co. Armagh, a lyric poet of distinction.—ANDREW MAGRATH a rambling disciple of Anacreon, and a good lyric poet well known in Munster, in the last century, by the name of the MANGAIRE SUGACH.—THADEUS, or TEIGE GAELACH O' SULLIVAN, another Munster bard of talents and celebrity, author of several excellent poems.—OWEN ROE O'SULLIVAN of Kerry, an elegiac and pastoral poet. He lived until 1784. —The Rev. WILLIAM ENGLISH of Cork, a facetious and satirical writer, who has left several poems of exquisite humour and originality.—EDMUND LEE of Cork, a pastoral and lyric poet.—PATRICK O'BRIEN of Newgrange in Meath, author of several odes and excellent songs.—JOHN COLLINS, a poet of the first rank, who lived to a recent period. Here this list must terminate, space not permitting mention of even half the bards of local celebrity throughout Ireland, during the last century. Amongst these men were many of great natural

more competent to vindicate them against the ignorance and prejudice by which they have been assailed, particularly during the last century. But their defence,

---

genius, several of excellent classical education, and some of superior learning. They are therefore not to be classed with the few gaelic rymers of the Highlands of Scotland, who have been described by their Lowland countrymen, as "rude and uneducated." The bards of Ireland were men of a very different character, but they were a proscribed and persecuted race, their very language interdicted, and yet from those outlawed bards, and in that denounced language, do we find specimens of poetic talent, which would do honour to any country. Had the unfortunate DERMODY been born a few years earlier, it is probable his name would appear only in the foregoing enumeration. The English tongue began to spread amongst the people of his native county, Clare, in the middle of the last century; and thus the talents which would have passed unnoticed, if confined to the language of his fathers, were universally admired in that of his adoption. If ROBERT BURNS had been an Irishman, and had lived at the period alluded to, his noble genius might have been displayed in the language of the country, from the same patriotic feeling which induced him to prefer the dialect of Scotland. But in that case what a different fate would have attended him. He would, no doubt, have obtained celebrity in the district of his birth, or sojourn, but beyond that, it is probable his name would never be heard, or only when enumerated with the rest of our neglected bards. His lot, however, was cast among a literary people. He wrote in a language which all Scotland understood, and he was brought forward by men of patriotism, genius, and learning. Thus he escaped the obscurity which would have inevitably awaited him, had he the fate to have been an Irishman.—Let it not be deemed presumptuous to say, that many a neglected Irish bard possessed genius equally entitled to admiration.

even in the humblest hands, must prove triumphant. What was their crime?—for, shame to humanity, in Ireland it was deemed a crime!—to love their country. What brought down on them the vengeance of the persecutor? their invincible attachment to the ancient faith, and to the ancient, though fallen, families of the land. If these be crimes, then were they guilty; if not, it is time to make reparation to the memory of these injured men, whose learning and genius would have been cherished and honoured, and held in " devout reverence" in any country under heaven except their own. Richly did they possess those brilliant qualities of mind, the exercise of which, in later and comparatively better days, have placed their more fortunate, though not more talented, countrymen *Curran, Sheridan, O'Leary,* and others, in the foremost ranks of mankind. But the bards were " mere Irish." They thought and spoke and wrote in Irish. They were, invariably, Catholics, patriots, and jacobites. Even their broad Celtic surnames they disdained to submit to the polish of Saxon refinement. Hence they have been erroneously considered, and by many of the educated of their country are still considered, as rude rural rhymsters, without any claim either to talents or learning*. So it was

---

* Several of the bards named in the foregoing note, were men of extensive learning. Of this fact, if space permitted, many instances could be adduced; one, however, out of justice

with the prince of Latin poets, when he first visited Rome. His countrymen could not discern the noble genius which lay hid under his rustic garb.

>   ————————rideri possit, eo quod
> Rusticius tonso toga defluit, et male laxus
> In pede calceus hæret.————— ———
> ——————————-at ingenium ingens
> Inculto latet hoc sub corpore.——
>   Hor.

But, lest the charge of national partiality may be alleged against the character here given, let us hear the description of a writer, who cannot lie under that imputation. Doctor Parsons, *an Englishman*, author of a curious antiquarian treatise, entitled the " Re-

---

to the individual cannot be omitted.—It is well known, that the late General Vallancey obtained much literary celebrity, both at home and abroad, and, in fact, first acquired the reputation of an Irish scholar, by the collation of Hanno, the Carthaginian's speech in Plautus, published *Vol.* ii. *Collectanea, p.* 310; but it is not so well known that that speech had been collated many years before, by *Teige O'Neachtan*, an excellent Irish poet, and author of the extempore epigram, Vol. ii. p. 120, of this collection. Vallancey had this collation in O'Neachtan's hand-writing, in his possession; and I am obliged (with regret) to add, that he never acknowledged the fact, but assumed the entire credit of the discovery to himself. A copy of this curious collation, from which Vallancey has materially deviated, is now before me, but is too long for insertion here. The autograph copy of *O'Neachtan*, dated 12 August, 1741, is preserved in the library of William Monck Mason, Esq., Dublin.

mains of Japhet," tells us, in that work, that about the middle of the last century he " spent several years of his life in Ireland, and there attained to a tolerable knowledge of the very ancient tongue of that country." Speaking of the bards, he says, " They repeat their poems in a stile that, for its beauty and fine sentiments, has often struck me with amazement; for I have been many times obliged, by many of these natural bards, with the repetition of as sublime poems upon love, heroism, hospitality, battles, &c., as can be produced in any language. Homer and Virgil have laid the ground of their noble tissue upon the basis of historical facts, and the Irish poets *of our times* write in the very same strain. It is the genius of the people, and their language is susceptible of it; more naturally than any other extant. There are numbers of them capable of composing extemporaneous eulogiums and poems of considerable length upon any subject, surprisingly elegant, and full of fine sentiments." Doctor Parsons, moreover, states that he was personally acquainted with the bards whom he has thus described, and whose names are already given in the margin. Speaking of these men, even James Macpherson, in his Dissertation on the poems of Ossian, says, " Their love sonnets, and their elegies on the death of persons worthy or renowned, abound with simplicity, and a wild harmony of numbers. The beauty of these species depends so much on a certain *curiosa felicitas* of expression in the original, that they must appear much to disadvantage in another language." Lord Byron and Sir Walter Scott have recorded their opinions of Irish poetry in terms which may enable us to conjecture what these distinguished men would have thought, could they have tasted the beauties of our bards in their original compositions. Many of the love sonnets and elegies alluded to by Macpherson will be found in the present collection, with some notices of their authors, whose names are thus brought to the remembrance of their countrymen, under a hope that this humble effort to awaken national attention towards these neglected sons of genius and their works, may be pursued by others better qualified to do justice to their memory.

For the course of education prescribed for the bards, in ancient and modern times, the reader is referred to the works in the margin*. The language invariably used in their compositions, was

---

* KEATING, and the anonymous Dissertation prefixed to the Memoirs of Clanricarde, Dublin, 1727.—In the early part of the last century, periodical meetings, or "Sessions," of the Munster bards were held at Charleville, and Bruree, in the counties of Cork and Limerick, where the aspirants for poetic celebrity, recited their productions before the assembly. They to whom the prizes were adjudged, in the various departments of poetic composition, were publicly crowned, and distinguished by other marks of honour. These poetic meetings were suppressed by the operation of the penal laws.

that of the country. To it they were attached for many reasons, independent of nationality. The most learned men of Europe, since the revival of letters, have been loud in its praise. Usher has ranked it among the first for richness and elegance, and Leibnitz and Lluyd have left on record their opinions of its value. The latter observes, that "The Irish have preserved their letters and orthography beyond all their neighbouring nations." The ancient language was very different from that spoken at the present day. It was divided into several dialects, of which the *Bearla Feine,* or *Phœnician,* was in highest estimation, and without a knowledge of that dialect it is impossible to understand the early poets. The introduction of Christianity, and Latin, had not that effect on this primordial language, which might be supposed. For a long period after, it suffered no material alteration. At length, in the sixteenth century, our learned men began to turn their thoughts to the subject; and if they had not been impeded by the jealous interference of the English, it is probable that it would have undergone a change similar to that of most of the other dialects of Europe. How far that circumstance is now to be regretted, by one who contemplates the present, and probable future political amalgamation of the interests of these islands, it may be difficult to determine. From the days of Henry VIII. the English rulers were bent upon the total annihilation of our national language, but time has shewn the folly of the undertaking. The late Bishop Heber, in his life of Bedel, has stigmatized it as "narrow and illiberal policy, which, though it has in part succeeded, has left a division in the national heart, far worse than that of the tongue." Most grants of lands from the crown, in the reigns of Henry and his successors to Charles I., contained special provisoes, for the disuse of the native, and the encouragement of the English tongue, But all these efforts would have proved abortive, were it not for the fatal disasters of the seventeenth century. Immediately before the civil war of 1641, a momentary gleam of hope lightened over this devoted language. The learned antiquaries of Donegal associated to collect and publish the remains of our ancient literature; but their patriotic intentions were unhappily frustrated by the succeeding troubles, and the language which had withstood the shock of so many ages, at length sunk in the general wreck. Thenceforth it was banished from the castle of the chieftain, to the cottage of his vassal, and, from having been the cherished and cultivated medium of intercourse between the nobles and gentry of the land, it became gradually limited to the use of the uneducated poor.* No wonder, then, that it should

---

* Although colloquially debased, many of the original characteristics of our language remain unimpaired. Its pathetic powers have been particularly celebrated. "*If you plead for*

have been considered harsh and unpolished when
thus spoken, but it was as unjust to estimate our

---

your life, plead in Irish," is a well known adage. But the
revilers of the people have not spared even their speech. Of
the species of abuse usually resorted to, a curious specimen may
be found in the prejudiced Stanihurst, (temp. Elizabeth,) who
assures his readers, that the Irish was unfit even for the prince
of darkness himself to utter, and to illustrate this, the bigotted
Saxon gravely adduced the case of a possessed person in Rome,
who " spoke in every known tongue except Irish, but in that
he neither would nor could speak, because of its intolerable
harshness." This notable story is said to have made such an
impression on the witch-ridden mind of James the first of
England, that he conceived as great an antipathy to our language, because the devil would not speak it, as he is known to
have had to the sight of a drawn sword. It was, however,
differently estimated by a celebrated personage of a later date,
even the renowned William Lilly, astrologer, celestial intelli-
gencer, and chamber prophet of the royal martyr, Charles the
first. That noted authority informed the world, that the Irish
language was like that spoken in heaven. " It is very rare,
yea even in our days, for any operator or master, to have the
Angels speak articulately; when they do speak it is like the
Irish, much in the throat."—How is it possible while reciting
these ludicrous specimens of prejudice and imposture, to avoid
reflecting, with bitter feelings, how often the best interests of
Ireland have been thoughtlessly sacrificed by its rulers, to the
extremes of bigotry, rapacity, and ignorance? Even in matters
connected with our subject, we are informed, that Queen Elizabeth was prevented from sending to Denmark for certain ancient
Irish records, said to be there, by the remark of one of her
council, that it would be better all such evidences of our inde-
pendence were annihilated. So late as the reign of Queen
Anne, we are told that the intention of that princess to promote
the cultivation of the Irish language, was frustrated by the

language by such a standard, as it would be to judge of the English by the jargon of Yorkshire. The measure of its vicissitudes was not yet, however, full. In the last century, the inquisitors of the Irish parliament denounced it as the dialect of that phantom of their political frenzy, popery. According to a favorite mode of native reasoning, it was resolved to reduce the poor Catholics to a state of mental darkness, in order to convert them into enlightened protestants. A thick cloud of ignorance soon overspread the land; and the language of

---

Duke of Ormond, who repeated in her presence, an unmeaning sentence of broad sounding words as a proof of its barbarity. At a later period, we find an Irish Catholic, in the fervency of his zeal, to make Ireland " thoroughly British," wishing that " the Irish language were entirely obliterated ;" and recommending that " if it were possible to pump St. George's channel dry, and unite the two islands physically, it ought to be done, at whatever expence."—*Moore's History of the British Revolution.* —On these wise projects, it need only be observed, that when the latter shall be achieved, and not until then, may the former be expected. What, it may be asked, is there in the Irish language to make worse men or worse subjects of those who speak it, than are the Welch and Highlanders, whose native dialects are cultivated and encouraged ? Among the foremost to answer in the negative, would have been his late Majesty, George the fourth. The warmest reception that monarch ever received from his numerous subjects, was expressed by an Irish " *Cead mile failte*;" and among the best bulwarks of his throne, were the bayonets of Ireland, pushed through the hearts of his enemies, under the broad voweled Celtic cry of " *Fag a ballagh*."

millions ceased to be a medium of written communication. To these circumstances, perhaps, may be attributed its preservation from the written corruptions which pervade the present Gaelic of Scotland. The bards of modern times were the principal scribes in Irish*. In it they were educated; to its orthography and grammatical structure they carefully attended; and in this last stage of its eventful history, it appears in their writings in a degree of purity, which, considering the disadvantages under which they laboured, is truly remarkable.

In our poems and songs, but particularly in those exquisite old tales and romances, which for originality of invention, and elegance of expression, vie with the Eastern stories that have so long delighted Europe, the beauties of our language are fully displayed. In lyrical composition, which forms so large a portion of the present collection, its superiority even over the Italian, has been repeatedly asserted. On this point, a late favorite melodist says, "I have in another place observed, that the Irish was superior even to the Italian, in lyrical com-

---

* In 1744, Harris, the editor of Ware's Antiquities, says, "There are no Irish types in this kingdom;" and so it continued for many years after. The first Irish type that found its way to Munster, was sent in 1819, by the writer hereof to his worthy friend Mr. Denis O'Flyn of Cork, an excellent Irish scholar, who erected a small printing press in his house, for the patriotic purpose of multiplying copies of some favorite Irish poems, as a means for their preservation.

position. I know a contrary opinion is held by many, *but by very few capable of judging as to both languages.*"* Voltaire has observed, that a people may have a music and poetry, pleasing only to themselves, and yet both good. But Irish music has been admired wherever its melting strains have been heard. Handel, and the first-rate composers of Italy, have been loud in its praise. If it be permitted to argue, as Sir William Jones did on the language and music of Persia, that the natural and affecting melodies of that people, must have a language remarkable for its softness, and the strong accentuation of words, and for the tenderness of the songs written in it, it would follow, that the original songs, so long associated with the Irish melodies, would prove equally pleasing, if more generally known. Many of them are contained in the present volumes, and they will be found replete with the simplicity and natural feeling

---

* *Reminiscences of Michael Kelly, London,* 1826. *Introduction.*—The veteran reminiscent again says, " General D'Alton, who was an enthusiast about Ireland, agreed with me that the Irish language was sweeter and better adapted for musical accompaniment than any other, the Italian excepted; and it is true, that, when a child, I have heard my father sing many pathetic airs, in which the words resembled Italian so closely, that if I did not know the impossibility, the impression on my memory would be, that I had heard him sing in that language."
—Such were the opinions of a popular and scientific melodist, who, as he says himself, was " capable of judging as to *both languages.*"—Swift's phrase, " Proper words in proper places," describes Irish song.

which will ever posses power over the human heart. Should these sweet original lyrics, therefore, attract the attention of future melodists, and be introduced on the stage, a circumstance, not at all unlikely, they may, when accompanied with their native melodies, and sung by our "sweet singers," prove no mean rivals to the dearly purchased warblings of Italy.

The metrical structure of ancient Irish poetry, must be considered with reference to its musical accompaniments*. The voice of the bard retrenched, or supplied, the quantity of long or short syllables, in order to adapt them to the sound or melody. This license required many rules to restrain it. Hence the hundred kinds of verse mentioned by *Ferceirtne* in the *Uraicepht* or " primer of the bards ;" and the declaration of *O'Molloy* in his prosody, that the rules

---

* Among the ancient Irish, the principal species of musical composition was termed AVANTRIREACH, (Abhbhantripeach) It consisted of three parts. *Geantraighe*, which excited to love; *Goltraighe*, which stimulated to valour and feats of arms ;. and *Suantraighe*, which disposed to rest and sleep. I find it described as follows, in a manuscript of considerable antiquity.—

Cṗı ꜰoṗ ᴀ neımhnıꜱhchıoṗ Cṗuıcıṗe, (eᴀbhon) cṗı cṗeıꜱhe le nonoṗuıꜱhchıoṗ, no le nuᴀıṛlıꜱhchıoṗ clᴀıṗṛeoıṗ, no ꜱᴀch ṛeᴀṗ cheoıl ᴀṗ bıch, (eᴀbhon) ꜱeᴀncṗoıꜱhe, (eᴀbhon) cṗoıꜱh cuıṗeᴀṛ cᴀch chum ṛuꜱoıꜱhe ; ꜱolcṗᴀıꜱhe, (eᴀbhon) cṗoıꜱh cuıṗeᴀṛ neᴀch chum ꜱolᴀ ; ṛuᴀncṗᴀıꜱhe, (eᴀbhon) cṗᴀıꜱh cuıṗeᴀṛ cᴀch chum cobᴀlcᴀ.—cṗoıꜱh, (eᴀbhon) ceol.

of Irish verse were " the most difficult under the sun."* The latter writer describes " a popular kind of poetry, much used in his time, called Abhrán," or " sweet verse." This he censures, as a deviation from the ancient rules; but it seems to have been devised as a middle course, between the strictness of the regular metre, and the license too generally taken by the voice of the bard. Some of our most admired lyrical compositions are in this measure. The *Octava Rima*, or eight line stanza of Italy, was borrowed from the Spaniards, who had it themselves from the *Troubadours* and Italians, perhaps not earlier than the end of the fifteenth century, and in it have been composed some of our finest songs.

The borrowed term " Minstrelsy" is used in the title of this collection, only because it is familiar to the public ear, for others more appropriate might be

---

* The Dán díreach, or " Direct metre," was the principal measure used in ancient Irish poetry. Each stanza of four lines, (or quartans) makes perfect sense in itself; and every line contains seven syllables, with concord or alliteration between the principal parts of speech. For the rules and requisites of Irish verse, see O'Molloy and Haliday's grammars; the unfinished translation, by the latter, of Keating's Ireland, p. 200, Dub. 1811; and the Transactions of the Gaelic Society, ib. 1808, p. 214, where the Scottish editors of " The post originals of Ossian," are charged with ignorance of all the rules of Irish metre. For further observations on Irish rhyme, see O'Conor's *Rerum Hib.* Vol. i., and for alliteration as used by the ancient Britons, Irish, &c. See Percy's translation of *Mallet's Northern Antiquities*, vol. ii. p. 147.

INTRODUCTION.   xxxvii

found in our language*. Aware of the influence of popular song on public morals, no verses, of even a doubtful tendency, have been admitted into the following pages; if some rigid moralist may not perhaps deem the *Chansons de boire* of our favourite bard CAROLAN exceptionable. It will be observed, that in the Irish originals all contractions are rejected, " pro faciliori captu, et modo legendi addiscendique hanc linguam."—*O'Molloy*. With the same view the letter h is invariably inserted in place of its usual representative the aspirate point. Against this it may be urged that that letter was not anciently written; and, moreover, that its insertion may create a difficulty in the way of the mere Irish reader's acquiring its true pronunciation in English. It is not, however, an innovation, for the first objection is proved groundless by various old manuscripts; and even supposing the latter entitled to considera-

---

* The Irish muses are expressly called banbee foghlama, filidheachda agus ceoil. Here we find poetry and music combined, as they generally were in the file or bard. The late Mr. Pinkerton, in a letter to Doctor Percy, 4 Sept. 1794, now before me, says, " I must confess myself thoroughly convinced that *Minstrel only implied Musician*." On this letter the Bishop writes, " Pinkerton's *attempt* to prove Minstrels only Musicians," on which he refers to *Putenham's Arte of English Poesie*, 1589, p. 9, where Minstrelsie expresses Poetry without any reference to Music. In the English translation of Favine, 1623, *Rymer* and *Minstrel* are synonimous. On these authorities I have used the term.

tion, it was deemed more important to facilitate the reading of the originals.

With respect to the origin and progress of the present publication, a few words may be necessary for the satisfaction of the reader. It has long been a subject of regret, with the writer, that the remains of our national bards, of those men who, according to James Macpherson, " have displayed a genius worthy of any age or nation," should be consigned to obscurity at home, while a neighbouring nation derived so much literary fame from a few of those remains, boldly claimed and published as its own. Several societies formed among ourselves, for the purpose of preserving our ancient literature, having successively failed, the task seemed abandoned to individual exertion. This consideration induced the writer to devote his few leisure moments to the collection of some of those neglected remnants of genius, with a hope that, at a future period, they might be rescued from the oblivion to which they were daily hastening. To this undertaking he adhered with a perseverance proportioned to his idea of its importance; and the first fruits of his humble labours are now respectfully presented to his countrymen.

A few valued and learned friends—the REVEREND MARTIN LOFTUS, late Professor of Irish in the College of Maynooth; the REVEREND DANIEL O'SULLIVAN of Bandon, who has enriched his native language with an inimitable translation of the " Imitation of Christ;"

and the late lamented JAMES SCURRY, author of valuable Remarks on Irish Dictionaries, Grammars, &c. in the Transactions of the Royal Irish Academy, favoured the writer, by kindly perusing most of his selections : and every care has been taken to insure that accuracy, which, without presumption, may be claimed for the following originals. Their preservation being his sole object, his intention at first extended only to their publication, with a few explanatory notes. He afterwards considered how far literal English translations would be an improvement of his plan. But the widely different idioms of both languages; the difficulty, or rather impossibility, of preserving the spirit of the bards; and the consequent injury to their works and memory, proved decisive against such a process. From a quarter, not previously contemplated, he was, at length, enabled to overcome the difficulty, and to present his literal essayings in the more appropriate garb of verse. Some literary friends of acknowledged poetical abilities, to whom he communicated his project, generously undertook the task. To the late THOMAS FURLONG, whose name, as a poet, is already familiar to his countrymen; HENRY GRATTAN CURRAN, ESQ., a youth richly endowed with the genius of his distinguished father; the talented friend of his country, the REVEREND WILLIAM HAMILTON DRUMMOND, D. D.; JOHN D'ALTON, ESQ., author of the distinguished prize Essay on the History of

Ireland, printed in the Transactions of the Royal Irish Academy; and EDWARD LAWSON, ESQ., whose talents and learning are well known; to these gentlemen the writer has to record his grateful acknowledgments, for the zeal with which they co-operated to render this collection worthy of public acceptance. In justice, however, to his respected friends, he must acquit them of any participation in the prose parts of the undertaking. For these, which were mostly written before the late conciliatory acts, and which, if now to be done, might, perhaps, remain for ever so, the writer alone has to entreat indulgence. In conclusion, he has only to add, that as his sole object was the preservation of even so much of the neglected poetry of his native land, he has presented the entire to the worthy publisher, Mr. ROBINS; and sincerely hopes it may not prove an unproductive gift to a man, whose liberal press and generous exertions in our national cause, at a late momentous crisis, deserve well of the people of Ireland.

MEMOIR OF CAROLAN.

ANECDOTES of genius have always been favorably received by the public; hence it is hoped, that the following detail of the life and compositions of this favorite Irish bard, may not be unacceptable to his countrymen. Though not hitherto published, the particulars may be depended upon as authentic, having been derived from the best sources of information now extant. It was originally intended, if space allowed, to introduce, under the general title of CAROLANIANA, many notices of the bard and his contemporaries, which might prove interesting, as illustrative of some old customs peculiar to Ireland, but these are reluctantly postponed for another opportunity.

TURLOGH O'CAROLAN, the well known subject of the present memoir, was the son of John O'Carolan*, a

---

* This surname, which is generally used without the Irish adjunct O, not occurring in the Topographical poems of O'DUGAN, or O'HUIDHRIN, or in any genealogical tables anterior to the fifteenth century, is supposed to have been assumed after that period by some branch of the *Mac Bradys*, a considerable clan of East Breifny, who were anciently called *Cearbhallach*, and who inherited large possessions in that territory. The extensive

respectable descendant of an ancient tribe of East Breifny, a district now forming part of the counties of Meath and Westmeath. He was born about the year 1670, at a place called Newtown, near Nobber, in the county of Meath.

---

tracts of Carolanstown, in the barony of Foure, co. Westmeath; and Carolanstown, near Kells, co. Meath, still bear the name. In 1550, Terence O'Kerrolan, rector of *Knogh*, co. Meath, was sued under Stat. 28 Henry VIII. for not keeping a Parochial School to " teche the English tong." He laconically pleaded, that he was always ready to " teche ;" but that no children would come to " larn." In the same year, an information was exhibited against *Edward O'Kerrolan*, for that he, being of " the Irish nation *de les O'Kerrolans*," held that benefice, within the English pale, contrary to *Stat.* 13 *Hen. VI.* His plea was, that he purchased a licence, 34 Hen. VIII. of freedom from the Irish yoke, and that he might enjoy the English laws, privileges, &c. In 1607, *Shane, (John,) Grana O'Carrolan*, " chief of his sept," became bound to the King in £100 and 100 marks, for the appearance of " certain of the Carrolans, his kinsmen." But having been afterwards himself committed prisoner to the castle of Dublin, the others, " affrighted, omitted their appearance," and his recognizance became forfeited. The king, (James I.) by concordatum, 24 july, 1614, remitted these forfeitures, because of " the many acceptable services performed by the said Shane Grana, in the late wars; and that many of the said persons are sithence dead and executed." These memoranda are taken from the Exchequer rolls of these respective years. This *Shane Grana* is stated to have been the grandfather of John, the father of the bard. His descendants were utterly deprived during the civil wars. Patrick Carolan, the bard's paternal uncle, appears, however, in 1691, to have possessed the lands of Muff, 300 acres, in Nobber parish, forfeited by Lord Gormanston, for adhering to JAMES II., and Neale Carolan, his second cousin, was, at the same time, in possession of the lands of Rabranmoone, 325 acres, in Stackallen parish, forfeited by Lord Slane.—*Returns of Forfeitures*, EXCHEQUER. The bard's father appears to have been totally stripped at this period. Numerous families of the name still reside in the districts here mentioned; and among them are many respectable householders and farmers.

Though gifted with a natural genius for music and poetry, he evinced no precocious disposition for either. He became a minstrel by accident, and continued it more through choice than necessity. "He was above playing for hire," says his friend, the venerable Charles O'Conor; who always respected him as one of those reduced Irish gentlemen, who were plundered of their birthright, during the troubles of the seventeenth century. He was not, therefore, one who could be humiliated by adopting the "idle trade." Respectably descended, he possessed no small portion of old Milesian pride, and entertaining a due sense of his additional claims as a man of genius, he always expected, and invariably received, that attention to which, in every point of view, he was so eminently entitled. At the houses where he visited, he was welcomed more as a friend than as an itinerant minstrel. His visits were regarded as favors conferred, and his departure never failed to occasion regret. He lived happy and respected; and under one of the greatest privations incident to humanity, this amiable and ingenious individual has shewn that true genius, properly directed, is able to triumph over difficulties, under which ordinary minds generally sink in despair.

But to return to our narrative. Carolan's father, with thousands of his countrymen, was reduced to a state of poverty, while the revolutionary puritans of England rioted through the plundered domains of their ancestors. Obliged to emigrate from his native spot, and aided by the friendship and advice of his countrywoman Lady St. George, he bid adieu to Meath, and settled at Carrickonshannon, in the county of Leitrim. This lady died soon after, but the ancient and respectable family, of M'Dermott Roe, then resident at Alderford, in the county of Roscommon, made ample amends for her loss. Our bard, who had by this time become a comely and interesting boy, of a mild and obliging disposition, attracted the attention of Mrs. M'Dermott. He soon became a favorite with that lady, and a frequent visitor at Alderford House; she had him instructed with her own children. He learned to read his native language, which, at that time, was universally taught. He also made some proficiency in English, and shewed an inclination for history. These particulars, and others which follow, were given by an intelligent old man of the name of Early, whose father lived for many years, during Carolan's time, at Alderford. To this respected family our bard was attached through life, by the tenderest ties of gratitude and affection. They were his earliest friends and patrons. With them he chiefly lived; under their hospitable roof he breathed his last, nor was he separated from them in death, for his ashes mingle with theirs in their ancient burial-place in the church of Kilronan. For them were composed some of his sweetest strains. The delightful tunes of " M'Dermott Roe;" " Mrs. M'Dermott Roe;" " Anna M'Dermott Roe;" and " Mr. Edmond M'Dermott Roe," prove how earnestly he exerted his musical talents in their praise.

About this period, our youth became acquainted with the distinguished Irish family of Belanagare, in the county of Roscommon; and commenced an intimacy, which ended only in death. Old Denis O'Conor, before the restoration of part of his ancient inheritance, by the Court of Claims, was obliged to quit the residence of his ancestors, and remove to a farm at Knockmore, near Ballyfarnon. Here this venerable descendant of Ireland's ancient kings, himself handled the plough, and inculcated maxims of humility and moderation to his family; observing, that although he was the son of a gentleman, they were to consider themselves but as the children of a ploughman*. This good man sympathized with the exiled family from Meath. They resided in his immediate neighbourhood. He considered them as fellow sufferers, and shewed them many acts of kindness. To our ingenious youth he became particularly attached, and furnished him with books of instruction. But the time had now arrived which was to terminate poor Carolan's book studies, and fix his destination for life. In his eighteenth year he was seized by the small-pox, and totally deprived of sight. In this melancholy state of privation the afflicted youth expressed a desire to learn the harp. His kind friend, Mrs. M'Dermott, procured a harper to instruct him, under whom he soon made pro-

---

* Inculcations of this nature were usual among the despoiled families of Ireland, at and after the period above alluded to. Of this, the following humorous instance has been handed down:— Daniel Byrne, well known in Dublin, in the seventeenth century, by the name of " Daniel the tailor," was the son of a forfeiting gentleman, who resided at Ballintlea, near Red Cross, co. Wicklow. Daniel was bred to the clothiering trade; and, having contracted for clothing the Irish parliamentary forces, under Cromwell, he made a considerable fortune. His son, Gregory, (whose descendants took the name of Leicester,) was created an English baronet in 1660. Soon after, as both were walking in Dublin, Sir Gregory said, " Father, you ought to walk to the left of me, I being a knight, and you but a private individual." Daniel answered, " No, you puppy, I have the precedency in three ways: first, I am your senior; secondly, I am your father; and thirdly, I am the son of a gentleman, and you are but the son of a poor lousy tailor." Of Daniel's wit, the following, among other instances, is related: William Dawson, of Portarlington, ancestor of one of our present noble families, one morning pressing him to a dram as they were going to hunt, said, " Take it off, Daniel, it is but a *thimble* full." " Yes, Willy," said the other, " I would take it, if it were a *hopper* full;" thus reminding the Squire of his own old occupation, which was that of a miller.

ficiency. Having finally determined to adopt it as a profession, his benefactress provided him with a horse and an attendant. In his twenty-second year he began his avocation, by visiting the houses of the surrounding gentry; and thus humbly commenced the career of one of the most celebrated of the modern bards of Ireland.

Among those places which he first visited, was *Letterfian*, the ancient seat of the *Reynolds* or *Mac Ranald* family, situate near Lough Scur, a beautiful lake in the county of Leitrim. The then proprietor, George Reynolds, Esq., was the direct representative of the chiefs of that once powerful sept, whose sway extended over the territory of *Muintir Eolais*, comprehending the present baronies of Leitrim, Mohill, and Carrigallen, in the north-east part of that county*. Here our youthful bard was welcomed with characteristic hospitality. Mr. Reynolds was fond of poetry, and had, himself, produced some pieces in his native language. Having asked Carolan whether he had ever attempted verse, and being answered in the negative,

---

* The last male descendant of the MAC RANALD family was the late George Nugent Reynolds, Esq. of Letterfian, so justly celebrated for his wit, talents, and patriotism. The remains of the extensive patrimony of this ancient and respectable family is now enjoyed by his sister, Mary, the widow of the late Colonel Peyton, at present married to Major M'Namara of the county of Clare, descended from one of the oldest families of that county, and one of its present representatives in parliament. Mrs. M'Namara is nearly related to his Grace the Duke of Buckingham and Chandos. The estate of Letterfian, being in fee, will no longer be possessed by a person of the name of Reynolds. It will descend to the son of Mrs. M'Namara, by Colonel Peyton, a young gentleman every way qualified to represent, and worthy to enjoy, the *Mac Ranald* property. For his great grandfather, *Toby Peyton*, Carolan composed a well known " Planxty," given in this collection.

he humorously observed, in the Irish idiom, " Perhaps, Carolan, you might make a better *hand* of your *tongue* than of your *fingers*." He then told him that a great battle had been recently fought between the " Gentry," or " Fairies," of Sigh-beg and Sigh-mor, (two hills in the neighbourhood,) and proposed it as a fit subject to try his muse upon*.

---

* LETTERFIAN House is situate in a pleasant valley, extending a considerable distance from south-west to north-east. In front of the house, and near to it, is a range of hills, extending nearly two miles towards Lough-Scur. Upon the highest part of this range, over Letterfian, is one of these ancient conical heaps of stones and earth, called motes or rathes, so common in Ireland, and which the popular voice says are inhabited by the *Daoine Maithe*, the " Good people," or " Gentry," for the country folk will not call them Fairies. This mote is called *Sigh-beg*. Westward of the house, and also near it, is a small lake; and at a distance appears the lofty hill or mountain of *Sigh-mor*, which presents an abrupt precipitous termination. On the highest brow of this precipice is another mote, called *Sigh-mor*, which the neigbouring *Seanachies* affirm is also thickly inhabited by another colony of " Good people." This mote, and the mountain on which it stands, are much celebrated in the popular poems and songs of Ireland. Tradition relates, that in ancient times a great battle was fought in the space between these hills, in which the celebrated *Fionn Mac Cubhail*, and his *Fionna Erionn*, were defeated. One of Fionn's heroes, who was killed in the engagement, is said to lie entombed in *Sigh-beg*; and a champion of the opposite party had his remains deposited in the centre of *Sigh-mor*. Some insist that it was over the body of *Fionn* himself the mote on *Sigh-beg* was erected. Under this idea, George Reynolds, Carolan's friend, caused an immense pile of lime and stones to be raised, in the figure of a man, which he called *Fionn Mac Cubhail*. This pile remained, for several years, a conspicuous object to the surrounding country; but it was, at length, prostrated by a storm. It was afterwards repaired by a gentleman, who had fallen into possession of that part of the estate; but it did not long resist the weather. Another storm laid it in ruins, and so it has remained ever since, and so it is likely to continue. For the people of the country assert, and

The poetic feeling, which had so long lain dormant, was at once awakened; and the great British poet never set about his "Paradise Regained" with more ardour, than did our Irish bard to describe this Fairy battle. Mr. Reynolds left home for a few days. When he returned, Carolan played and sung for him the words and music of his celebrated "Fairy Queens." His generous friend, delighted at so unexpected a proof of the bard's genius, on the spot predicted his future celebrity; and, among other favors, presented him, when departing, with a horse for his attendant. This composition, which begins, "Impeáɼán moɼ cháinic eidiɼ ná ſiȝhche," presents a romantic and pleasing picture of Fairy strife; but it is chiefly remarkable as the first poetical production of Carolan. Soon after this he composed his well known "Planxty Reynolds," for his friend; whose first cousin, Gracey Nugent, he also commemorated in the fine song which bears her name, and which is contained in the present collection.

---

firmly believe, that the storms by which it was overthrown were raised by the "Good people" of the mote, and that it was only in compliment to Mr. Reynolds, who was "one of the old stock," that these aerial beings suffered the building to stand so long after its first erection. But when it was rebuilt, they, having no respect for the then proprietor, soon raised the storm by which it was again prostrated.

It is further related, that after the battle already mentioned, a long continued warfare was kept up between the aerial inhabitants of *Sigh-beg* and *Sigh-mor*. The queens of these *Sighbrugha*, or Fairy palaces, espoused the cause of the different parties, whose chiefs were interred in their respective quarters; and when the mortal combatants ceased to fight, the quarrel was perpetuated by many bitter engagements between their immortal allies. One of these conflicts was that proposed by Mr. Reynolds, as a fit subject to exercise the muse of Carolan.

To those acquainted with the popular opinions of the Irish, it will not appear strange that our bard, like the old Scottish poet, Thomas of Ercildoune, or the Rhymer, was supposed, in his youth, to have held communication with the " good people." Near his father's house was a mote or rath, in the interior of which, one of their queens was reputed to have held her court. This mote was the scene of many a boyish pastime, with his youthful companions; and after he became blind, he used to prevail on some of his family, or neighbours, to lead him to it. Here he was accustomed to remain for hours together, sometimes stretched listlessly before the sun. He was often observed to start up suddenly, as if in a fit of ecstacy, occasioned, as was firmly believed, by the preternatural sights which he witnessed. It happened, in one of these raptures, that he called hastily on his companions to lead him home. He immediately sat to his harp. His fingers wandered confusedly over the strings; and, in a little time, he played and sung the air and words of his sweet song, "A bhrīghib bheuṟách iṟ ḃuiṫ áń bhéiṗṟe," addressed to Bridget Cruise, the object of his earliest and tenderest attachment*.

---

* For Bridget Cruise, Carolan composed several songs; and of these, perhaps the best is given in this volume, p. 14. The following is an anonymous translation of a few sweet Irish stanzas, addressed, in her name, to the bard.

Air—Tender and plaintive.

O! tempt not my feet from the straight path of duty,
   Love lights a meteor but to betray!
And soon would'st thou tire of the odourless beauty
   If grew not esteem upon passion's decay.
Then cease thee! ah cease thee, to urge and to plain!
I may not, I cannot, thy suit is in vain;
For filial affections a daughter restrain,
   And worthless were she who had slighted their sway.

Some say that this was his first production. At all events, it proved so unexpected, and so captivating, that it was confidently attributed to nothing less than fairy inspiration. To this day, the country people point out the spot from which he desired to be led home. They gravely state that he once related the vision which he then beheld, but was so overcome with terror, that he entreated of his friends not to question him further on the subject; and that he could never again be prevailed upon to repeat what he had witnessed. Fear and superstition are ever ingenious to deceive themselves. Carolan's silence became confirmatory proof. He took no trouble to correct the popular reports; and, perhaps, he was not wholly uninfluenced by vanity in suffering them to remain uncontradicted.

Some of his earliest efforts were called forth in praise of

O how could'st thou trust for connubial affection
    The bosom untrue to its earliest ties?
Or where were thy bliss when on sad recollection
    I'd sink self-condemned, self-abashed from thine eyes?
Then cease thee! ah cease thee! 'tis fated we part!
Yet if sympathy soften the pang to thy heart,
I will own to this bosom far dearer thou art
    Than all that earth's treasure—earth's pleasure supplies.

But where am I urged by impetuous feeling!
    Thy tears win the secret long hid in my breast.
Farewell! and may time fling his balsam of healing
    O'er wounds that have rankled and robbed thee of rest.
Yet lose not! ah lose not each lingering thought
Of her who in early affection you sought,
And whose bosom to cheer thee would sacrifice aught
    But love to a parent the kindest and best.

How many domestic afflictions would be spared, if the youthful and unsuspecting fair were more generally influenced by the amiable sentiments expressed in the foregoing lines.

the M'Dermott Roe family. Henry, the only son of his friend and patroness, having married " Nanny," the daughter of Manus Roe O'Donnell of *Cahirnamart*, (now Westport) in the county of Mayo*, Carolan produced his fine Epithalamium, entitled, " Anne and Henry Oge." A trifling circumstance, connected with this composition, may serve to convey an idea of the importance formerly attached to these bardic effusions. Carolan, as may be seen, placed the lady's name before that of her husband. This gave great cause of umbrage, even to his kind patroness, because her daughter-in-law's family was considered inferior to her own, and the bard was excused, only on account of the politeness which he submitted was due to the sex. The issue of this marriage was a daughter, Eliza, who became the wife of Robert Maguire of Tempo, Fermanagh, a most distinguished family of the North of Ireland. For this gentleman, Carolan composed his famous " Planxty Maguire ;" Colonel Con Maguire, his brother, he celebrated in his fine song, beginning " Cuchonꭺchꞇ mhꭺc bꞃíꭺın ;" and " Bryan Maguire," their father, was another tribute to this ancient and noble race†.

---

* I have been assured, by an old *Fin-Scealuighe*, that " O'More's fair daughter," or " The Hawk of Ballyshannon," was composed for Charles O'Donnell, the brother of " Nanny," and not for O'Reilly, as stated, p. 113 of this volume. This information I find corroborated by accounts derived from the M'Dermott Roe family.

† TEMPO was the only house in the North that Carolan is said to have visited. During one of these visits, Colonel Maguire contrived that he should be conveyed to the county of Louth, where the blind bard, Mac Cuairt, then resided. They were brought together without their knowledge. Mac Cuairt was considered the better poet—Carolan the better musician. After playing for

Mrs. M'Dermott continued to reside at ALDERFORD. Her son Henry, soon after his marriage, built the house of GREYFIELD, on another part of the estate, where he lived, in the old hospitable style, for many years. Here Carolan past some of the happiest days of his life*. It is related that whenever he wished to retire from the noise and bustle of company, he generally directed his attendant to provide him with a pipe and a chair, and to lead him to the garden, where he used to remain, absorbed in thought, or modulating some of those favorite pieces, which have, ever since, been the delight of his countrymen. His presence never failed to attract visitors to Greyfield. It happened, on one occasion, that several of the neighbouring gentry, the MAGUIRES of TEMPO, O'ROURKE, MAC CONMEE, the NUGENTS of Castle Nugent, and others,

---

some time, on their harps, Carolan exclaimed, "Iſ bínn, boʒ, bɼeḋʒᴀch ᴀ ɼhınneᴀɼ ᴄu," "Your music is soft and sweet, but untrue." On which the other promptly replied, "Iſ mınıc ᴅo bhıḋheᴀn ᴀn ɼhıɼınne ɼeın ɼeᴅɼbh," "Even truth itself is sometimes bitter," alluding to his rival's performance, which, though correct, was not always sweet or pleasing to the ear. The bards soon recognized one another. On this occasion, Mac Cuairt composed the "Welcome," printed in this volume; and the excellent Northern poet, Pat Linden of the Fews, in the county of Armagh, who came up to see Carolan, wrote another pleasing poem to commemorate his visit to that part of Ireland.

* GREYFIELD House is now occupied by Hugh O'Donnell, Esq. the elder representative of the ancient chiefs of one of the most illustrious tribes of Ireland. This gentleman, who is particularly addressed as "THE O'DONNELL," is the eldest male descendant, in a direct line, from Rory, Earl of Tirconnell, brother of the celebrated "Red Hugh," who, by the talents he displayed in his struggles to emancipate his native land from the trammels of English usurpation, in the reign of Elizabeth, proved himself one of the most illustrious heroes that Ireland ever produced.

arrived when Carolan was absent. As they expected to meet the bard, a messenger was sent after him to Castlekelly, in the county of Galway, where he had just composed his fine song of " Mild Mable Kelly." On his return he called on Mr. Kelly at Cargins, near Tulsk, in the county of Roscommon, an old and hospitable friend, whom he celebrated in his " Planxty Kelly." Proceeding forward, he stopped at Mr. Stafford's, near Elphin; and the famous " Receipt for Drinking," or " Planxty Stafford," will long commemorate his affectionate reception there. On his arrival at Greyfield, he composed *Mhaire an Chulfhin,* or " Fair-haired Mary," for one of the visitors, Mary, daughter of M'Dermott, " Prince of Coolavin," and wife of Owen O'Rourke, who lived on the banks of Lough Allen, in Leitrim*. The compositions here enumerated, have been always reckoned amongst the happiest of his effusions.

Carolan imitated the Troubadours, without knowing that he did so; and, perhaps, like them, too, " feigned or fancied himself in love." His amatory verses are numerous. Some will be found in the following pages, and on them we may safely rest his claims as a poet. Although his knowledge of English was imperfect, he once ventured on a few verses to his own fine air the " Devotion," composed for a Miss Fetherstone. This was an act of poetic gallantry, as the young lady did not understand Irish. These verses, though " in bad English," are subjoined, as a literary curiosity, from an old transcript. They are sufficiently

---

* A person lately remonstrating with a descendant of this gentleman, on his extravagance, amongst other things told him that he " ought to have sense;" " Sense," replied the indignant Milesian, " know, that an O'Rourke scorns to have sense."

ludicrous, but claim the indulgence of the modern reader, as the production of a blind Irish bard, in the seventeenth century, and in a language foreign to him. Perhaps other foreigners, who attempted English composition, have not succeeded much better*.

---

* On a fair Sunday morning *devoted to be*,
Attentive to a sermon that *was ordered* for me,
I met a fresh rose on the road *by decree*,
And though mass was my notion, my devotion was *she*.
    Welcome, fair lily white and red,
    Welcome, was every word we said;
Welcome, bright angel of noble degree,
I wish you would love, and that I were with thee;
I pray don't *frown* at me with *mouth* or with *eye*—
So I told the fair maiden, with heart full of glee,
Though the mass was my notion, my devotion was *she*.

See *Vol.* ii. *p.* 411, *note.*—Although Carolan delivered himself but indifferently in English, yet he did not like to be corrected for his solecisms. Of this, a humorous instance has been handed down. A self-sufficient gentleman of the name of O'Dowd, or Dudy as it is sometimes pronounced, once objecting to his English, asked him why he attempted a language of which he knew nothing. "I know a little of it," was the reply. "If so," says the other, "can you tell me the English for *Bundoon?*" (a facetious Irish term for the seat of honor,) "Yes," said the bard, with an arch smile, "I think the *properest* English for Bundoon is *Billy Dudy*." This repartee turned the laugh against the critic, who was ever after honored with the unenviable sobriquet of *Bundoon Dudy*.

Carolan possessed strong satirical powers, but seldom exercised them. Inhospitality he never pardoned. Being once at the house of a Mr. Jonine, or Jennings, a farmer in Mayo, where he was sparingly supplied, he addressed his host in the following bitter stanza, to which many would be found to respond *Amen:*

Mo mhallacht go bráth, air an ghloine ghrána, gann,
Is go mo mearad ná rin an lámh, nár chuir a leachlán an.

As usual with most men of genius, Carolan's friends and admirers increased with his fame. Amongst the foremost of these was THEOBALD, the sixth VISCOUNT BOURKE of MAYO, celebrated in the popular song of " *Tighearna Mhaigheo*." Mr. Walker, in his Memoirs of the Irish Bards, on the authority of Charles O'Conor, has attributed the air of this excellent song to one Keenan, and the words to a person of the name of Murphy. On this authority, I have been guided in the present publication; although it is, by some, asserted that both the words and air were composed by Carolan*. Against this, however, an argument may be deduced from some passages not reconcileable with the independent spirit at all times manifested by the bard. It is certain, however, that he was a favorite with Lord Mayo, whose ancient baronial residence, near Castlebar, he frequently visited. Another noble patron of our bard was RICHARD, the ninth VISCOUNT DILLON of CASTELLO-GALLEN in Mayo, from whom he experienced the kindest attentions; and whose favors, like all others, he gratefully repaid by music and song. For his lordship, and family, Carolan composed three favorite pieces, known by the titles of " Lord Dillon," " Lady Dillon," and

---

* Mr. Walker's anonymous correspondent is circumstantial in his denial of this. But his assertion that the song " had its existence perhaps long before Carolan was born," is clearly erroneous. In the original, Lord Mayo's christian name is THEOBALD; his lady, MARY; and their children, *Theobald, Suibhan,* i. e. *Joan* or *Judith, John, Betty, and Biddy.* On consulting Lodge's Peerage, it will be found that no Viscount Mayo had a lady or children of these names, but Theobald, who was born in 1681, (when Carolan was but eleven years old,) and who died in 1741, two years after the bard. This proves that the song was not composed *before* Carolan's time. Mr. O'Conor's authority, however, ought, in my opinion, to be decisive, against his right to " *Tighearna Mhaigheo*."

"Fanny Dillon." The first, celebrates the noble and generous actions of his lordship; the second, those of his lady; and the last, the virtues and accomplishments of their daughter, the Lady Frances, a young lady of great beauty, and most amiable disposition. She was, subsequently, married to her own cousin-german, Charles Dillon, who afterwards succeeded her father in his title and estates. With these, and the other principal inhabitants of Connaught, Carolan passed his life, for he seldom stirred out of that province. He was an universal favorite amongst them; and amply has he returned their kindnesses and partiality, by celebrating the virtues, and perpetuating the names of families and individuals, who would, otherwise, have been consigned to oblivion. He generally gave his tunes and songs the names of the persons for whom they were composed[*]. The number of his musical pieces, to almost all of which he composed verses, is said to have exceeded two hundred. Several are irrecoverably lost, and of the verses not one-half is supposed to be remaining. On many of these compositions, some light may be thrown by considering them locally; and for that purpose, it will be necessary to accompany our bard through the several counties of the province.

In MAYO he spent much of his time, and his unwearied

---

[*] His compositions, which do not bear the names of individuals, have generally his own prefixed, and are known by the titles of "Carolan's Concerto," "Devotion," "Dream," "Elevation," "Farewell to Music," "Fairy Queens," "Frolick," "Lamentation," "Nightcap," "Parting of Friends," "Planxty," "Port Gordon," "Last Will and Testament," "Ramble," "Receipt," "*Siothchan ar Thus*," or "Peace at First," and "The Feast of O'Rourke." Most of these are deservedly popular.

muse paid his friends there many a grateful tribute. Besides those already mentioned, we have remaining his " Thomas Burke," " Isabel Burke," and " Planxty Burke," composed for a respectable family of that name near Castlebar; " Mr. James Betagh," and " Fanny Betagh," of Manyn; " John Moore," of Bryes; " Mrs. Costello,' " Mr. Costello," of an old family which has given name to a barony in this county*. Colonel Manus O'Donnell;" " Counsellor Dillon," " Rose Dillon," both of the noble house of Lough Glyn; " Doctor Harte;" " George Brabazon;" " Bridget O'Malley;" " Captain Higgins," a brave old soldier, well known in his day. " Mrs. Garvey," of Murisk, at the foot of the REEK, near Westport, an excellent old lady, for whom the bard composed two distinct tunes, both bearing her name. " Peggy Browne," " Mrs. Palmer," " Frank Palmer," and " Roger Palmer," members of an opulent family in Tyrawly.—In the district of GALWAY Carolan was but little acquainted. Long before his time, the natives of this " English nook," lost the old national partiality for the " charms of song," and were thus described by an indignant bard—

" Ᵹaillimh ᵹan ᵹhcobhailᵹ, iƒ reaρbh leo ρan."

---

* Mr. CANNING, late Prime Minister of England, was maternally descended from this ancient and respectable family. His mother's maiden name was COSTELLO. Her father was a younger brother, who settled in Dublin early in the last century, and engaged in the woollen trade. His accomplished daughter, afterwards Mrs. Canning, and latterly Mrs. Hunn, went on the stage; at which, the feudal pride of her friends, in Connaught, was so hurt, that they never wished even to hear the circumstance mentioned. Two of Mr. Canning's near relatives, Charles and James Costello, Esqrs. now resident in Galway, the writer of this is proud to class among his most intimate friends.

The only Galway families whom he appears to have noticed, were the old Milesian stocks of O'Daly of Dunsandle, O'Kelly of Castle-Kelly, and the Anglo-Norman baronets of Glinsk; for whom he composed his "James Daly," "Anne Daly," "Mable Kelly," "John Kelly," "Patrick Kelly," and "Sir Ulick Burke."—In SLIGO he was more conversant; and to several branches there, both of English and Irish descent, many pleasing productions of his muse were dedicated. Amongst these, are his "O'Conor Sligo," "Edward Corcoran," "Margaret Corcoran," "Nanny Cooper," "Charles Coote," "Sir Edward Crofton," "Mr. James Crofton," "Mrs. Crofton," of Longford, "Miss Crofton," "Edward Dodwell," "Maud O'Dowd," "Mrs. Fleming," "Doctor Harte," "Colonel Irwin," "Loftus Jones," "Planxty Jones," "Abigail Judge," "James Plunkett," and "Kian O'Hara," or the "Cup of O'Hara*,"

---

* He composed a few verses for John Harlow, Esq. of Ramelin, a gentleman of good fortune, and fond of amusement, who erected a "Sporting Lodge" at Temple House, which, during half the year, was resorted to by the principal gentry of the country. O'Hara, remonstrating with the bard on this composition, said—" Turlogh, you did wrong to place that *Bullocker* Harlow on a level with me." " I did so," was the reply; " but that can be easily remedied." He then supplied an additional stanza for the " Cup of O'Hara;" of which I could only obtain the following couplet:

" 'Y cṙuaʒh nach ʒlár placa bhi paiṙce aṙ mo ṙeóiʒ,
Ḱuaiṙ a chuiṙ me Ƭeon hařboe chomh aṅò le Ciaṅ oiʒ."

This satisfied the Milesian aristocrat. A description of one of John Harlow's entertainments at Temple House, by James White, a cotemporary poet, is described by Mr. Walker's anonymous correspondent, as " the *ne plus ultra* of all the subjects that the wit of man has ever devised to excite and continue the loudest peals of laughter." This production has, as yet, escaped our research.

some of which will be found in the following collection. But it was in his favorite county of ROSCOMMON, that Carolan always found and felt himself most at home, and for the natives there, particularly the old Irish, and, above all, the ancient and princely stocks of O'Conor, and M'Dermott, he poured forth some of his sweetest strains. Of these, we have the various compositions before enumerated for the M'Dermott Roe family, and also his "O'Conor Faly," "Young O'Conor Faly," "Mrs. O'Conor," "Mrs. O'Conor of Belanagare," "Denis O'Conor," or "Donagha M'Cathail oig," (his early friend,) "Doctor O'Conor," "Maurice O'Conor," "Michael O'Conor," "Planxty Conor," "Planxty Drury," "John Duignan," "Mrs. French," of the respectable house of French Park, "Robert Hawkes," "Nelly Plunket," and "Planxty Stafford," or as more generally called "Carolan's Receipt;" all of which are well known to the lovers of Irish song. To conclude with LEITRIM, there remain "Toby Peyton," "Bridget Peyton," "Molly St. George," (his father's old friend,) "Maire an Chulfhion," and others contained in the subjoined list*. One popular song, in particular,

---

* To the several compositions of our bard already enumerated, the following, produced at various times and places, are to be added:—" Doctor Delany," "Bishop of Clogher," "Catherine O'Brien," "Mary Maguire" of Fermanagh, (afterwards the bard's wife), "Madam Cole," "Lady Iveagh," wife of Brian Magennis, Viscount Iveagh, "Captain O'Kane," or O'Cahan, of a distinguished Antrim family, (a sporting Irishman, well known, in his day, by the name of *Slasher O'Kane*), "Lord Louth," Bermingham Baron of Athenry, "Lord Massareene," "Lady Massareene," "Madame Maxwell," "Miss Murphy," "John Nugent" of Colamber co. Westmeath, brother to Gracey Nugent," "Mrs. Nugent," his lady, "Phelim O'Neill," "Mrs. O'Neill," "Miss Eliza O'Neill," "Miss Mary O'Neill," "Catherine Oolaghan," (Nolan), "David

"*Cathlin Tiriall*," Carolan is said to have composed for a young lady, Miss Catherine Tyrrell, whose father resided near Mohill; and whose grandneice, a Miss Byrne, is still living near Drumsna in this county. I cannot, however, but date this fine old song long before his time. Perhaps, as other bards certainly did, he supplied words for the air, which caused the latter to be attributed to him. Many of his compositions may, doubtless, have escaped the most minute research; but sufficient are here enumerated to transmit his name, as a man of musical genius and a poet, to posterity.

It would be impossible to trace our bard through all his wanderings during a long and restless life. They were chiefly confined to Connaught, where his friends were so anxious for his society, that messengers were continually in quest of him, and he was hardly seated in one place, until he was followed by an invitation to another. Ulster he seldom went to, and then only to the Maguires of Tempo. The puritanical habits, and anti-Irish feelings of the Scotch and English settlers in the North, were but little calculated to conciliate the esteem of such a man as Carolan. In 1720 he went to Donass, in the county of Clare, the seat of Charles Massey, Dean of Limerick, who was recently married to Grace, the daughter of Sir Charles

---

Poer or Power" of Cahirered, co. Galway, " Mrs. Poer," his lady, " Planxty Reilly," " Conor O'Reilly," " Myles O'Reilly," " John O'Reilly the Active," all of the great Cavan family of that name, " Major Shanly," " Mervyn Spratt," " Mrs. Sterling," " Mrs. Waller," " Mr. Waller," " Mr. William Ward." Many curious anecdotes, connected with these, and other productions of Carolan, are necessarily omitted in this already lengthened detail.

Dillon of Lismullen, in the county of Meath. Here he was kindly entertained by his countrywoman; and his grateful muse celebrated the nuptials, by two pleasing compositions, which bear the names of " Dean Massey," and " Mrs. Massey." To this visit we are indebted for the only original portrait of Carolan now extant*. From it the engraving prefixed to this volume has been taken. It corresponds with every description we have of the bard. His countenance appears open, kind natured, and intelligent, though the " sovereign vital lamp" was for ever extinguished.

While celebrating the living, Carolan did not forget the

---

* Dean Massey wishing to retain some memorial of a man whose genius, and amiable manners, excited at once his admiration and esteem, caused this portrait to be painted by a Dutch artist, who was then in the neighbourhood. It continued in possession of the family until the death of the late General Massey, who prized it so highly, that he carried it with him wherever he went. Upon his death, in Paris, in 1780, the picture was brought back to Ireland; and, in 1809, was sold to the celebrated WALTER COX, editor and publisher of the *Irish Magazine*. Mr. Cox having afterwards presented it to THOMAS FINN, Esq. of Carlow, that excellent and patriotic gentleman kindly communicated it to the writer, who expressed a desire to have it engraved and preserved as a national relic. With that view, he caused an accurate copy to be taken, which he presented to an ingenious Dublin artist, Mr. MARTYN, on the sole condition that it should be well engraved. Mr. Martyn published his engraving in 1822, (of the same size as the original, which is painted on copper, about 8 inches by 6,) and dedicated it to the MARQUESS WELLESLEY, then Lord Lieutenant of Ireland. GEORGE PETRIE, Esq. of Dublin, whose acquaintance with the history and antiquities of this country, is, perhaps, only surpassed by his knowledge of the arts of painting and sculpture, in which he so eminently excels, thinks it probable that the original portrait was painted by VANDER HAGEN, a distinguished Dutch artist, who was, at that time, in Ireland.

dead. Some of his elegiac productions are well known, particularly those on the death of his wife, and of his friend M'Cabe*; which have been newly translated for the present work. In addition to these, we have his " *Cumhadh*," or Lamentation, for Owen Roe O'Neill, the celebrated Irish general; the " Lament," for the famous Catholic lawyer, Terence M'Donogh of Sligo; and the " Dirge on the death of Owen O'Rourke," for whose lady he had previously composed his " *Mhaire an Chulfhin*." These are favorable specimens of his talent for this species of composition. But, as he was by nature of a gay and lively turn, so he delighted more in that strain than in the sad and mournful. The few of the latter, however, which remain, display many genuine touches of natural feeling. The bard composed as he felt, and his elegiac efforts are alike creditable to his head and his heart.

But the time was now drawing nigh when Carolan was himself to become a subject for the elegiac muse. In the year 1737, his health, which had been long declining, gave

---

* The bard, M'Cabe, was the frequent companion, and humble friend, of Carolan. He was a man of some talent, well skilled in his native language, and had a tolerable knowledge of Greek, Latin, and English. He played sweetly on the harp; but as a poet, or musician, he was, to use the words of a contemporary, " what the titlark is to the cuckoo," when compared with his friend. M'Cabe was a practical humourist, and many anecdotes are related of his wit and pleasantry. He composed an Elegy on the death of Carolan, whom he outlived many years. Having obtained a license to teach, as a " Popish schoolmaster," he earned a scanty subsistence in his old age, and, finally, died in want. Similar to his, was the fate of hundreds of talented Irishmen, during the horrible period of Protestant ascendency and persecution, men who, in any other country, or under other laws, would have proved ornaments to society, and to human nature.

evident symptoms of approaching dissolution. At Tempo, finding himself growing weak, he resolved to proceed to Alderford, the house of his old and never-failing friend and patroness, Mrs. M'Dermott, who, though then nearly in her eightieth year, enjoyed excellent health and spirits. By her, in his youth, nearly fifty years before, he was supplied with his first harp and his first horse; and to her, in the decline of life and health, he turned for a sure asylum, and a kind and affectionate reception. Having composed his " Farewell," to Maguire, he proceeded on horseback to his friend Counsellor Brady's, near Balinamore, in Leitrim, where he rested for a few days. He then continued his journey, accompanied by several of the neighbouring gentry, and a concourse of the country people, among whom he was always held in the highest veneration, towards Lahire, the seat of Mr. Peyton. Here he stopped for a few moments, and, with tears, took leave of his friends. During the remainder of his journey, it is not improbable that his mind was occupied by thoughts somewhat similar to those afterwards expressed by his countryman, Goldsmith*:—

> In all my wand'rings round this world of care,
> In all my grief (and God has given my share,)
> I still had hopes, my long vexations past,
> Here to return, and die at home at last.

---

* Oliver Goldsmith was born, and until his fifteenth year resided, not far from where Carolan spent the greatest part of his life. Although but ten years old at the death of the bard, it is evident that he was well acquainted with his genius and character. This may be deduced even from the trifling Essay on " Carolan the blind," which appears in his works; and which, if really written by Goldsmith, confers no great credit on his memory. This inge-

At Alderford he was received with the warmth and welcome, which have ever characterised Irish friendship. After he had rested a little, he called for his harp. His relaxed fingers for a while wandered feebly over the strings, but soon acquiring a momentary impulse, he played his well known "Farewell to Music," in a strain of tenderness and feeling, which drew tears from the eyes of his auditory. This was his last effort. Nature was subdued; and the dying bard was carried in a state of exhaustion to his room. He lingered for some time. The woman who attended him, and who lived until about the year 1787, used to relate, that to revive or stimulate decaying nature, he was occasionally indulged with a *taste* of his favorite beverage, *Usquebaugh*. His natural vivacity, and good humour, never forsook him. A few hours before his death, while in the act of stretching forth his hand for the cup, as he humourously said, to give it his farewell kiss, he rolled out of bed on the floor. The female attendant alluded to, stated that after she had replaced him, he observed, with a smile, " Maudy, I often heard of a person falling when going to the field, but never knew one to fall while lying but myself." His last moments were spent in prayer, until he calmly breathed his last[*]. When his death was

---

nious man was descended from one of our " Clerical families," who were generally a prejudiced class; and his historical works, at least, prove that he never entirely laid aside the prejudices of early education.

[*] Carolan's death was thus recorded by his devoted friend and admirer, the venerable Charles O'Conor.—" On Saturday, 25th March, 1738, TURLOGH O'CAROLAN, the talented and principal musician of Ireland, died, and was interred in Kilronan, the church of the Duignan family, in the 68th year of his age. May the Lord

known, it is related that upwards of sixty clergymen of different denominations, a number of gentlemen from the surrounding counties, and a vast concourse of country people, assembled to pay the last mark of respect to their favorite bard. All the houses in Ballyfarnon were occupied by the former, and the people erected tents in the fields round Alderford House. The harp was heard in every direction. The wake lasted four days. On each side of the hall was placed a keg of whiskey, which was replenished as often as emptied. Old Mrs. M'Dermott herself joined the female mourners who attended, to weep, as she expressed herself, "Over her poor gentleman, the head of all Irish music." On the fifth day his remains were brought forth, and the funeral was one of the greatest that for many years had taken place in Conaught. He was interred in the M'Dermott Roe's vault, in their chapel, at the east end of the old church of Kilronan.

On opening the grave, in 1750, to receive the remains of a Catholic clergyman, whose dying request was to be interred with the bard, the scull of the latter was taken up. The Hon. Thomas Dillon, brother to John, Earl of Roscommon, caused it to be perforated a little in the forehead, and a small piece of ribbon to be inserted, in order to distinguish it from similar disinterred remnants of mortality. It was placed in a niche over the grave, where it long remained an object of veneration, several persons having

---

have mercy on his soul, for he was a moral and religious man."—See *Cat. Stow. MSS.* vol. i. p. 146, for the original Irish. Doctor O'Conor adds, "This memorandum is in the handwriting of Carolan's friend, the late Charles O'Conor of Belanagare, who ever spoke of him in terms which reflected back upon his own character, the lustre which they shed on that of the last of the Irish bards."

visited the church for the sole purpose of seeing this relic of a man, so universally admired for his musical talents. At length, in the year 1796, it disappeared. A person on horseback, and in the garb of a gentleman, but supposed to have been a northern Orangemen, came to the church, and desired to see it. It was brought from the niche, and, watching his opportunity, he discharged a loaded pistol at it, by which it was shattered to pieces*. Then, damning all Irish papists, he rode away. Some neighbouring gentlemen pursued him as far as Cashcargin, in the county of Leitrim; and from their excited feelings at the moment, it was, perhaps, fortunate that he escaped. This brutal act could be perpetrated only through the demoniac spirit of party rage which then disgraced this unhappy country.

Thus far I have endeavored to trace our national melodist and his compositions, without reference to any former printed accounts; but fear that many of the particulars detailed may be considered trifling, and possibly most of them unimportant. They possess, at least, one quality, and, perhaps, only one, to recommend them, which is that

---

* Notwithstanding this act, and although the people of Kilronan show some fragments which they assert to be those of the scull, yet it is confidently stated that it may be seen, perfect and entire, in the museum at Castlecaldwell, co. Fermanagh, having been presented to Sir John Caldwell, by the late George Nugent Reynolds, Esq., who took it privately from Kilronan for the purpose. This, however, may be doubted. Mrs. M'Namara, the sister of Mr. Reynolds, does not believe it, never having heard it mentioned in her family until lately; and thinks it must be some other pericranium which her brother, who was a facetious gentleman, imposed on the connoisseur, by way of joke, for that of Carolan. A cast of the Castlecaldwell relic is about being sent to the Phrenologists of Edinburgh; but, probably, the portrait prefixed to this volume, would prove more satisfactory to those gentlemen.

of being new to the reader. That the death of Carolan has caused a chasm in the annals of Irish song, is a fact which has been sensibly felt and deplored by his brother bards in many a heart-moving lay. When we consider the difficulties which this ingenious man had to encounter, his loss of sight, the consequent want of adequate education, and, above all, the retrograde state of society in Ireland, during the greater part of the time which he lived, he will be found entitled to no small portion of praise and admiration. As a musical genius, he is universally acknowledged to rank with the foremost of modern times. His character has been often drawn. As a poet and musician, it is well delineated in Walker's "Memoirs of Irish Bards," by that author's anonymous correspondent. But there are, in that communication, some errors, particularly respecting his moral character, which require observation. He is described as a reckless reveller, whose genius required the constant stimulus of inebriating liquors to rouse it to exertion. Now I have been assured by old people, who knew some of Carolan's contemporaries, that nothing could be more unjust or untrue than such a representation. On this head, the solemnly recorded evidence of Charles O'Conor, may be considered decisive. bu miazhalca azuy ba cpáirech, " He was moral and religious," says that venerable and virtuous man, who was long and well acquainted with him, and whose testimony is surely preferable to any anonymous information. It is not, however, pretended that he was a mere water drinker. On the contrary, he always delighted in cheerful society, and never refused the circling glass. Perhaps few individuals ever heightened " the feast of reason," or enriched it with " the flow of soul," in a greater degree, than Carolan.

To him Ireland is indebted for upholding its ancient

character for music and poetry, and the debt yet remains to be paid. In every part of the world his strains are heard and admired; and our countrymen, in foreign climes, feel justly proud of their national bard. But how has he been requited at home? His humble grave may indeed be traced; but "not a stone tells where he lies." The indignant exclamation of Johnson is not even yet applicable to us:—

> See nations slowly wise, and meanly just,
> To buried merit raise the tardy bust!

A musical commemoration of the bard was celebrated in Dublin, in 1809. It was chiefly composed of his own popular pieces, and, with the impetuosity natural to Irishmen, was held twice in the same week, but never since repeated. His fame, however, depends not on "piled stones," or musical commemorations. He lives in his own deathless strains. And we may safely predict, that as long as the charms of melody shall hold their sway over the human heart, so long will his countrymen remember and revere the name of Carolan.

MEMOIR OF THOMAS FURLONG.

SINCE the commencement of this work the writer has had to lament the death of an old and valued friend—the translator of CAROLAN'S REMAINS, and of other ancient relics, which enrich these volumes. He is here induced to lay before the reader a few particulars of the short career of that talented individual, and to those who sympathise over the fate of resident Irish genius, the brief and unpretending detail may not be wholly uninteresting. For some of these particulars he is indebted to a tribute which appeared soon after Mr. Furlong's death, in several periodical publications, from the pen of J. B. Whitty, Esq., the popular author of " Tales of Irish Life,"* and other

---

* These admirable pictures of Irish Society have been translated into French, and reprinted in America. The author's

esteemed productions. This gentleman, who was long and intimately acquainted with the poet, knew how to appreciate his merits, and was eminently qualified to do justice to his memory.

This offering of disinterested friendship is prefaced with a few pointed observations on the reproachful apathy of Irishmen towards the encouragement of native genius; and the truth of the statement cannot be controverted. "Scotsmen," says the ingenious writer, "have erected a monument to BURNS, and they celebrate the anniversary of his birth: they differ as widely in politics as my countrymen, but still they do justice to each other; every man of them considers himself honored in the fame of their literati. Alas! the case is very different in Ireland: they have erected no monument to their Carolan or their Goldsmith—their Grattan or their Curran. They have no cheering anniversary—no moral landmark, to guide or stimulate their rising genius; all is sluggish and thoughtless —a dead flat surface—an uninviting uniformity—a cheerless gloom. My heart swells with indignation at this national apathy; it looks like Irish ingratitude; there is in it an implied want of national pride—a cruel indifference to the best of all claims—those of intellect. The circumstances of the times cannot justify this; it exists still. If

---

extensive knowledge of the History and Antiquities of Ireland, and the sound philosophic views which he has taken of its situation and affairs, ancient and modern, render a history of the country, on which he is now engaged, an object of national consideration. I cannot conclude this note without acknowledging my obligations to two intimate friends of the deceased, Messieurs MICHAEL GILLIGAN and JOHN FERRALL, merchants of Dublin, for their kind and interesting communications respecting him.

you disbelieve me, go to Drumcondra church-yard, and ask the shade of Furlong. His fate singularly illustrates the foregoing remarks.*

" This 'sleepless boy, who perished in his pride,' had no claims to notice but those which genius furnished; but these were of an order which gives an immortality to his name, despite the neglect of his countrymen. He was, in the words of Ferguson, 'one of God Almighty's nobility.' He derived no intelligible dignity from his ancestors, but he reflects back upon them a kind of posthumous vitality; he rescues them from the oblivion of the grave, and bestows upon them a lustre not the less brilliant or lasting, because it is derived from reflected rays. He owes them nothing; they become in death his debtors."

"Thomas Furlong was born in the county of Wexford, and that noble portion of Ireland has also the honor of of giving birth to Thomas Moore. Furlong's father was a respectable farmer, and our poet was born in the year 1794, at a place called Scarawalsh, a romantic part of the country, midway between Ferns and Eniscorthy. His education qualified him for the counting-house; and, at fourteen, he was apprenticed to a respectable trader in the Irish metropolis. The ledger, however, had less attraction for him than the muses; but though he ' lisped in numbers,' he did not let his passion for poetry interfere with his more useful and more important duties. Through life he retained the friendship of his employer; and when that gentleman died, some years ago, he lamented his fate in a pathetic poem, entitled *The Burial.*

---

* It is but justice here to state, that a handsome monument has been recently erected by Mr. Furlong's friends to his memory. But this, I rather fear, will be considered only as a solitary exception to the general charge.

This was one of Mr. Furlong's earliest productions, and no reader of taste will be displeased at finding here the following impressive stanzas:

'Oh! if the atheist's words were true,
  If those we seek to save,
—Sink—and in sinking from our view
  Are lost beyond the grave!
If life thus closed—how dark and drear
Would this bewildered earth appear,
  Scarce worth the dust it gave.
A tract of black sepulchral gloom,
One yawning, ever-opening tomb.

' Blest be that strain of high belief,
  More heaven-like, more sublime,
Which says, that souls that part in grief,
  Part only for a time!
That far beyond this speck of pain,
Far o'er the gloomy grave's domain,
  There spreads a brighter clime,
Where care and toil, and trouble o'er,
Friends meet, and, meeting, weep no more.'

" At length he was enabled to indulge without obstruction in his love of literature. MR. JAMIESON, an eminent distiller of Dublin, and a man of enlarged and liberal views, gave him a confidential situation in his extensive concerns. Here he remained until the period of his death, and it does honor to Furlong, as well as to his worthy patron, that Mr. Jamieson wept like a child the day of his funeral."

While at school, our youthful poet produced a poem of considerable length, in blank verse, which it appears he had some intention of offering for publication: but probably not wishing to trust solely to his own judgment, and perhaps having no friend on whose opinion he could safely rely, he adopted the prudent advice of the Roman critic, and laid it aside for some years. At length, in 1815, our distinguished countryman, Thomas Moore, having visited

Dublin, the young aspirant for poetic fame embraced the opportunity. He boldly submitted his poem to the dangerous ordeal of Mr. Moore's perusal, and solicited his patronage, should he consider it worthy of publication. That gentleman expressed his opinion of this juvenile performance in the following letter:—

"I have read the poem which you did me the honor to entrust to me, and think highly of the talent and feeling with which it is written; but I should deal unfairly with you, were I to promise you much success from the publication of it. There is nothing less popular at the present day than blank verse; as some proof of which, I need not perhaps tell you (for your subject and his are somewhat similar,) that the "EXCURSION" of WORDSWORTH, one of our finest geniuses, lies unbought and unread on his publisher's shelves. If, however, notwithstanding this discouragement, it should still be your wish to try the fate of your poem in London, I shall be happy to give it all the aid and recommendation in my power. "Your's, &c.
"Mr. Furlong, &c. "THOMAS MOORE."

Notwithstanding the kind offer contained in this letter, the idea of publication was abandoned, and it is supposed the poem was committed to the flames. Mr. Moore's attestation, however, to the talent and feeling with which it was written, seems to have stimulated the author to fresh exertions, for he soon after produced the "MISANTHROPE," a poem which was published by COLBURN, LONDON, 1819. "This poem," says one of the periodical Reviewers, "is now before me, and though of a didactic nature, it abounds with beauties, and shews that, even young as the author then was, his powers of versification were of a very superior order. His epithets are chosen with great happiness and propriety, and his arguments are managed with surprising skill. In this poem there is much of GOLDSMITH's sweet simplicity, though POPE's style was evidently the model on which it was formed. The description of an occurrence at Wexford, in the rebellion of 1798, shews that our poet knew every avenue to the human heart. The blood runs cold as we read it." A second edition of the Misanthrope was published in Dublin in 1821. About that time the author printed a few stanzas, which he entitled, " Lines written in a blank page of LADY MORGAN'S 'ITALY.'" He soon after received the following letter from that highly-gifted and patriotic Irish lady, whose talents do honor to her native land.

" In acknowledging the receipt of your letter, and the very interesting little volume which accompanied it, I beg to assure you that I am sensibly alive to the approbation of minds, honest, enlightened and liberal, as that of the author of the 'Misanthrope' appears to be. Such testimonies, in favor of my intentions, at least, have always been a sufficient counterbalance to the paid scurrility of hired critics—and from whatever quarter they come, they are both precious and gratifying.—Your poem, written in the blank page of 'Italy,' has been read and admired by persons of more judgment than her whom it must naturally most interest. Feeling and writing as you do, I trust you will not neglect ' The goods the gods provide you.' I shall always be happy to hear of your literary exertions, without entertaining a doubt of their success.

"29th March, 1822,   "I am, &c.
"Kildare Street.   "SYDNEY MORGAN."

These testimonies, from the most distinguished writers of his country, must have been highly gratifying to the feelings of Mr. Furlong, and notwithstanding his natural diffidence, perhaps tended to inspire him with greater confidence in his own abilities. About this time he contributed largely to the *New Monthly Magazine,* London. In 1822 he projected the *New Irish Magazine,* printed in Dublin. In 1824 he published the " PLAGUES OF IRELAND," one of the most caustic satires that ever appeared on this side of the channel. The following year, when the *Morning Register,* a popular Dublin newspaper, was started, on the Catholic interest, Mr. Furlong wrote those inimitable parodies, which gave it a decided character; and which, having ran the rounds of the English press, were subsequently copied into the American Journals. About the same time he became a contributor to *Robins's London and Dublin Magazine*. Decidedly one of the most powerful pieces of ridicule in the English language is his poem on Daniel O'Connell, entitled, "The Leader," which appeared in that publication. When asked why he wrote those severe lines on the indefatigable patriot, who was known to admire him, and who publicly termed him " A thorn in the side of the enemy." He replied, " O'Connell is of too much value to Ireland to let him spoil himself: he must sometimes feel the rod." Though our poet did not speak in public, his pen was incessantly and powerfully employed in favor of the great question of *Emancipation*, which then agitated the country. On that subject, his writings, both in prose and verse, are numerous; and his services were considered so efficient, that on the success of the measure, his portrait was published with those of O'Connell, Shiel, Steele, Barrett, Wyse, and other leading members of the Catholic Association.

His poetical pursuits were not, however, entirely interrupted by his patriotic and political labors. During the years 1825 and 1826 he was occasionally employed on the *Doom of Derenzie*, a descriptive poem, which was published, after his death, by Robins, London, 1829. This poem was warmly eulogised by his friend and brother poet, the late Rev. Charles Maturin, with whom he had been long on habits of the closest intimacy*. It was thus spoken

---

* From among several familiar letters of this talented individual to Mr. Furlong, the following is selected for its brevity, and its allusion to the above poem :—

" Wednesday,—I trust the melancholy circumstance of my poor father's death will excuse my not writing to you lately.—I am

of in some of the London periodicals of the day. "The Doom of Derenzie was only passing through the press when the author died. The poem is of considerable length, and of a somewhat domestic character; it addresses itself to the most salutary feelings of the human heart, and possesses a power and an interest, which the most romantic fictions of the day could not communicate. The hero is a character quite new to us; neither Lady Morgan nor Mr. Banim has rendered us familiar with an Irish fairyman; and, we believe, this is the first instance in which his portrait has been given to the English public. As a mere tale, this poem possesses all the advantages of an ingenious fiction; and to this is superadded the charms of the most exquisite poetry—breathing the finest pathos and the sublimest sentiments. Mr. Furlong was a poet in the exact sense of the word: his soul seems to have glowed

---

confined with an inflammation in my eyes, for which I am undergoing a severe mercurial course; but if you can have the charity to sit with a blind invalid, come and drink tea with me this evening from seven till ten. Bring your poem with you. I write this with great difficulty. You see I have some chance of fame in being ranked with, 'Blind Thamyris and blind Mæonides,' though I confess it is the last particular in which I should wish to resemble those worthies.   "Faithfully your's,
"C. R. MATURIN."

The writer did not long survive this letter. He died with a broken heart, after having been made the dupe of a party of religious bigots in Dublin, who, with all the bitterness of sectarian zeal, prevailed on him to preach a series of shallow " Sermons against Popery," for which he was laughed at by many, and pitied by all. This bigotted coterie, from the "mitred prelate" to the bible-reading votaries of the tea-table, afterwards suffered the man of genius to die in comparative want. When Sir Walter Scott, after his arrival in Dublin, visited Mr. Maturin's widow, he burst into tears on beholding her situation. This affecting incident does honor to the feelings of that distinguished man.

with a passionate love of nature; and he painted as he felt, vividly and correctly. Were merit alone a sufficient recommendation, the 'Doom of Derenzie', we are certain, would become popular." The reviewer has given several extracts, from which he says, " Our readers will perceive how truly poetical the whole must be. The limits of these pages render it necessary to omit those passages, and refer to the poem itself, which will amply reward the perusal of every reader of taste."

Mr. Furlong's last poetical efforts were the translations of CAROLAN'S REMAINS, and other ancient poems and songs contained in this collection. When his aid was first solicited, the writer had the same difficulty with him, as with others, to prove that any productions of value were extant in the Irish language. Acquainted only with the English words associated with our native airs*, he smiled incredulously at the asserted poetical excellence of the original lyrics, and even questioned their existence.

---

* The vulgar ballads, composed in English, during the last 150 years, are a disgrace to our sweet and simple melodies, to which they have been so cruelly and unnaturally united. This trash, which modern *collectors* have dignified with the title of "National Irish Song!!!" displaced the native lyrics so effectually, that the memory of the originals was soon wholly erased in the Anglicised parts of Ireland. Mr. Furlong was, therefore, fully excusable for his literary scepticism on a point with which men of more years and experience were equally unacquainted. It is considered scarcely necessary here to state, what every reader is already aware of, that Mr. Moore's words to our "Irish Melodies," form a splendid exception to the foregoing *general* censure. "Poetry," it has been truly observed, " is the soul of melody." Hence these beautiful lyrics will command admiration to the latest posterity. Our patriotic countryman, T. Crofton Croker, Esq., is now engaged on the subject of Anglo-Irish Song. He will separate the ore from the dross; and from his talents and research, much may be expected in this department of national literature.

It was true, he admitted, that he had often heard them spoken of, and sometimes praised, but that he considered as the mere boasting of national prejudice. "If," said he, "they possess any merit, I cannot conceive how they could have remained so long unknown." After several explanations, however, and an examination of some of these neglected originals, his opinions began to change. He at length confessed that he discovered beauties of which, until then, he had been wholly unconscious; and finally entered on the undertaking, with an ardour and perseverance which continued to the hour of his death. In his translations he endeavored to express himself as he conceived the bard would have done, had he composed in English. He was "true to his sense, but truer to his fame." But as the public will now have to judge of the merit of his labors, it is not intended here to anticipate its opinions, by any premature expression of our own. On the principle, that none but a poet should attempt to translate a poet, his translations may be entitled to attention; and on them his friends are not unwilling to rest his poetical character.

A short time before Mr. Furlong's death, he attended a public dinner in Dublin, at which the health of our patriot bard, Thomas Moore, was drank with the usual enthusiasm. Mr. Furlong, having been called upon, spoke as follows:—

"It is impossible to speak of MOORE in the ordinary terms of ordinary approbation—the mere introduction of his name is calculated to excite a warmer, a livelier feeling. We admire him not merely as one of the leading spirits of our time; we esteem him not merely as the eager and impassioned advocate of general liberty—but we love him as the lover of his country. We hail him as the denouncer of her wrongs, and the fearless vindicator of her rights. What a glorious contrast does he offer to the spiritless, slavish race that have preceded him. We have had our poets, the Parnells, the Roscommons, and the Goldsmiths, distinguished and celebrated in their day; but these, Irishmen as they were, scorned even to name the ill-fated land of their birth. It remained for Moore to tread the unbeaten path, and believe it, his example will not be lost upon others. The fine mind of the nation is already unfolding itself. Irish literature is no longer unfashionable. The demand increases, and the supply is certain. There is an exuberance of talent in the country, literally a waste of genius. Justly has Ireland been called " The Land of Song," the very atmosphere is poetical—the breezes that play around us seem the very breathings of melody. The spirits of our ancient bards are looking down, inviting the youth of the soil to participate in their glory. How could Moore, when speaking of Ireland, be otherwise than poetical? how could he touch on such a subject without catching an added spirit of inspiration? Ours is, indeed, a country worth loving—worth struggling for—aye, worth dying for. Who can look on it with indifference? The land of the beautiful and the brave—the land of the minstrel, the saint, and the sage—the home of all that is lovely and endearing.—

> Green are her hills in richness glowing,
> Fair are her fields, and bright her bowers;
> Gay streamlets thro' her glens are flowing,
> The wild woods o'er her rocks are growing;
> Wide spread her lakes amidst laughing flowers,
> Oh! where's the Isle like this Isle of ours?

Such has been the source of Moore's inspiration."

On this occasion Mr. O'Connell, who presided, pronounced a glowing eulogium on the talents and patriotism of the speaker, declaring him, in his opinion, second only to the inimitable poet whom he had so eloquently described. Soon after this, Mr. Furlong's health, which had been long declining, suddenly grew worse. A general weakness pervaded his frame, accompanied with a total loss of appetite. His disorder, although he had the best medical assistance which Dublin could afford, proceeded rapidly, and, after a short confinement to his bed, he died on the 25th of July, 1827, in the thirty-third year of his age. He was interred in the churchyard of Drumcondra, in the vicinity of Dubin; and over his grave, which lies near that of the celebrated antiquarian, GROSE, his friends have erected a handsome monument, which bears this inscription :—

TO THE MEMORY OF
THOMAS FURLONG, ESQ.
in whom the purest principles of
Patriotism and Honor
were combined with
Superior Poetical Genius,
This Memorial of Friendship
is erected by those who valued and admired
His various Talents, Public Integrity,
And Private Worth.
He died 25th July, 1827, aged 33 years.
MAY HE REST IN PEACE.

The following lines were the last which issued from the pen of Mr. Furlong, written a few days before his death :—

THE SPIRIT OF IRISH SONG.

Lov'd land of the Bards and Saints! to me
There's nought so dear as thy minstrelsy;
Bright is Nature in every dress,
Rich in unborrow'd loveliness;
Winning is every shape she wears,
Winning she is in thine own sweet airs;
What to the spirit more cheering can be
   Than the lay whose ling'ring notes recal
The thoughts of the holy—the fair—the free
   Belov'd in life or deplor'd in their fall?
Fling, fling the forms of art aside,
   Dull is the ear that these forms enthral;
Let the simple songs of our sires be tried,
   They go to the heart—and the heart is all.
Give me the full responsive sigh,
The glowing cheek and the moisten'd eye;
Let these the minstrel's might attest,
And the vain and the idle—may share the rest.

PART I.

REMAINS OF CAROLAN.

It was a good old custom, observed in former days, to introduce works of learning and genius by "commendatory verses." Shakspeare, Milton, Dryden, Pope, and other exalted names have not disdained to preface their productions with these passports to fame. The rhymes of honest Andrew Marvell, beginning—

"When I behold the Poet blind, yet bold,"

yet survive, and generally precede "Paradise Lost." In imitation of this laudable custom the ensuing Ode is placed before the Remains of Carolan. It is the production of one of those men of genius with whom Ireland has at all times abounded, but who are as little known to the good people of England, or even to the would-be English of Ireland, as if they had never existed: because, "they were born Irishmen and men of genius," and wrote in a language rendered unfashionable by those acts which enjoined our ancestors to purify their "upper lippes" with steel, to enable them to "speke Englishe" with effect.—This ode in our opinion exceeds even Marvell's rhymes, and bids fair to last as long. For the present it will serve to introduce Carolan to the reader, and shew the estimation in which he was held by his cotemporaries. Envy, the old and natural infirmity of the Poetic tribe, recoiled within itself in his presence; and his praises were resounded by his brother Bards, with the undissembled homage always paid to superior genius.

Fáilte do Chearbhallán.

Séamas Mac Cuarta ró chán.

Dá mhilliún déag fáilte bhíaoibh
  O árus Mheadhbha, inghean Eochaidh,
  Go feadrann Oirghiall, glúnmhar, grínn,
  Le 'r bh'ionmhuin éuchta Choneculuinn.

Dá maireadh Conchobhar a n-Eamhain Mhacha,
  Dhur d-tupur a n-iár ní'r bh'áithreach;
  Ní pachfadh an líog-lóghmhar air ais,
  No go g-créuchtraidhe Uladh fá'n Maigneis.

Cheithre Néill Theamhra na d-treas,
  Conn agus Cormac cómhdheas,
  Ní léigfeadh an Cárrmhogall ag éin
  D'fhuil Abhaimh, acht ag Ardrígh.

WELCOME TO CAROLAN.

AN ODE, BY JAMES COURTNEY,[1]

TRANSLATED BY THOMAS FURLONG, ESQ.

Oh! millions of welcomes for thee,
Chosen bard of the fair and free,
From the mansion of Meavè[2] thou comest in pride
To where Orgial's flow'ry fields[3] spread wide.
Dear to Cuchullin, that dreaded name,
Bright and high in the rolls of fame.

If Connor still in Emania reign'd
   Brilliant would be thy cheer,
Long would the sacred gem be retain'd,
   High priz'd and precious, and dear.
All Ulster upon its beauty might gaze,
And the land be bless'd by its scattering rays.

The four Nials[4] of Tarah's embattled pile,[5]
   Con and Cormac[6] of regal birth,
Would not give up the prize, the pride of the Isle,
   To the proudest foe upon earth.
Oh! glorious and great in the tented field
Must the monarch be who might make them yield.

Cárbuncáil Teamhra na b-triach;
Maigneir Uláidh na n-beargh-sciath;
Orpheur chlainne Cathaoir ó dhear,
A's meabhair na h-Eorpa gan chómhmear.

Geall ceóil ó'n n-Apia n-oir
Go Toirbhealbhach anois do ráinic;
Prionnsa na naoi Músa rá mhear
Do sheálbhuigh air b-túr Parnassus.

Gach buine sheinneas rá a luíbheann grian,
Is bá n-áirmhínn go muir b-Toirrian;
O Thoirbhealbhach do gheibh 'na láimh,
A n-aoibhneas, a n-ór 's a n-arán.
    An t-abhrán,
Tá an t-arán 'n a láimh go bás má sheinnid le céill,
Gach rolla d'á b-tug athair na-n-grás d'Ollahamh na b-téub;
An cumadóir árd-so shárigh an chruinne le céim,
'S ba chubhaidh bho páilte bharr air bhá mhilíún déucc.

Rich jewel art thou of old Temor, of kings,
   Darling of Ulster of red red shields—[7]
Where's he who like thee can strike the strings?
   Where is the voice that such music yields?
Bard of Clan Cahir,[8] the race renown'd,
Light of our isle, and the isles around.

The prize of harmony's sent from afar,
   My Turlogh that prize is thine,
It comes from Apollo, the old world's star,
   The guide of the sacred Nine :
And each bard that wanders o'er earth and sea,
Seems proud to learn new lays from thee.

Oh! yes! from thee, thou son of the song,
   Full many a strain may they borrow,
'Tis thine in their mirth to entrance the throng,
   Or to sooth the lone heart of sorrow :
Then welcome to Orgial's flowery fields,
Thou darling of Ulster of red red shields.

Maire Maguidhir.

Cearbhallán ró chan.

Mo léun 'r mo chrádh gan mé 'r mo ghrádh,
 A n-gleanntán áluinn sléibhe;
Gan neach b'ár g-cairde bheith le fághail,
 'Ifáit air bith 'n ár n-gaobhar ann :
Ifígh na n-grás, cá níoh bhamh tráchtadh ort,
 A chiúin-bhean náireach, bhéusach ?
'S gur b'é do ghrádh-sa tá tré mo lár
 'Ifá sháighiottaibh chráidhte, ghéura !

Is moch air maidin, do ghluaireas an ainfhir,
 Agus a cúilín ag earadh léithi,
Mar rósa brithlean tá rgéimh an leinbh,
 A'r gach ball di ag teachd le chéile ;
A taébh mar an g-cnorodal, a béilín meala.
 Dár liom, budh bhinne 'ná guth téuda,
Séimh a leaca, a brághaid mar an eala,
 A'r a gruadh air bhath na g-caor-chon.

MARY MAGUIRE.[1]

BY THOMAS FURLONG.

Oh! that my love and I
From life's crowded haunts could fly
To some deep shady vale by the mountain,
Where no sound might make its way,
Save the thrush's lively lay,
And the murmur of the clear-flowing fountain;
Where no stranger should intrude
On our hallow'd solitude,
Where no kinsman's cold glance could annoy us;
Where peace and joy might shed
Blended blessings o'er our bed,
And love! love! alone still employ us.

Still sweet maiden may I see,
That I vainly talk of thee,
In vain in lost love I lie pining,
I may worship from afar,
The beauty-beaming star,
That o'er my dull pathway keeps shining;

Loime a's léun a's díoghbháil céille,
  Air bhuachaill éudtrom ró dheas,
D'iarrfadh sreidh air bith le n-a sháith chéile
  Acht sneadh fíor d'á pógadh :
Dár brígh mo bhairtidh b'fearr liom agam,
  Cailín geanamhuil, sreireamhuil,
'Ná lán na leabtha dhe stróinse caitíche
  'S ná'r bheag a díol do'n bh-fóghnadh.

But in sorrow and in pain,
Fond hope will remain,
For rarely from hope can we sever,
Unchang'd in good or ill,
One dear dream is cherish'd still,
Oh! my Mary! I must love thee for ever.

How fair appears the maid,
In her loveliness arrayed,
As she moves forth at dawn's dewy hour,
Her ringlets richly flowing,
And her cheek all gaily glowing,
Like the rose in her own blooming bower;
Oh! lonely be his life,
May his dwelling want a wife,
And his nights be long, cheerless, and dreary,
Who cold or calm could be,
With a winning one like thee,
Or for wealth could forsake thee, my Mary.

Fáinní Biadhtacha.

Ceárbhallán ró chan.

Má fiafruigtheár dhíom cá rachfad, triallfaidh mé go
  Mámionn,
Féuchain an tsapuidhe is áoibhne cáil;
Már tá'n ríogán sin Fánní, inghín dheise Ghearáilt,
Plánndá is binne, ghrinne, 's is dílse de mhnáibh :
'S é thaoileás gach barún tíre agus talamh,
  Trách nach m-bídheann 'n a n-gár go bh-fuighe fád-
    rán bár ;
Airís trách bhídheann 'n a d-taichíghe, eirghíd a g-cróibhe
  's a n-áigne
A's deir rád liom de phreib go m-bídheann rád slán.

'S í phéinic na finne, an péarla breágh leinbh,
  A's féuchadh gach duine an cár már is cóir ;
Gur 'n a h-éadain tá'n lile, geimhreadh ná gile,
  Is tá gach níbh breith buille agus báinn air an pór :
Féuchfaidh mé mo ghliocár, péir már tá m'oideár,
  Eirghím ár, 's ní dheirim níbh acht an chóir :
Líontár suás na cannáidhe, fúd fá chuairim Fánní !
  Sláinte cháiptín Ghearáilt cóibhche beidheám d'á h-ól.

FANNY BETAGH.[1]

BY THOMAS FURLONG.

My path I shall name not to any,
  All know 'tis to Mannin I steer;
I seek the bright home of fair Fanny,
  I go her gay accents to hear:
Young Fanny so gentle, so tender,
  Whose glance with enchantment is crown'd,
Whose smile, like the sun in its splendor,
  Spreads blessings and brightness around.

O Gerald! thy daughter's young beauty
  Leaves many a proud one in pain;
To praise the bright maid is my duty,
  But why do I try it in vain?
Come friends! while the moments are going,
  The joys that they bring let us share,
And drink in a bumper o'erflowing,
  To Fanny the flower of the fair.

bpigbitt cpur.

Cearbhallán pó chan.

A ṡaétcair a'ṡ a chuiṡle, na ṡṡéiṡ-ṡí chóiḃche me-ṡi,
D'ṡéiḋiṡ ṡo ḃ-tiocṡaḃh ṡṡaṡa ó Chṡíoṡḃ,
Ṡo m-beiḃhinn-ṡi aṡuṡ tu-ṡa, n-éinṡheachṡ ṡan tuiṡṡe,
Aṡuṡ nach tú ḃ'ṡaiṡ oṡnaḃh ann lar mo chṡoíḃhe:
Ní ṡéuḋaim-ṡi cobla aén oiḃhche ṡo ṡoscaiṡ,
Acht aṡ ṡmuaineaḃh oṡt-ṡa an tṡath ṡin ḃo ḃṡíḃhim;
Aṡuṡ ṡéiṡ mo bhaṡamhla 'ṡ tú an ṡéiṡín ṡuaiṡ Paṡiṡ
O bhénuṡ, aiṡ a ṡṡṡioṡaḃh ṡo bṡath an Tṡoíḃhe.

A bhṡíṡhitt bheaṡ, bheaṡ, a bhéilín meala,
Le'ṡ ṡaébhaḃh leat-ṡa ṡeaṡa chṡíche Ṡail,
'Ṡ ṡuṡ bh'éiṡeachtaíche ṡach ṡcaiṡ ḃ'a léiṡhteaṡ ḋúinn
    aiṡ ḃeiṡe
Bhénuṡ, lúnó, ḣélen a'ṡ na Ḋéiṡḃṡe an aiṡh,
A ṡṡéimh ṡúḃ 'ṡ a n-ṡlaine n-éinṡheachṡ ṡan eaṡbaḃh,
Iṡ eaṡal liom ṡo ḃeimhin ṡuṡ aḃ aṡaḃ-ṡa ta,[2]
Méuṡa caéla, ḃeaṡa iṡ tṡéiḃhtíche aṡ ṡeinneaḃh
    An ṡéiḋh-phoiṡt chliṡḃe aiṡ chaoín-chṡuit ṡhaímh.

BRIDGET CRUISE,[1]
BY THOMAS FURLONG.

Oh! turn thee to me my only love,
   Let not despair confound me,
Turn! and may blessings from above
   In life and death surround thee.
This fond heart throbs for thee alone,
   Oh! leave me not to languish,
Look on those eyes whence sleep hath flown,
   Bethink thee of my anguish;
My hopes—my thoughts—my destiny—
All dwell, all rest, sweet girl, on thee.

Young bud of beauty for ever bright,
   The proudest must bow before thee;
Source of my sorrow and my delight—
   Oh! must I in vain adore thee?
Where, where, through earth's extended round,
Where may such loveliness be found?
   Talk not of fair ones known of yore;
Speak not of Deirdre the renown'd,[3]
     She whose gay glance each minstrel hail'd;
   Nor she whom the daring Dardan bore
From her fond husband's longing arms;
Name not the dame whose fatal charms
     When weigh'd against a world prevail'd:—

Tá na céuda fear cliste, an-éclipr air meirge.

Ys̄eul é nach g-ceileann fáigh na druidhe,
Méud úb gan earbaidh, ag éagnach a leath-troim,
A ghéag óg na m-bachall m-bán agus m-buidhe :
'S í géagán na m-ban í, breágán na bh-fear í,
  Geug ag a m-bídheann taithneamh, cáil agus gnaóidh,
Mhéuduigh ar sml, agus do luíghe aduigh ar n-gean,
  A'd bhiaigh-ri le real, ó d'fág tu-ra an tír.

Tá m'intinn air meárbhall, agus m'intleacht d'á dallabh,
  Le trom-chiach le fada, ló agus d'óidhche,
'N-diaigh do bhinn-bhriathar m-blarda, na g-cruinn-
  chíocha ngeala,⁴
  Na g-craébh-fholt m-breágh, n-daichte, ir breághbha
    air bich fíob ;
Do ghrír-leaca thana, bhéurradh faóireamh do lucht
  galar,
  D'fágbhair pian mór air fhearaibh, trath de do dhíth ;
Má'r binn libh le n'aithrir, 'r í an féirín a chanaim,
  Nach aóibhinn do'n d-talamh 'n ar tharlaigh, 'r í
    brighitt.

To each some fleeting beauty might fall,
   Lovely! thrice lovely, might they be;
But the gifts and graces of each and all
   Are mingled sweet maid in thee!

How the entranc'd ear all fondly lingers,
   On the turns of thy thrilling song;
How brightens each eye as thy fair white fingers
   O'er the chords fly lightly along:
The noble, the learn'd, the ag'd, the vain,
Gaze on the songstress and bless the strain.
How winning, dear girl, is thine air,
How glossy thy golden hair:
Oh! lov'd one come back again,
   With thy train of adorers about thee,—
Oh! come, for in grief and in gloom we remain,
   Life is not life without thee.

My memory wanders! my thoughts have stray'd—
   My gath'ring sorrows oppress me;
Oh! look on thy victim, bright peerless maid,
   Say one kind word to bless me.
Why! why on thy beauty must I dwell,
When each tortur'd heart knows its power too well;
Or why will I say that favor'd and bless'd
   Must be the proud land that bore thee?—
Oh! dull is the eye! and cold is the breast
   That remains unmov'd before thee.

Leiġioṡ ġaċ ġalaṅ aṅ t-uirciḋe.

Sul fá n'eirġiḋh tú air maidin bioḋh do ḃeár-láṁh uait ríṅte,
Mar a ḃ-fáġh tu do ḃuiḃéal de'n ḃiotáile ḃpríoġṁháir;
Sul fá n-déanaiḋh tú do ċoirreaġaḋh cuir ġraiḋeóġ fá do ċpríoḃhe ḃhe,
Má'r maiċh leat 'r a' t-ráoġhal-ro ḃheiċh buan, fulláin, beóḋh,
Eirġiḋh ġo tápaiḋh aġur fáiġ oṁt do ḃhfírtiḋh,
Ná fán le do ḃheappaḋh, do ġhlanaḋh nó do ċíopaḋh,
Nó ġo ġ-cuiriḋh tú boġ-ċhappaing fá do rġáirteaċh' 'r do ṗhioḃán
De'n n-Uirċiḋhe mar Ṅeatar, do ċhoiġġear ġaċ ioċa,
A'r ó mhaidin ġo h-oiḋhche cuirṁeat ceileaḃháir a'd ġhlóir.

Ir iorṁláinte an t-uirċiḋhe léiġheárar aġur rhlánuiġheár
Ġaċ tinnear aġur aicid ḋ'á leanann riol Aḃháṁh ;

WHISKEY IS THE POTION THAT CAN CURE EVERY ILL.[1]

BY THOMAS FURLONG.

At the dawning of the morn, ere you start from the bed,
Try and clear away the vapours which the night has shed,
  If drowsy or if dull,
  At the bottle take a pull,
And comfort thro' your bosom the gay draught shall spread:
  Moist'ning, cheering, life-endearing,
  Humour-lending, mirth-extending—
Be the whiskey ever near thee thro' the day and the night;
  'Tis the cordial for all ages,
  Each evil it assuages
  And to bards, and saints, and sages
    Gives joy, life, and light.

Oh! whiskey is the potion that can cure every ill,
'Tis the charm that can work beyond the doctor's skill;
  If sad, or sick, or sore,
  Take a bumper brimming o'er,
And sprightliness and jollity shall bless thee still:

Ní'l ursaid le dochtúir nó le poitecéirídhe gallda,
Acht ól lán gála dhe gach maidin a'r gach oidhche.
An biotáile beandurghthe do choirpic Ncomh Pátruice,
Ná cuiridh é g-comprád le fíontaibh na Fráinne,
Le burgundíbhe na Fráince, nó hoc na n-Almáinne,
Le plum nó le h-Appác do tháinic thar sáile,
O'r ocaid mhór báir iad do loirgeas ár g-croidhe.

Má tá maill amháire ort nó durrán ann do chluasaibh,
Coilic ann do gháile nó greas-lorgadh ruail ort,
Gút ann do chorsaibh nó arrang ann do ghualnibh,
Ól naoi n-uaire deoch Uircíbhe 'r an ló.
Glanraidh do rorg, beidhir argeantach, úr-chroidheach,
Meanmnach, clirce 'r ní chuirridh ruacht ort,
Ann rin gheabhair codla, rocarracht a'r ruaimhneas,
Ní tháobhrfaidh tú aicíd, tinneas nà buaidhreadh,
Go m-beidh tú deich n-uaire chomh rean leir an g-ceódh.

Still seducing, glee-producing,
Love-inspiring, valor-firing—
'Tis the nectar of the Gods—it is the drink divine;
Let no travell'd dunce again,
Praise the wines of France or Spain,
What is claret or champagne?—
Be the whiskey mine.

Oh! bright will be your pleasures, and your days will be long,
Your spirits ever lively, and your frame still strong;
Your eyes with joy shall laugh,
If heartily you quaff,
Of the liquor dear and cheering to the child of song:
Gout-dispelling, cholic-quelling,
Agues-crushing, murmurs hushing,—
To the limbs all old and feeble it will youth restore;
And the weak one who complains,
Of his weary aches and pains,
If the bottle well he drains,
Shall be sick no more.

Pliuingsrtigh an stafaroaich.

Cearbhallán ró chan.

Má's tinn nó slán do chárlaibhear séin,
  Ghluaiseas tráth 's do b'feárr-de mé,
Air cuairt chum t-Seóin chum rócamháil b'fazháil,
  An Stararoach breágh, sárda nach znách zan chéill :
A's a b-tácá án mheóbhán-oíbhche do bhíobh rinn ag ól,
  Agus air maidin árís án cóirbiál ;
'S é mheas sé ó mhéinn mhaith zur bh'é rúd an gléus
  Le Cearbhallán caoch do bheóbhúghádh :
    Seal air meirge, seal air buile,
    Fleubábh téud 's ag dul air mire,
An fáisiun sin do chleachtamáir ní tgársám leis go
  deóigh !
Deirim árís é, agus innrim do'n b-tír é,
Má's maith libh do bheith sáoigh'lach bíbhíbh choíbhche
  ag ól.

PLANXTY STAFFORD.[1]

BY THOMAS FURLONG.

When in sickness or in sorrow I have chanc'd to be,
My hopes my dear Stafford were plac'd in thee,
    For thy friendly care and skill,
    And thy drink more cheering still,
Left the jolly-hearted bard from each evil free:
At midnight all merrily our cups went round;
Our joys in the morning the gay cordial crown'd;
    For the past had plainly shewn,
    That in this, and this alone,
Old Turlough unfailingly true comfort found:
        Drinking, drinking,
        Never thinking,
        Roaring, raking,
        Harpstrings breaking,—
Oh! this is my delight—'tis the life for me;
    Then let glasses overflowing,
    Still o'er the board keep going,
    Bright gleams of bliss bestowing
              On the sons of glee.

Go m-budh fada, buan-ṡhaoġ'lach do bheiḋheas tú beóḋh,
  A aén-mheic Ṡheóin mheic Thomáis bháin,
Spalpaire an úr-chroíḋhe d'ḟillfeaḋh air an t-súgraḋh,
  'S go bh-fuil na chúig chóige lán de do ġráḋh :
    Fear is ġrinne a g-céill s'a d-tuigsin,
    Chuirfeaḋh na cléir go léir air meirge ;
Deir sé gur b'é mo liaigheas anois leanmhuin de go deóiġh :
  Is follusach do'n t-saóġheal, go d-teannfainn le'm
    chroíḋhe é,
An Stárardach breaġh siansamhuil, ó 's é mhiann bheith
  choíḋhche ag ól.

Oh! many joyous years may my friend still see,
This—this my fond pray'r to the last must be;
  Let the country all around
  With my Stafford's praise resound,
As the lover of wild merriment and harmony:
    Filling, quaffing,
    Joking, laughing,
    Ever pleasing,
    Never teazing,
Still plying the gay bard with the song-fraught wine;
   Oh! Stafford dear thou art,
   To this old but honest heart,
   Aye! its fondest, warmest part
      Throbs for thee and thine.

Éadbhart O'Corcrain.
Cearbhallán ró chan.

Nach é Eadbhart O'Corcrain an furránach glégheal,
  An leómhan breagh, roineanda, roilbhir, céillidhe?
De'n n-uairle ghrinne do geineadh ó ghaedhlaibh;
  A'r nach raoitheamhuil, cuideachtamhuil, oineachamhuil tréidheach é?
Air a chuairt chum na h-áite beidh báire air gach machaire,
  Olam a shláinte, grádh mo chroidhe an preabaire;
Cá bh-fuil fear a bhárrtha ó'n n-Gráinrigh go Gaileng?
  Béurfar gleóidh do na páirtidhibh agus árus do shean-daoinibh—hóm bó!

Beidh againn tróirt, feóil agus beatha-uisge,
  Airgiod, ór agus dóbracha ceapairidhe,
Gin, rum, fion, pórter agus córg air n-áicidhidhe;
  Beidh téuda b'á n-dóighthcheadh, 's ní bheidh brón chóidhche fearóa orrainn:
'S nach é Eadbhart an tréan-fhear budh tréidhíche bhídh luimneach;
  Ceannfuirt gach péidhtich, ré b'feuchfadh a g-cómhrac iad;
A shamhuil ní'l a'n-Eirinn, a't dá n-déurfainn-ri a Fasgan,
  Agus cómhdeachán Dé leis an déagh-mhac fin hannruidhe.

EDWARD O'CORCORAN.[1]

BY THOMAS FURLONG.

O, Corcoran, thy fame be it mine to proclaim,
    All meet thee, all see thee delighted!
As the bards tell the tale, thou hast sprung from the Gael,[2]
    A race that should never be slighted:
On thy dear native plain we behold thee again,
    And thy coming is cheering to many;
For from Gallen to Grange,[3] tho' we turn and we range,
    We will find thee unequalled by any.

What crowds shall resort, to our feasts and our sport,
    The silver and gold shall be flowing,
And the heart-cheering wine, that liquor divine,
    In bumpers around shall be going;
Our harps they shall ring, and our minstrels shall sing,
    For the hero of Limerick[4] is near us,—
Search the nations around, and his like won't be found,
    Heaven bless him and spare him to cheer us!

Seón hArt.

Cearbhallán ró chan.

Páchpaidh me-ri ruar an uair ro gan bhréig,
  Mar a bh-fuil an ragaipt geanamhuil, bappamhuil de
    uairlibh gaodhal,
Fear le g-claoidhteap tapt, fear le tgaoilteap gappaidhe,
A'r air Sheaghan O'hairt uadh cheart do labhpam
    féin :
Fear de'n n-aicme rcaipeadh fion go péidh,
  Agus painnreadh é go ffar le mac an cheóil 'r an
    léighinn ;
Dá m-beidhinn 'r an Róimh mar b'ait liom, 'r go m-biadh
    mo bhóta inghlactha,
Ir fior go n-déanfainn Carbog mór dhíot féin.

Stiobhard ceart do mhac na glóire é féin,
  Go m-budh buan é bh-fad, ir mac de'n n-órd é go léir ;

DOCTOR HARTE.[1]

BY THOMAS FURLONG.

In this hour of my joy let me turn to the road,
    To the pious one's home let me steer ;
Aye ! my steps shall instinctively seek that abode,
    Where plenty and pleasure appear.
Dear Harte with the learned thou art gentle and kind,
    With the bard thou art open and free,
And the smiling and sad in each mood of the mind,
    Find a brother's fond spirit in thee.

To the lords of the land we can trace back thy name.
    But a title all bright is thine own,
No lives have been lavish'd to prop up thy fame,
    For it rests on calm goodness alone.
Could they deign in old Rome my fond suffrage to hear,
    To that spot for thy sake should I roam ;
And high in the conclave thy name should appear,
    Known, honour'd, and lov'd as at home.

Ní'l-son beán ná leánbh áir eárbáidh teágáis
  Nách n-déánfádh reánmhóir mhór dóibh le céill,
Agus láigheás de phreáb áir áicid, glórthá á bhéil;
A pléáróid bheás is máith do bhótá thoil uí Néill,
Ní'l-son uáir ná tráth d'á bh-fáighinn uáim áir chách,
  Nách n-ólfáinn suás gán sráf do shláinte bhreágh,
  shéimh.

To thy master in heaven a true steward art thou,[2]
    From thy lips his high mandates we hear;
And the young and the aged submissively bow,
    When thy voice comes in peace on the ear.
Oh! good is thy fame in the land of O'Neill,[3]
    Kind heir of the race that is pass'd,
Let others, when drinking, still falter or fail,
    I'll pledge thee, dear Harte, to the last.[4]

Laoidh Uí Mhórdha,

do

Seabhac bheal-aith-Seannaigh.

Cearbhallán ró chan.

Súd í seirín deágh-bhan n-áilne,
  Uadh Chonchúbhar O'Plaghallaigh go Sléibhtibh
    Mháille,
An písh-bhean óg is millse póg,
  Is air mghean uí Mhórdha thráchtaim:—
Gáel na písh-pheár láidir,
  Is fáide léigseadh cíos air cáirde,
A phlannda an t-séin 's na g-craébh-pholt n-dáithte,
  Is tú do luadhaim a'm pháibhtibh.
Is truagh gan mé agus géug na bh-páinneadha,
  Air oileán na g-caér 's gan aén neach lámh linn,
Acht sinne bheith ag ól ó oidhche go ló,
  'S ag seinneadh go reólta air chláirsich

O'MORE'S FAIR DAUGHTER;
OR,
THE HAWK OF BALLYSHANNON.
AN ODE,[1]—BY THOMAS FURLONG.

Flower of the young and fair,
   'Tis joy to gaze on thee;
Pride of the gay green hills of Maile,
Bright daughter of the princely Gael,
   What words thy beauty can declare?
   What eye unmov'd thy loveliness can see?
Fond object of the wand'rer's praise,
Source of the poet's love-fraught lays,
   Theme of the minstrel's song,
Child of the old renown'd O'More,
   What charms to thee belong!
Happy is he who wafts thee o'er
     To yon green isle where berries grow—
Happy is he who there retir'd,
   Can rest him by thy side,
Marking with love's delicious frenzy fir'd
     Thy young cheek's changing glow,
And all the melting meaning of thine eyes;
While round and round him far and wide,
On the shore, and o'er the tide,
   Soft strains of music rise,

Áen do bheith agam-sa 'n a Táibhleis,

A's gan ceád aici an oiread sin do chásadh,

Acht bain agus cup fíos go miannmhar, maiseach,

Gan chomhrác, gan ghrusaim, gan náire.

Nach aoibhinn do'n t-é úd d'fheudsadh a mealladh,

Geug na m-bachall bh-fáinneach,

Siúr na ríogh a ríos ó Theamhair,

Do síolruigh ó Chonall Cearnach;—

Molaim thú féin fá'n péim sin do ghlacais,

A bhéigh-inghín chársaidh Mhánuis,

'S tú seabhac na h-Eirne a's bheal-áith-seanncaigh,

Agus miann gach miann tar mhnáibh tú;

Tá a réimh-chúm gléigeal air ghnéidh na h-ealá,

Air chuan na mealá ag snámhadh,

'S a carinn-phoilt chraébhach' síos go talamh,

Ag filleadh 's a carsadh go fáinneach,

A súil mar dhrúcht 's a gnuadh breagh, cailce

Mar bhénus ag teacht ó'n n-dáimh-thóinn;—

'S é shaoilim féin gur b'í péulc na maidne,

A's go m-bidheann gach duine a n-grádh léi.

Varying thro' each winning measure,
Soothing every sense to pleasure,
Wild intense delight imparting,
Pain-touch'd rapture, sweet tho' smarting;
He to whom such joy is given,
Hath, while here, his share of Heaven.

 Happy is he who hath gain'd thy love,
  Happy is he who hath won thee;
 Thy princely sires look from above,
  And smile in their pride upon thee:
The race of Tarah, the men of name,
First in the gory fields of fame.
Oh! fair one! wherever thou art,
There is light for the eyes and balm for the heart;
The desire of desires, the essence of all,
That can torture, or soften, or soothe, or enthrall.
Thy step is life and lightness,
And thy glance hath a thrilling brightness;
 Thy waist is straight and slender,
  And thy bosom gently swelling,
Outdoes the swan's in whiteness,
 When she starts from her tranquil dwelling,
 And breasts the broad lake in splendor.
Sweet girl these locks so wildly curl'd
 Have snares and spells for many;
Oh! far may we range thro' this weary world,
 And find thee unmatch'd by any.

Tá reabhac na h-Éirne a n-éinḟheacht linne,
　Go céillíḋe, garta, rárta,
Aruamh go fóil nach beapnaiḋ circe,
　Acht ag bronnaḋ óir 'n a ṁáṁaibh;
Tá a rúil mar ḋrúcht go nuaḋ ar lile,
　'S a gnúis mar clóḋ-ṁín Ṗápptair
Aṁáre 'n a ḋeóiġ ní ḃearnaiḋ ri-re,
　Acht buan ag brortúġaḋ cáil' ṁáith';
Tá cuach ḃeinn'-Éadair ag éalóġaḋ linne,
　Síos go ḃeal-áth-reannáiġ,
Agus reaḃac na h-Éirne ag triall ar g-coinne,
　Mar rún ṁiliṡ ḃeach na béaltoine;
A chiúin-ḃean ḃéurach, réiṁḣíḋe, ṡocáir,
　Uaḋ ó' aiṡdeár thug cumann agus áilne,
Ní ḟuil éan ar chraéḃ iṡ caoine binneaṡ,
　Ioná cuach a b-teár do ḃáil-ri.

Art thou a thing of earth,
 A maid of terrestrial birth ;
Or a vision sent from on high
 In peerless beauty beaming—
Like those shapes that pass o'er the poet's eye,
 When he lies all idly dreaming.

Rejoice ! rejoice ! with harp and voice,
 For the hawk of Erne is near us ;[4]
She comes with a smile our cares to beguile,
 She comes with a glance to cheer us :
Not lov'd and lovely alone is she,
But bounteous as high-born dames should be.
On she moves while the eyes of all,
Hail the ground where her footsteps fall ;
 Sweet are her tones as the treasur'd store,
  Which the weary, weary bee
 Culls from the flowers he lingers o'er;
  When he wanders far and free ;
Sweeter far than the cuckoo's lay,
That rings on the ear on a summer's day :
 But come, let this the rest declare,
  In this bumper flowing o'er,
 We pledge the fairest of all the fair—
  The daughter of old O'More.

Feidhlim ua Néill.

Cearbhallán ró chan.

Gluaisfidh mise feasda, fusar ann san n-aisdear,
  Nach air Fheidhlim ua Néill bheurfaidh mé an
    chuairt,
An t-óig-fhear de'n bh-fréimh, b'ar chóir do bheith ccéim,
  Sud é mo sgéul agus ní náire liom a luadhadh:
Sgafart geanamhuil, bárramhuil, cráidhbheach, suairc,
  Nach léigfeadh neach b'ár cheart d'á cháirde uile
    uaidh;
Líontar suas na sgálaidhe, 'nois dár liom is fearr iad,
  Léigidh chugat an t-sláinte úd Fhéidhlime uí Fluadh.

Ní'l tróst air an d-talamh nach bho-san budh duál;
Péir már bhíodh air buile 's a dáimh chuige ghluaif,

PHELIM O'NEILL.

BY THOMAS FURLONG.

At length thy bard is steering,
  To find thy gay hearth again ;
Thy hand, thy voice so cheering,
  Still soothes him in grief or pain :
Thy sires have shone in story,
  Their fame with friendly pride we hail ;
But a milder, gentler glory
  Is thine—my belov'd O'Neill !

Still cheerful have I found thee,
  All changeless in word or tone,
Still free when friends were round thee,
  And free with thy bard alone :—
Fill up the bowls—be drinking—
  'Tis cheering still woe or weal ;
Come pledge with lips unshrinking,
  The dear—the belov'd O'Neill !

Ceól, póit, agus aiteas, a'r gártha rúain,
'Y gach órd 'n a reólta teacht 'n a bhail gach uair,

* * * * * *

* * * * * *

Léigim dho-ran fearda, ir leór damh ṁn do theardas,
Nach é Feidhlim óg an fear a ta mé luadhadh.

Of blameless joy the centre,
  Thy home thro' each night hath been,
There might the wanderer enter,
  And there the blind bard was seen:
There wit and sport came blended,
  In careless song or merry tale;
But let my praise be ended—
  Who loves not my lov'd O'Neill.

pianngstighe peaton.

Cearbhallán pó chan.

Lámh leir an g-Céir tá an pollaire fárta,
Tubóid óg Péaton ir ré tá mé pádh,
　Ir uaral 'r ir raoitheamhail,
　Ir gruagach 'r ir gnaoidheamhail,
'S ní léigpeadh ré a mharladh air cáirde.

Go m-budh buan é 'gur raoghlach 'n a rhláinte,
O fuair re buadh air a námhaid,
　'S a rciúradh, 'g a ngreadadh,
　'S a m-bualadh, 'g a larcadh,
Má'r cloidheamh no bata 'n a lámhaibh.

Bráinaich 'g a g-ciopadh, do ló agur d'oidhche,
A'r bhainpeadh ar phoic dhiomarach léimneach,
　Na céuda rópd fiona
　Dá n-ólpadh na raoithe,
'S é Tubóid óg Péaton do dhiolpadh.

PLANXTY PEYTON.[1]

BY THOMAS FURLONG.

Let our Peyton's health go round, my boys,
For him be our bumpers crown'd, my boys,
    Who has horsewhip and sword,
    Or a cellar well stor'd,
When the foe or the friend can be found, my boys:
For Toby's the soul of sport, my boys,
His home is our gayest resort, by boys,
    Where the toasts fly round,
    And all care is drown'd,
In brimmers of sparkling port, my boys.

Then joy to Keash-Corran's lord, my boys,
Still sharp and bright be his sword, my boys;
    And thro' life as he goes,
    May each hour that flows,
New feelings of pleasure afford, my boys:
On his steed may he swiftly steer, my boys,
When the upstart Saxon is near, my boys;
    And often and long,
    Amidst jest and song,
May we gather to taste of his cheer, my boys,

Madam Crofton.

Cearbhallán ró chan.

Is miann liom trachtadh air óig-mhnaoi,
 Agus dar liom féin gur chóir sin,
Madam Crofton shúgach, gheanamhuil,
 Bean le'r bh'ionmhuin ceól.

'S í do líonfadh an dram damh
 Gach oidhche, gach uair a's gach am ceart,
Leanbh beas na g-cam-bhlaoibh
 Is uaisle 'gus is ceannsa cáil.

Mar tá, betíbhe shéimh na g-creébh-sholt n-daithte,
 Is geal a píob 's a brághaid bhil,
Is deas a béud, réimh aleaca, 's é béarrfaibh ról Eabha,
 Gur binn, beacht, grinn, ceart chanaibh sí gach ceól.

MADAM CROFTON,[1]

BY THOMAS FURLONG.

With delight may I praise a fair dame that is dear
To the lovers of music, of mirth, and good cheer;
'Tis my joy in each change the fond theme to renew,
From thy bard, lovely Crofton, this tribute is due,
           This tribute is due.

Sweet dame of the brilliant and soft curl'd tresses,
Whose hand with the goblet thy minstrel still blesses;
Young, gentle, and generous, and sprightly, and kind,
All faultless in person, and spotless in mind,
           And spotless in mind.

How blooming thy cheek, thy young bosom how fair,
How rich the long locks of thy beautiful hair;
That neck so proportion'd, so snowy in hue,
And the smile that each spirit can soothe or subdue,
           Can soothe or subdue.

Cailín báidheach, cráidhbheach, clúiteach,
 bean le'r bh-feárr-de cáirde rhúgach;
Ní bh-fuighe áen-neach bár de'n d-tárr
 bheidheár a chóidhche 'g a cóir.

Uch! is fíor gur náemhtha an duine,
 Fuair mar chéile í-rí,
'S an tráth bheidheár betídhe gheanámhuil fínte air leabá
 Rábháil de air an gcúplá t-réimh gach óidhche a's gach lá.

May the gay lovely Bessy still sit by thy side,
May thy spouse ever smile on his beautiful bride
As a friend ever dear, ever lov'd as a wife:
Oh! pure be thy pleasures, and long be thy life,
     And long be thy life.

Marbhairiad ṅ-i Ċorcaraiġ.

Cearbhallán ró chán.

Ṅach aoibhinn do'n tsársaire bheidheár 'ġ a meallaḋ,
Plannda leinbh na mín-chroḃ m-bán;
'S í ġráḋ a'r sṗéis do'n n-uaisle ġhrinne, cailín suairc na ġruaiġe finne,
Sud é mar deirim, aġus nach air is miann liom tráċt?
Ós m-biaḋ an péim-ro linn aġ Ġaoḃlaibh mar buḋh chleaċtaċ,
Ṅí ṗéadamaoid codla d'oiḋche ná do lá,
A ṡúil bhreaġh, mhóḋ'mhail, mhór na maire, bhéilin cheólmhair, oide ġach tuiġsi,
Pheġiḃe ḋear na b-péarlaḋa, séun ort aġus áġ!

A chúmhail na b-prionnsa Sráinneach, lúb na d-tuillis bh-ráinneach,
Moch líontar fíon dúinn, aġus bioḋmaoid-ne choiḋche a sláinte 'ġ a h-ól;

PEGGY CORCORAN.[1]

BY THOMAS FURLONG.

How happy the youth who can win the soft smile
    Of Peggy the gentle, the lovely, the young,
The life of each circle, the light of the Isle,
    The joy-beaming star of whom minstrels have sung.
Tho' the Gael in their glory should start up again,
    To strike the proud soul of the foeman with fear;
The chieftains, unheeded, might wait for a strain,
    If Peggy, sweet Peggy, the charmer were near.

The nobles of Spain have been seen at her side,[2]
    They have paus'd in delight on her beauty to gaze—
But come, fill the wine, be the goblet supplied,
    And each string that I touch shall ring loud in her praise.

Ṅach meanra do'р cinneaḋh an t-áileacán leinbh,
 Fuair bárr rgéimh' na cruinne, nach í ir coimрiaráiche cáil?
Craébh an áigh agur í ra bhláith uile, grruaḋh gan ſmál
 'r í ir ſinne, grunne,
A lúb an t-réin, a phláir na n-Gaoḃal, a'r a n-uairle,
 céile a ccuímhneaḋh!
Ṅach rin prionnraḋha ar gach péigiúin, a g-campa le chéile,
 Faoí'n airḟip gheal, rhéimh n-í Chorcaráin?

Young branch of prosperity, blossom of bliss,
 Bright cheek without blemish, fair form without fault,
If thy bard hath one task that is dear, it is this—
 To name thee, to praise thee, sweet girl, as he ought.

Seón Ó Neas.

Cearbhallán ró chan.

Oig-bhean mhín, róir orm bídeann, róil, na rcóil, óch! mo chur de'n t-ráeghal,

Ir leór liom mar tаóim crearpalta ag an m-bár,

Nach mé tá gonta, greadtha ag rearcabh.

Ag ráigheadaibh de do ghrábh :—

O rinne tú an feall, agus nach d-tiucrabh tú liom,

Mar dúbhrar leat air maidin, ríor rá'n n-gleann,

Rcaóibh bhuan-mhallacht rcaóilim leat-ra go deacrach,

Agus ní ní mhairreab, ir mé Seón Ióner.

Oig-ghair na n-dlaóibh n-ór-chartа, m-buíbhe,

Ir brónach a taóim a'r toitear, díothach gan bhrígh

Mar bhíbhear gach uile bhuime ar eólar na rlíghe,

Nach me tá moladh cruitneacht' ór-bhuíbhe an ríghe;

JOHN JONES.[1]

BY THOMAS FURLONG.

Oh! fair one relieve me—come! pity my pain,
   'Tis thine to restore me, then fix not my doom;
Struck, tortur'd, and wounded, I mourn here in vain,
   For helpless despondency points to the tomb.
Oh! think of thy promise—but promises fail—
   Yet if one gentle feeling thy bosom still owns,
Bring back the sweet moments we spent in the vale;
   Restore them! or death is the choice of John Jones.

'Dear maid of the brilliant rich ringletted tresses,
   How gloomy each scene in thy absence appears;
Thy presence no more the fond wanderer blesses,
   No more thy soft voice he exultingly hears.

Tá tú binn, fúgach, geanamhail, grinn,
  Múinte, maiseach, pathamhail, maérbha dar liom,
Is tú miann gach maire, is tú piar gach flatha,
  A pígh-bhean, is leat an t-úbhall gan painn.

Dar an dómhnaich, má ghníbhis, biab-sa go bráth,
  A g-cómhgar na fúighe mar a m-bíbheann an corman sán,
Mo luíbhe, mo shuíbhe, mo sheasamh, ag éisteacht na n-ánb,
Fáire! fáire! fút, a mhaíghbean bhán,
'S go m-béibhinn-si trí óibche ag ól fínte air stól,
Chúghab tagaim óch! go mín no go mall,
Agus nach aoíbhinn an fháill,
  A shiúr, pachsainn leat a nún tar an b-toinn.

Thy charms, the charms of all others outshine,
  They might touch the proud bosoms of kings on their
    thrones :
Oh ! lov'd one, the world of beauty is thine,
  Thou hast humbled and broken the heart of John Jones.

Yet fairest depart not, I still shall pursue thee,
  Like echo attending the voice whence it grows ;
At dawn, and at dusk, I will watch thee and woo thee,
  Nor rest in the moment that brings thee repose.
In crowds and in loneliness still I'll be near thee,
  For still this fond heart thy supremacy owns ;
In silence and absence I'll think that I hear thee,
  Then dearest come, come, to thy lover John Jones.

Gráinne Mhaolṡiún.

Cearbhallán ró chan.

Is miann leam tráchtadh air bhláith na finne,
Gráḋaim an ainnṡir is rúgáiche,
'S gur b'í rug báirr a g-cáil 'r a d-tuigsin
Air mhnáibh breágha, glice na g-cúigeadh:
 Cia b'é bhiadh na h-aice d'oidhche 'r de ló,
 Ní baeghal do fad-ṫuirse choidhche na brón,
 Aṫ an fiogḣán t-séimh is aoibhne méinn,
 'S í cúl na g-craébh 'r na bh-fainneadha.

A taébh mar áel, 's a píob mar ghéis,
'S a gnáoí mar ghréin an t-sámhraidh,
Nach tarcaidh bho'n t-é d'ár geallaḋ mar spréidh
Bheith aici-si, geug na g-cam-ḃlaoidh:
 Is ruaire 's is rámh do ráidhte geanamhuil,
 Is áluinn, deas do ṡúil ghlas,
 'S é chluinim gach lá ag each 'g a aithris,
 Gur fáinneach, cas do chúl tais,

GRACEY NUGENT.[1]

BY THOMAS FURLONG.

Oh! joy to the blossom of white-bosom'd maids,
    To the girl whose young glance is endearing,
Whose smile, like enchantment, each circle pervades,
    She who makes even loneliness cheering.
Oh! he that beholds thee by night or day,
    He who sees thee in beauty before him,
Tho' stricken and spell-bound may smile and say,
    That he blesses the charm that's o'er him

Her neck is like snow—rich and curling her hair,
    Her looks like the sun when declining;
Oh! happy is he who may gaze on the fair,
    While her white arms round him are twining:
Her words are all joyous—and mildly the while
    Her soft blue eyes seem glancing;
And her varying blush and dimpled smile,
    With those eyes and tones are entrancing.

Sud mar a deirim leis an óig-mhnaói t-séimh,
bh-fuil a glór ní 'r binne 'ná ceól na n-éun,
Ní'l ranr ná sneann d'ár smuáinigh ceann,
Nách bh-fághthár go cinnte as Grásr.

A lúb na féud, is bláith-bheár deúd,
A chúil na g-craébh 's na bh-fáinneadha,
Gidh ionmhuin liom féin thú, scádaim de'n rgeúl;—
Achd d'ólfainn gán bhréig do shláinte.

Then joy to young Gracey, the gentle dame,
   'Tis bliss on one's pathway to meet her;
Where! where's the proud spirit her voice cannot tame?
   Oh! where is the sound can be sweeter?
'Tis soothing the song of the birds to hear—
   But her tones are yet more thrilling;
But where's the bowl?—let the bowl be near,
   And I'll finish the theme while filling.

Máible ṡeiṁh n-í Ceallaiġ.

Cearḃallán ró chán.

Cia b'é bh-ḟuil ré a n-dán do,
  A láṁh-ḃeas bheiṫ ḟaoi na ceann,
Is deiṁhin nach eagal bás do,
  Go bráth ná 'n a ḃeóḋ ḃeiṫ tinn,
A chúl ḃeiṫ na m-bachall bh-ḟáinneach, bh-ḟionn,
  A chuim mar an Eala ag snáṁaḋ air an d-tonn,
Gráḋ 'sur spéis gach gárṡaiḋ, Máible ṡéiṁh n-í
  Cheallaiġ,
Déud is deise leagaḋ ann a rus a céim.

Ní'l ceól b'á ḃinne ḟós d'ár seinneaḋ,
  Ná'r bh'eólġhach ḋi-si thuigsin 's a ráḋ ann gach céim
A gnuaḋ mar rós ag drithleaḋ, is buan 'n a g-cóṁharpa
  an lile,
A ḃorg is mine, gláise 'ná bláith na g-craeḃ:
'S é deis ollḋaṁh molta chláir ṡíl Néill,
Go g-cuirṡeaḋ na corpaḋa chooola le ráṗ-ġhuiṫ a béil,
Ní'l aṁhús ann a ruil bhṗeaġ, lonnach,
Acht óltar linn go sṗíñ do ṡláinte mhaiṫ ṗéin.

MILD MABLE KELLY.[1]

BY THOMAS FURLONG.

Oh! blest is the youth by kind fortune selected,
 Who clasps to his bosom my own blushing maid,
By him may the warnings of fate be neglected,
 Nor sickness nor sorrow his joys shall invade.
How richly, how softly thy young tresses fall,—
 Thy shape seems more light than the swan's on the wave,
The love, the delight, the gay idol of all,
 The spur for the sluggard—the spell for the brave;
Oh! mild Mable Kelly, how lovely art thou,
Thy skill in each strain let the minstrels avow—
  Thy soft cheeks disclose
  The mix'd lily and rose,
And thy breath comes like blossoms just plucked from the bough.

The bard of the chieftain—the bard of O'Neill—
 Will say that thy song seems more sweet to his ear,
Than the murmur of waterfalls heard thro' the vale,
 When the heart-parching heats of the summer are near.

O d'éagadar na mná mánla
  Air a d-tráchdadaoís an domhain go léir,
Measaim nach bh-fuil 'n a n-áit aguinn
  Acht Máible le clú ann gach céim.
Annsacht gach duine a g-cáilidheachd 's a g-céill;—
  Is ághmhar do'n bh-filidh a fágháil d'á n-déis,
Cúl na g-cnáebh is finne, lúb na d-téud is binne,
  Fnuadh na géise gile, a brághaid a's a taebh.

N'íl áen d'á bh-feiceann an t-srói-bhean mhaireach,
  Nach éirghidheann mar na geiltibh, a m-barradhaibh na g-cnáebh,
A's an t-é nach léur do an choingeal, lán de sbéis an leinbh,
Is fearr tréighthe a's tuigsi dhe náirsún Gáedhal :—
Is fí is deise cos, bas, lámh agus béul,
  Péighne rosg, a's folt ag fás léi go féur,
Tá an bháire-fi linn ag sárúghadh luchd gréinn,
  Fá padh go bh-fuair mé an fháill, is ághmhar liom é.

Oh! gaze but for once!—in that soul speaking eye—
　　Shew! shew me the spot where suspicion could reign;
But come! fill the glass, fast around let it fly—
　　And here's mild Mable Kelly again and again!.
There were maidens all lovely, in days that are o'er,
Whom the warm and the young might to madness adore;
　　　　But there never was one,
　　　　Whom the sun shone upon,
That could match Mable Kelly the light of our shore.

Oh! who can behold this young flourishing flower,
　　And still in dull soul-sinking coldness pass on;
Even he doom'd to blindness till death's dreary hour,
　　Must own all her beauty till feeling is gone.
Oh! fairest of maidens—gay flower of the Gael!
　　All bright is thy fame o'er the bounds of the land!
But here stands the bumper—and ne'er may we fail
　　To pledge the mild Mable with heart and with hand.
Till life's latest moment how blest shall I be,
To sing, oh! my mild Mable Kelly, of thee;
　　　　And proud may I deem
　　　　My heart-soothing theme,
For the praise of the loveliest falls upon me.

cupán uí h-eagnra.

Cearbhallán ró chan.

Dá m-béidhinn-ri a muich a 'n-Arainn,
   Nó a' n-gár-ghleann na réud,
Már a n-gluaireann gach rár-long
   le cláiréid a'r le méad,
b'reárr liom é már rhárámh,
   Agur rághaim é dhamh réin,
Cúpán geal Uí h-Eaghra
   Agur rághláil lán le mo bhéul.

Cad é b'áill liom 'g a chur a g-céill,
   'r a liacht áigh maith 'n a dhéigh,
'r gur b'é deir olldhámh na h-áite,
   Dár mo lámh-ra ní bréug,
Thoirdhealbhach bhriain ághamháil,
   Tárr tráth rárói mo dhéin,
Go n-ólram ár an t-rár-chupán
   Sláinte bhriágh Chéin.

THE CUP OF O'HARA.[1]

BY THOMAS FURLONG.

Oh! were I at rest
   Amidst Arran's green Isles,
Or in climes where the summer
   Unchangingly smiles;
Tho' treasures and dainties
   Might come at a call,
Still, O'Hara's full cup,
   I would prize more than all.

But why would I say
   That my choice it must be,
When the prince of our fathers
   Hath lov'd it like me:
Then come, jolly Turlough,
   Where friends may be found;
And our Kian we'll pledge,
   As that cup goes around.

Marbhairiad Inghin Sheoirse bruin.

Cearbhallán ró chan.

A Mhárgharíad brún, is dúbhach do fhágbhair mé,
  Mo luighe 'r an n-uaigh 's gan cúmhdach mná orm féin,
Fuil 'g a gcaoileadh bham-ra a d-tús a's a n-deireadh gach lae,
  A's a Inghín Mheic Suíbhne, a rúin dhil, tárthaigh mé.

Ghluaiseas 'nunn dar liom fá 'n tráth-so a n-dé,
  Fá 'n g-coill chroím, go cinnte b' árd mo léim;
Mo leabhrán gríann ag innsin fáth gach rgeil,
  Is eagal liom gur mhill do ghrádh-ra me.

'S í Mair'iad an ainbhear sheímh is caoine glór,
  Is binne a béul 'ná guth na d-téud a's 'ná na fídh-cheóil,

PEGGY BROWNE.[1]

BY THOMAS FURLONG.

Oh! dark! sweetest girl, are my days doom'd to be,
While my heart bleeds in silence and sorrow for thee:
In the green spring of life to the grave I go down,
Oh! shield me and save me, my lov'd Peggy Browne.

I dreamt, that at evening my footsteps were bound,
To yon deep spreading wood where the shades fall around;
I sought, 'midst new scenes, all my sorrows to drown,
But the cure of my sorrow rests with thee, Peggy Browne.

'Tis soothing, sweet maid, thy soft accents to hear,
For, like wild fairy music, they melt on the ear—[2]
Thy breast is as fair as the swan's clothed in down;
Oh! peerless, and faultless, is my own Peggy Browne.

Is gile taobh ná an eala shéimh théibheann air linn gach ló,
  'Gus a mhaiseach, bhéusach, ghasta, thpéibhtheach ná diúltaibh mé.

Dul eadar an dair 'sa croiceann, 'sé mheasaim gur cruadh an céim,
  Dul eadar mé agus rúin-searc agus grádh mo chléibh,
Air chur mo lámh tháiri air maidin le bánúghadh an lae
  Fuair mé an tsapaibhe dubh ag gleacaibheacht le grádh mo chuim.

Dear! dear is the bark, to its own cherish'd tree,
But dearer, far dearer, is my lov'd one to me:
In my dreams I draw near her, uncheck'd by a frown,
But my arms, spread in vain to embrace Peggy Browne.

Seoirse bracroy.

Cearbhallán ró chán.

A Sheóirse bhradroin go mairidh tú ráeghalach, slán,
Gradh gach duine a's a leinbh is aoibhne cáil
Lámh an oinich ó m-b'fusur dúinn fíon do fhaghail,
Is gártha an chuideachd 's an n-ionnad a m-bidheann
  do ghradh.

  Hí ho! rud é an preabaire,
    Hóm bo! Plur na ngarsuidhe;
  Spórt, gleódh, corg ar n-aicididhe,
  Feóil, beóir, ceól agus cearpuidhe,
  Cláirseach, Fideléir, gair ag Piobairidhe;
    'S é báire Chunparce é, lár a chige 'stigh
  Barr-shlat Ghailleng é, gradh mo chroidhe-sa leis,
  Sar-mhac dathamhuil é, carthannach, firinneach.

GEORGE BRABAZON.[1]

BY THOMAS FURLONG.

Oh! Brabazon, long may you live, brightly blooming,
 Thou darling of all, easy, open, and free;
Thou guide of the cup, while the wine is consuming—
 How happy's the circle that's favor'd by thee.
  High ho! he's the fellow that's hearty,
  High ho! he's the pride of each party:
In sport, and in mirth, and in feasting abounding,
The flower of Kinratty, where strings are resounding;
He's the top branch of Gallen, the joy of the ladies all,
First in the fight, and not last at the lively ball;
The friend of all fun, and the foe of frivolity,
Jolly George Brabazon lives but for jollity.
    High ho!

I would rather than Spain with her herds and her treasures,
 Than Rome, where the steeds and the coaches abound;

b' feárr liom ná bómlácht á'ṛ ná óṛ ríȝhe ná Ṛráinne,
Eáchṛáiḋhe áȝuṛ cóiṛḋiḋhen á Ṛlóimhe á'ṛ án Ṗáṛá leiṛ,
A'ṛ ná Ḋúnmóṛ mheic Ceóṛuiṛ áȝuṛ Ṅóṛáill mheic
Ṛláȝhnáill,
Ḃheiṫh áȝ ámháṛc áiṛ Ṛheóiṛṛe áȝ táḃháiṛt óiṛ 'ná
mháṁáiḃh uáiḃh.
Ḣi hó ! ṛúḋ é án ṛolláiṛe,
Ḣóm bó ! ḋuḃh-ṛhlán ḋuine ṛáói,
Ḣim hám ! ṛláinȝṛiḋh meṛṛiment,
Ṛinȝ, ḋánce, ḋṛinc, hiṛ heálṫh áḃouṫ,
Iṛ ṛáṁh, iṛ ṛoineáncá é, tá ṛé cúiṛtéiṛeách,
'Ṛ é bláiṫh á chineáḋh é, ṛácháṁ ḋ'á ḋhúnṫche
leiṛ ;
Táinte ṛonuiṛ áiṛ, áȝh áȝuṛ oineách áiṛ,
A'ṛ báṛṛ máiṫh uile-ḃhṛeáȝh ȝo ḋ-tuitiḋh áiṛ.

Than Norrall and Dunmore, with their sports and their pleasures,'
To see thee again deal thy bounty around.
    High ho! he's the youth that is sprightly,
    He smiles on the world, and looks on it lightly:
Then fill up again! see, our cups are all sinking,
We'll sing and we'll dance while his health we are drinking;
He's the boast of his race! gentle, winning, and affable,
Eager for all that's good-humour'd and laughable.
To his mansion I'll go, where still pleasant I've found him,
Oh! may blessings on blessings, for ever surround him.
            High ho!

bpigitt ḟ-ic ui Mhaille.

Cearbhallán ro chan.

———

A bhrigḣitt n-ic uí Mhaile, is tú d'ḟáig mo chroidhe cráidhte,
Ta arraingeadha báis tré cheart-lár mo chroidhé,
Táid na mílte fear a ngrádh le na h-éadan chiúin, náireach,
'Sgo d-tug sí bárr breaghdhachta air chír-Eirill, má's fíor.

Maidin chiúin, cheódhmhar, d' ar éirgheas 's an bh-fóghmhar,
Cía casfaidhe ann sa' ród orm, acht stór geal mo chuím,
'Nuair bheárc me air a clóḋh geal, do rgardar fuil t-rróna,
A's fuair mé trí póga d'fóir air mo rhaoigheal.

BRIDGET O'MALLEY.[1]

BY THOMAS FURLONG.

Dear maid, thou hast left me in anguish to smart,
And pangs, worse than death, pierce my love-stricken heart;
Thou flower of Tirerell, still, still, must I pine,
Oh! where my O'Malley blooms beauty like thine.

On a mild dewy morn in the autumn I rov'd,
I stray'd o'er the pathway where stray'd my belov'd.
Oh! why should I dwell on the bliss that is past?
But the kiss I had there, I must prize to the last.

The sunbeams are beauteous when on flower beds they play,
And sweet seem young roses as they bloom on the spray;
The white-bosom'd lilies thrice lovely we call,
But my true love is brighter, far brighter than all.

Níl nead air bith is áilne, 'ná grian ós cionn gáirdín,
 'S na pógá breághdhá b'fárás amach ar an g-craóibh:
Már rúd a bhídheás mo ghrádh-sa, le deire 's le
    breághacht,
A chúl chiurgh na bh-fáinneádhá, bh-fuil mo ghean
    ort le blíádháin.

Buáchaill deás óg me, tá triáll chum mo phórtá,
 Ní buán a bh-fád beódh me, muná bh-fágh mé mo
    mhiánn:
A chuirle a's a stórách! fágh péidh águs bídh pómhám-
    sa,
Go déighéánách diá dómhnáich air bhóithribh Páth-
    liámh.

Is me-si tá thíos, leis an b-pótáro dhéánádh;
 Ní choblaim an óidhche acht ag orná ighioll go trom;—
Ná'r fhághbháidh me an ráéghál-so, go m-béidheád a's tú,
    chéád sheárc,
Air leábá chlúmh eánláich a's mo lámh fáói do
    cheánn.

L

I'm young, and a bridegroom soon destin'd to be,
But short is my course, love! if bless'd not with thee:
On Sunday, at dusk, by Rath-leave shall I stray,
May I meet thee, my sweetest, by chance on the way.

In gloom, and in sorrow, my days must go by,
At night on my pillow in anguish I sigh;
Hope springs not—peace comes not—sleep flees from
    me there—
Oh! when comes my lov'd one, that pillow to share.

Seághan Glas.

Ceapbhallán fó chan.

Dá bh-feicfeá-sa Seághan Glas, is é dul chum an aonaich,
A's gnádh gach leinbh a m-brollach a léine;—
A's, a cháilíneadha an t-sléibh', sin agaibh Seághan
    Glas.

'S é deir bean d'á bheirse, d'á b-feiceann é n-éinfheacht,
Gho bh-fágh mé mo mhilleadh! gur b'é rúd mo chéile;
A's, a cháilíneadha an t-sléibh', sin agaibh Seághan
    Glas.

Ní úghdar gan dántaibh, ní cláirseach gan téudaibh,
Ní'l eárnadh ann a chnámhaibh gan beárnadh le
    bréagaibh,
Ní'l ann acht fámaire fánach, a fágbhadh gan chéile,
Má bhpistear a chnámha, ní'l fáth dho 'g a fhéunadh;
    A's, a cháilíneadha an t-sleibh', sin agaibh
    Seághan Glas.

SHANE GLAS.[1]

BY THOMAS FURLONG.

Have you gaz'd at Shane Glas as he went to the fair,
How lively his step, and how careless his air,
 With his breast full of favours from many a lass;
Oh! there's not a sweet girl that appears on the green,
But simpers and blushes wherever he's seen;
They cry he's the boy, our darling and joy,
Still ready to sport, or to court, or to toy,
 Then maids of the mountain there's for you Shane Glas.

Without verses, no poet can boast of the name;
Without music, no harper the title can claim—
 No lover, thro' life, without quarrels can pass;
The gallant whose head is not smash'd for the fair,
Is a boaster unworthy their favours to share:

Dá bhfeicfeá-sa Ḟailbh, a'ṡ í dul chum an aonaiġ,
  Brógaḋ ḋaichte uirṫi, a'ṡ aprún gléigeal,
    A'ṡ, a chailíneaḋa an t-sléibh', ṡin agaibh
      Ḟeaġġan Glar.

'Ṡ í iṡ ṡamhail dí ḃénuṡ, ġeaġ na porġ ngial
  'Ṡ a ġruaḋh air laraḋh, 'ṡa leaca maṡ chaépa;
    A'ṡ, a chailíneaḋa an t-sléibh', ṡin agaibh
      Ḟeaġġan Glar.

Dá chíoch chruinne, naċ'ṗ fionnaḋh 'ṡ naċ'ṗ feuchaḋh,
  A Ohia! ġan me-ṡi aġuṡ i-ṡe n-éinḟheacht,
  A b-tom nglar coille, ġo n-déaniṡamaoiṡ péiḋteach,
    A chara mo chroíḋhe! nach ann ṡin do ḃéiḋheaḋh an
      ṡult?
    A'ṡ, a chailíneaḋa an t-sléibh', ṡin agaibh
      Ḟeaġġan Glar.

Then Shane is the lad, that his bruises has had,
For the girls and drinking have made him half mad,
 Then maids of the mountain there's for you Shane
 Glas.

Have you chanc'd on your way handsome Sally to meet,
With her gown snowy white, and her nice little feet,
 When she's bound to the fair, or returning from
 Mass;
With her smile so bewitching, her glances so bright,
And her bosom so temptingly fair to the sight :
Oh! might I but find, the sweet girl to my mind,
In yonder green holly-wood gently reclined,
 What joy would it bring to the heart of Shane Glas.

seamus pluinceaD.

Cearbhallán ro chan.

Seamar óg Pluincéad, bronntóir an fhíona,
  Fuair oideas air cheoltaibh, spórt agus aoibhneas,
Air laitin, air Ghréigis, 'r air Ghaoidheilg bhreagh,
  líomhtha,
Grádh na m-ban n-óg é, an t-óig-fhear glan, saoithea-
  mhail.

Is feárr 'ná rin féin, a mhéinn a'r a mhaithios,
  Guaire níor chug buadh air, a' n-uairreacht a
  bheartaibh,
Go m-budh fada saoghlach, beódh é, gan bhrón air bith
  na earbaidh,
'N a árd-fhlaith mhór bhéurradh ól fada do Ghaspaibh.

JAMES PLUNKETT.[1]

BY THOMAS FURLONG.

Oh ! where shall thy like, my lov'd Plunkett, be found,
Thou soul of each circle when mirth reigns around,—
Let the learned thy skill in each language declare,
While fond sighs speak the feelings and thoughts of the
  fair.

Oh! kind is thine heart, as each tongue can avow,
In sports and in pastimes unrivall'd art thou ;
Long long be thy days, and unclouded by care,
And plenty be thine—that of plenty can share.

Say who has not heard of mine own favor'd youth,
The lov'd one whose looks beam with genius and truth ;
Oh! many is the maiden, and beauteous to see,
Who pines all in silence, my Plunkett, for thee.

An g-cualaibh sibh tréighthe an tréun-mharcaich shúgaich,
  Mar a tá an Pluincéattach gléigheal, breágh, éudtrom, lúchmhar;—
'S é dubhairt gach maighdean bhéurach, m-bíodh na céuda bhi ag umhlughadh,
  Mo léun! gan mé a's tú, mar aén air ar n-glúinibh.

Ní'l rin maighdean bhéurach, ó Eirne go Gaillibh amach,
  Dá g-cualaibh riamh a thréibhe, nár'p mhéinn leó bheith 'n-aice realt,
A g-cóilltibh bhuin-an-phiodáin tá an ruppánach, breágh, roineanta,
  Mheallradh na caitiníbhe air chúl na g-craóibheacha.

Not one from Loch-Erne to Galway around,
But longs for my hero ! my swain so renown'd ;
Thy groves, Buninedin, are shady and fair,
They are bless'd and belov'd—for my Plunkett is there.

Ησηριδη cooper.

Ceαρbhαllαn ρó chαn.

'Y nín, mαιγeαch, mαnlα, γocαιρ, milιγ, cραιbhcheαch,
Zαn zhρuαιm α'γ αδhnαιρeαch δο zhnúιγ bhρeαzh, α ρúιn!
Γúιl zhlαγ αz zαιρeαδh, δ'úρ-leαcα ιγ αιlne,
Γúδ leαc nα cαιnce, α zhραδh δhιl, αz cnúch;
'Y ρíορ-δheαγ δο zhnαóι zhlαn, ιγ leαδhαιρ δο ρhíοb zheαl,
'Y cuιρeαδh nα mílce leαc γínce αnn γαn n-úιρ!
'Y cú γzαnnραδh zαch béιche, α chúιl chαιγ nα z-cραέbh-
  γholc,
'Y δlúιch-δheαγ δο δhéuδ chαóιl, α'γ δο cheαnnγαcht
  bhρeαzh, chιúιn.

'Y γolluγαch 'γ ιγ léuρ, οιγnαδh α z-cροίδhe zαch αέn,
bhίδheαnn αz αmhαργ γcέιmhe zheαl-ρέιlcιοnn nα m-bαn;

NANCY COOPER.[1]

BY THOMAS FURLONG.

Oh! lov'd one how temptingly fair is that face,
    On which thousands have gaz'd but to sigh;
How winningly smooth seems each motion of grace,
    When thy shape of soft brightness glides by:
Tho' some in thy absence a throb may excite,
    When near thee their triumph is o'er,
They shrink in thy presence—they fade in thy light,
    They droop and look lovely no more.

Those brilliant grey eyes with these tresses all curl'd—
    That bosom where love holds his throne;
Dear! these are thy dowry for what were a world
    To him who could call them his own.

'S deas do chos 's do lámh, is geal do bhpollach bán,
Och! 's tú los 's do chpádh, na céuda láech meap!
A phéupla shlad scéimh mhna deapa' an t-sáeghail,
'S tá tú tláith tais a 'd mhéinn,—acht 's eigean damh-sa
        stad;

'Nois, a chuid 's a ghpádh, mo bheannacht leat do ghnáth,
A Mansidh Cooper bhreagh na m-bán-chíoch n-deas.

Of millions the beauty seems blended in thee—
But why on this theme should I dwell?
Thro' life there's but sadness and silence for me—
Farewell! Nancy Cooper! farewell!

Marbhna Cheapbhaillaigh air bhás a Mhná Máire ní Ghuidhir.

Intleachc na h-Éireán, na Gréige, 'r na Rómha,
Bíodh uile a n-éinfheachc, a' n-áen-bheirtín rómhamsa,
Ghlacfainn mar fhéirín, tar an mhéid-sin de na seodaibh,
Máire ó'n n-Éirne a'r mé bheith 'g 'á pósadh.

Is tuirseach, tinn, tréith-lag me féin gach trathnóna,
'S air maidin ag éirghiabh, mar b'eag uaim mo nuabhchéar,
Dá bh-fagháinn a nois tréuda, 'r gach ráibhbhreár b'ár nósabh,
Ní ghlacfainn 'n a béigh-sin áen bheán le pósabh.

CAROLAN'S MONODY ON THE DEATH OF HIS WIFE MARY MAC GUIRE.[1]

BY THOMAS FURLONG.

Were heaven to yield me in this chosen hour,
   As an high gift ordain'd thro life to last,
All that our earth hath mark'd of mental power,
   The concentrated genius of the past :
Were all the spells of Erin's minstrels mine,
   Mine the long treasur'd stores of Greece and Rome—
All, all with willing smile I would resign,
   Might I but gain my Mary from the tomb.

My soul is sad—I bend beneath my woe,
   Darkly each weary evening wears away ;
Thro' the long night my tears in silence flow,
   Nor hope, nor comfort cheers the coming day.

Fuair mé seal a' n-Eirinn go h-aedhrach a's go
   sóghamhuil,
Ag ól le gach tréan-fhear, bhíoh éireachtach, ceólmhar,
Fágbhadh 'n a dhéigh-sin, leam féin mé go brónach,
A n-deireadh mo shaeghail, 'r gan mo chéile bheith beódh
   agam.

M' intleacht mhaith, aerach, ní fhéudaim a cumhdach,
M' intinn, 'n a dhéigh-sin, is léur go bh-fuil smúiteach,
Go deimhin a'ó dhéigh-si, ní fhéudaim bheith súgach,
A Mháire na céille, ann san t-saeghal bhíoh go clúiteach.

Wealth might not tempt—nor beauty move me now,
　　Tho' one so favour'd sought my bride to be—
Witness, high heaven!—bear witness to my vow—
　　My Mary! death shall find me true to thee.

How happy once! how joyous have I been,
　　When merry friends sat smiling at my side;
Now near my end—dark seems each festive scene—
　　With thee, my Mary, all their beauty died.
My wit hath past—my sprightly voice is gone,
　　My heart sinks deep in loneliness and gloom,—
Life hath no aftercharms to lead me on—
　　They wither with my Mary—in the tomb.

Uaill-chumhaidh Chearbhallaín os cionn Maigh Mheic Aíb.

Nach í so an chuairt easbadhach, do lasaidh mé th'péir mo shiúbhail!
Air uaigh mo chárad, 'r me faleadh na n-déar go h-úr;
Ní bh-fuair mé agám mo tháithneamh, a'r padharc mo shúl;
Acht cruaidh-leac dhaingean, a'r leabadh de'n g-cré bhíodh cúmhang.

Ní tréan me a' labhairt, 'r ní mhearaim gur cúis náire,
Is caóibhean bhocht scoithte me, ó chailleas mo chúl báine,
Ní'l péin, ní'l peanaid, ní'l galar chomh cruadh, cráidhte,
Le h-éag na g-carad, nó scaradh na g-cómpánach.

CAROLAN'S LAMENT OVER THE GRAVE OF MAC CABE.[1]

BY THOMAS FURLONG.

Oh! what a baffled visit mine hath been,
　How long my journey, and how dark my lot;
And have I toil'd thro' each fatiguing scene,
　To meet my friend—and yet to find him not?

Sight of my eyes!—lost solace of my mind!
　To seek—to hear thee—eagerly I sped;
In vain I came—no trace of thee I find—
　Save the cold flag that shades thy narrow bed.

My voice is low—my mood of mirth is o'er,
　I droop in sadness like the widowed dove;
Talk, talk of tortures!—talk of pain no more—
　Nought strikes us like the death of those we love.

Mairbhna Cheapbhallaig.

Mac Lib ró chan.

Mo bhrón! mo mhilleadh! mo chinneas 'r mo bhuaidhreamh tráth!
Do cheól-chruit mhilir, gan bhinneas, gan rudirceas bán!
Cia bhéanras aiteas do'n ghárraidh na ceól go buan,
Ór ríor, a chárraid, gur leagadh thú a g-cómhra chruadh?

Tráth eirghidhim air maidin, a'r bheárcaim an tir ráoi-chiach,
Agus shuidhim air na cnocaibh, go bh-feicim an dubh a n-iar,
A Aén-mheic Mhuire! furtaigh do 'm chár a'r piár!
'Y go n-beárnadh loch rola, de amhárc mo rhúl a'd bhiadh!

MAC CABE'S ELEGY ON THE DEATH OF CAROLAN.

BY THOMAS FURLONG.

Woe is my portion! unremitting woe!
  Idly and wildly in my grief I rave;
    Thy song, my Turlogh, shall be sung no more—
Thro' festive halls no more thy strains shall flow:
    The thrilling music of thy harp is o'er—
    The hand that wak'd it moulders in the grave.

I start at dawn—I mark the country's gloom—
  O'er the green hills a heavy cloud appears;—
Aid me, kind Heaven, to bear my bitter doom,
  To check my murmurs, and restrain my tears.

Oh! gracious God! how lonely are my days,
  At night sleep comes not to these wearied eyes,
Nor beams one hope my sinking heart to raise—
  In Turlogh's grave each hope that cheer'd me lies.

A bfuigh na g-carad! nach airdeach na cúrsadha é?
Ag luidhe bhamh air mo leabadh nach g-coblann mo
  shúil aen néull!
Táid piantá deacrach' dul tarsna tré lár mo chléibh;—
  'S a Thoirbhealbhaich uí Cheárbhalláin, 's biombáidh
  liom tú fínnte g-cré!

Guidhim-si Naomh Doiminic, Naomh Proinsias, a's
  Naomh Clára,
'S na h-iliomad Naoimh, fsói bhídhean na eachrach
  neamhdha,
Fá fháilte thabhairt d' anam Thoirbhealbhaich ann a
  n-arus,
'S a liacht port saoitheamhail do sheinn sé air an
  g-cláirsigh.

Oh! ye blest spirits, dwelling with your God,
   Hymning his praise as ages roll along,
Receive my Turlogh in your bright abode,
   And bid him aid you in your sacred song.

NOTES.

NOTES.

NOTES.

WELCOME TO CAROLAN.

¹ JAMES COURTNEY, better known to the Irish reader by the name of DALL M'CUAIRT, the author of this Ode, was a native of Louth, and an Irish poet of repute in the days of Carolan. Several poems of his composition are preserved in the manuscript collection of the editor. Many of them are possessed of considerable merit, and highly deserving of publication.

² *" From the mansion of Meavè."*

A celebrated queen of Connaught, and one of the heroines of Irish lore. She flourished about the beginning of the Christian era, and was co-eval with Connor, King of Ulster, (who reigned in the palace of Emania, which was situate about one mile west of the present city of Armagh,) Cuchullin, Connall Kearnach, Fergus Mac Roy, and other heroes famed in our history.—Mr. Macpherson in the beautiful, but supposititious, translations from his imaginary Ossian, makes Cuchullin, who died in the beginning of the first century, cotemporary with Fingall who died in the third. Yet these " translations" are quoted by Mr. Pinkerton and others, as true history !

3 "*Orgiel's flowery fields.*"

Orgiel, Oriel, Uriel, an ancient territory, comprehending the present counties of Louth, Monaghan or Mac Mahon's country and Ardmagh.—*Ware.*

4 "*Tarah's embattled pile.*"

Tarah, or Teamor, was the royal seat, and court of legislation of the kings of Ireland, until about the year 560. The edifice was erected on the well-known hill which bears its name, in the county of Meath, where there are yet to be seen remains of several circular entrenchments, or foundations. We have more than once walked over this venerable spot, so famous in Irish classic lore, with sensations which it would be as difficult for an Irishman not to feel, as for an Englishman to estimate. It is related that his present Majesty, during his visit to Ireland, passing in view of the hill of Tarah, declared himself proud of his descent from the ancient Monarchs of the land. Such a declaration was worthy of a king, and complimentary to a faithful people.

5 "*The four Nialls.*"

Monarchs of Ireland. The first surnamed "of the nine hostages," commenced his reign, A. D. 379. The fourth fell in a desperate conflict with the Danes, A. D. 919.

6 "*Con and Cormac of regal birth.*"

Also Monarchs.—The first is well known in history by the appellation "of the hundred battles." The last assumed the government, A. D. 254. He combined the study of philosophy with the cares of government. Some of the writings of this heathen prince are still extant.—*See Annals IV. Masters, p. 86.*

7 "*Ulster of the red red shields.*"

The provincial arms, generally attributed to Ulster, are —On a field or, a lion rampant, double queued, gules.

The knights of the red branch — Cuṙaḋha na craoibhe ruaiḋhe of Ulster, are much celebrated in our ancient annals,

⁸ *" Bard of Clan Cahir."*
Cahir, son of Fergus, king of Ulster, whose descendents settled in the south of Ireland. The Etymon of Kerry is *Cahir riaghta*, the kingdom of Cahir.

⁹ The last stanza of this ode is called Abhran, versicle, or combination. Irish poems frequently conclude with a similar stanza, which in general contains a recapitulation of the principal heads of the composition. These terminations are also found in Spanish and Arabic poetry.

MARY MAGUIRE.

¹ The poetical effusions of Carolan contained in this volume, commence with the love verses addressed to his future partner through life. They are sweet and simple, and breathe the soft language of tenderness and affection. It is observable that in these stanzas, he avoids any mention of the favourite pleasures of the bottle, which will be found so frequently alluded to in his other compositions.

Mr. Walker, in his Memoirs of the Irish Bards, informs us that Mary Maguire was "a young lady of a good family in the county of Fermanagh," and that she " proved a proud and extravagant dame : but she was the wife of his choice; he loved her tenderly, and lived harmoniously with her."—His beautiful monody on her death will be found in this collection of his poems.

Many of Carolan's airs are lost, though the words remain; while numerous sweet airs have been preserved, whose original words are now irrecoverable. The difficulty of adapting

English verse, in any variation of metre, to the "complicated modulations" of several of his surviving melodies is generally acknowledged. The attempt has been often made, but seldom with success. His lively style, so different from the slow plaintive strains of our ancient music; the rapidity of his turns; his abrupt changes and terminations, so unexpected yet so pleasing, could be followed only in the language in which he thought, composed, and sung. In the selection of airs, therefore, for such of these translations as are not adapted to the original music, the choice has been in general determined by the nature of each composition.

The translation of "Mary Maguire" will call to the recollection of our musical readers the fine old air, Catherine Ogie, to which there are also English and Irish words, beginning—

"Dear Nelly I'm afraid that your favor I'll not gain.

Ann ɼᴀ m-bᴀıłe ɼo 'n ᴀ bh-ꝼuıł cú ᴀò chómhnuíòhe."

FANNY BETAGH.

[1] Daughter of Captain Gerald Dillon, and wife of James Betagh, formerly of Mannin, in the county of Mayo, a residence long distinguished as the seat of old Irish hospitality. The latter gentleman was head of a branch of the ancient family of his name, descended from the Danes, and, for centuries before the Anglo-Norman invasion, settled at Moynalty in the county of Meath. Francis Betagh, the last heir of that illustrious house, was most iniquitously deprived of his patrimonial possessions after the Restoration of Charles II. though, like many of his similarly treated countrymen, he adhered with "desperate fidelity" to the fortunes of that ungrateful monarch. The particulars are related in the History of Ireland, by Hugh Reily, Esq. chancellor of James II. where they may be perused with benefit by future confiscators. " Perhaps," says my

valued friend and kinsman, the late proprietor of Mannin, alluding in a strain of happy irony to this circumstance, "Francis Betagh was deprived to gratify the Irish, by the extirpation of the last of the Danes, and that it was reserved, *parva magnis componere*, for Charles to finish what Brian had begun." The usurpers of Moynalty are forgotten, but that injured and venerated family will be remembered while a pulsation of Irish feeling shall remain in the land. A passage in Mc Gauran's well-known *Plearaca na Ruarcach*—" O'Rourke's noble feast," alluding to this family, has been thus translated by Swift—

" The Earl of Kildare,
    And Moynalta his brother,
Great as they are, I was nursed by their mother."

The air to which the present little song has been translated is well-known by the name of Cáilín beág chruibhte ná m-bó. "The pretty maid milking the Cow," literally, "The pretty cow-milking maid."

BRIDGET CRUISE.

[1] We have seen in the preliminary Memoir of Carolan, that Bridget Cruise, was the first object of his affections. Though she entertained a correspondent feeling for him, yet, by some fatality, their union never took place. The ode, which bears her name, has been always considered one of the tenderest and most harmonious of all his works. "I have often listened," says the venerable Charles O'Conor, " to Carolan singing his ode to Miss Cruise. I thought the stanzas wildly enthusiastic, but neglected to preserve them." Mr. Walker calls it his "chef d'œuvre," and says, "it came warm from his heart, while his genius was in full vigour." It has been the fate of Irish

poetry, from the days of Spenser to the present time, to be praised or censured by the extremes of prejudice, while the world was unable to decide for want of the original poems, or translations of them. The present Ode may now, for the first time, be compared with other specimens of our Bard, and though it may not, perhaps, be considered as entitled to the first place, yet it will always maintain a respectable rank amongst his poetical compositions.

² cᴀ, should be cᴀɪb, the third person plural of the verb, required by the preceding nominatives.

³ "*Speak not of Deirdre the renowned.*"
Deirdre, a female much celebrated by our poets. She was the heroine of "The tragical fate of the Sons of Usnach," an Irish tale of the days of Connor king of Ulster, and the foundation of Mr. Macpherson's *Darthula*.

⁴ nᴀ ʒ-cpuínn-chíochᴀ n-ʒeᴀlᴀ should, according to the strict rules of grammar, be no ʒ-cpuínn-chíoch n-ʒeᴀl; but this licence was taken by our bard, for the preservation of the metre.

---

¹ WHISKEY IS THE POTION.

This humorous whiskey *lilt*, has been generally, but, as I apprehend, improperly ascribed to Carolan; lest, however, I may be mistaken in this opinion, I have judged it proper to include it among his Remains. It is now, for the first time, published; and, it may be considered strange, that in this whiskey-loving isle, this land of cheer, and song, and merriment, so curious an antidote against care, should have remained so long unknown. But perhaps it was unnecessary; the enticing beverage was but too copiously used without it. It is here translated to the characteristic air of " Carolan's Receipt;" and as a genuine "Chanson de boire," stands, in our opinion, unrivalled.

Tradition has preserved the following account of its composition. The jolly-hearted bard, whoever he was, in one of his excursions, visited an old friend, whom he found confined to his bed, more under the pressure of melancholy feelings, than of any bodily ailment. He immediately drew near the bedside, took his harp, and played and sung the music and words of this inimitable song. The effect was instantaneous—irresistible. The melancholy spirit fled. The dispossessed started up, joined the festive board, and was "sick no more."

[1] PLANXTY STAFFORD.

Or, as more generally called, " CAROLAN'S RECEIPT," is one of our bard's most celebrated compositions. " He commenced the words," says Walker's anonymous correspondent, " and began to modulate the air in the evening, at Boyle, in the county of Roscommon; and before the following morning he sung and played *this noble offspring of his imagination* in Mr. Stafford's parlour at Elphin." It is to be observed, that the first stanza only was composed by Carolan, the second, p. 24, now, for the first time printed, was by his friend Mc. Cabe, who sometimes, with Carolan's permission, added verses to his songs. In the present instance, the Irish reader will immediately perceive the difference. The Stafford family is most respectably descended. They were " transplanted" by Cromwell, from Wexford to Roscommon, where they had a grant of lands, trifling in comparison to those which they lost in their native county. These lands remained with their descendants, until after the enactment of the penal laws; when a profligate younger brother, "conformed" to protestancy, and deprived the elder, who was the father of Carolan's friend, of the estate. It soon after passed away from the family.

Mr. Stafford, having on a certain occasion, requested Carolan to prolong his stay, the facetious bard is said to have made the following humorous reply:

Ɛo τιʒh ꝺo chɑpɑɩꝺ mɑ chéɩꝺh τú,
Cuɑɩρτ ꝼhɑꝺɑ ní h-í ɩꝼ ꝼeɑꝶꝶ ;
Pɑɩρτ ꝺe'ꝺ chɩon beɩρ leɑτ uɑɩꝺh,
Iꝼ ɑꝺhbhɑꝶ ꝺ'ꝼuɑchɑ ɑn τ-ɩompóʒhɑꝺh ʒeɑꝶꝶ.

If to a friend's abode thou should'st repair,
Pause, and take heed of lingering idly there ;
Thou may'st be welcome—but, 'tis past a doubt,
Long visits soon will wear the welcome out.

EDWARD O'CORCORAN.

[1] The air of the old song, called the "Farmer," which was written by a Catholic priest, who certainly, while composing it, was not dreaming of the "church establishment," will be found to answer this translation.

[3] "*Thou hast sprung from the Gael.*"

Gael and Gadelian, which frequently occur in Irish poetry, mean the ancient Milesians of Ireland. From one of these families was descended the gentleman for whom the present song was composed.

NOTES.   111

³ "*From Gallen to Grange.*"

The first of these places is a barony in the county of Mayo, the latter a village in Ahamlish Parish, lower half-barony of Carbry, county of Sligo.

⁴ "*For the hero of Limerick is near us.*"

This line requires no comment. The siege of Limerick, its capitulation, the articles of surrender, and their flagrant violation, are already known throughout the civilized world. Edward O'Corcoran was one of the heroes who " covered themselves with glory" in that memorable struggle. His name has been consecrated by the muse; but many a brave and noble spirit, his companion in arms, fell in the contest, whose name is unknown to posterity.

—— Omnes illacrimabiles
Urguentur ignotique longâ
Nocte, carent quia vate sacro.
HORAT iv. 9.

DOCTOR HARTE.

¹ Doctor Harte was Titular Bishop of Achonry, an Episcopal see in the West of Ireland. The virtues, persecutions; and sufferings of the Catholic clergy of Ireland, not only endeared them to all of their own persuasion, but excited the commisseration, and gained them, almost generally, the esteem of every liberal and enlightened Protestant in the kingdom, even before the relaxation of the penal code. Carolan, " constitutionally pious," was enthusiastic in his attachment to the clergy of his faith. Their praises frequently occupied his muse, and gave birth to some of his noblest conceptions in music and poetry. The anonymous, but excellent, correspondent of the

Author of the Memoirs of the Irish Bards, alluding to his poem to Doctor Harte, says, " it has often excited sentiments of the most fervent piety."

Ⓢtiobhᴀρd ceᴀρt do mhᴀc nᴀ ʒlóiρe é ƒein

² " *To thy Master in heaven a true steward art thou,*"
is no less an idea of the most exalted devotion, than of the most elevated genius." He adds, " It is a loss to the public that this truly virtuous dignitary had been so insensible to all emotions of self-love, as to have the first of Carolan's compositions for him entirely suppressed."—This, however, was not the case. The copy here given has been had from the dictation of an aged man, by whom it was recited with all those feelings of virtuous enthusiasm so peculiar to the Irish.—It has been translated to the air of " My lodging is on the cold ground."—*See Moore's Irish Melodies, No. II. p.* 100.

³ " *Oh! good is thy fame in the land of O'Neill.*"
The province of Ulster which has been particularly denominated the Land of O'Neill, being the territory of that princely family.

⁴ The O'Harte's are an ancient and noble family of Ireland. In the topographical poem of the famous John O'Dugan, beginning " Tριᴀllᴀm timcheᴀll nᴀ ƒóblᴀ," Fines obeamus Iernes, O h-Ꙋiρt ρíoʒhðhᴀ " O'Harte the Noble or Regal," is the first family of Meath mentioned after Maelseachlan the monarch. This was anterior to the Anglo-Norman visitation.

Though Carolan's attachment to the Catholic clergy was unbounded, yet he sometimes had occasion to make them feel the severity of his satirical powers. Having once visited the Friars of Rossreill, a monastery beautifully situated on the banks of Lough-Corrib in the county of Galway, he is said on departing to have addressed them as follows:

Má'r ionmhúin leac na bráichpe,
bíbh leó 50 ráta, rocáip;
Cabhaip bóibh 5ach níbh iappaib,
'Y na h-iapp áen níbh opcha.

Would'st thou the friendship of the friars secure,
Be civil—be submissive—be demure!
Breathe not a word that may their ways condemn—
Grant all they ask, but nothing ask from them.

O'MORE'S FAIR DAUGHTER;
OR,
THE HAWK OF BALLYSHANNON.

[1] The music of this ode has never, that I know of, been published, although it is, undoubtedly, one of the finest specimens of our bard's composition,

It was composed, with the words, on the following occasion. The son of O'Reilly, returning from Leitrim, accidently met the "Fair daughter of O'More," near her father's residence. Struck by her beauty, the youth remained "spell-bound," gazing in silent amazement at the charming object before him. Love took possession of his soul, and the new inmate, always fertile in expedients, soon suggested a pretext for accosting the maiden. Feigning fatigue, he approached her, and requested a cup of water with so gentle, so engaging an address, heightened by the external graces of a fine person, that a correspondent feeling was instantaneously excited in her bosom. He enjoyed her conversation for a few moments only, and then, for the first time in his life with regret, continued his course homewards. On arriving at his father's house, he there found his old favorite, Carolan, who had just made one of his annual visits. The bard, whose eyes, as he used humourously to say of himself, "were transferred to his ears," perceived his youthful friend unusually thoughtful and pensive; and from as thorough an acquaintance with every chord of the human heart, as with every string of his own harp, he at once suspected the cause. After some anxious inquiries, and a few good-natured sallies, the secret was imparted; and the bard, in a little time, produced the words and music of the present ode. They only who have ever felt as young O'Reilly did, can duly appreciate the enthusiasm with which he received them. Shortly after, invited to an entertainment at the house of O'More, the youthful lover took the opportunity of reciting the ode, accompanied by the music of the harp, music of which, perhaps, no modern can form an adequate idea. The effect on the young lady, who happened to be in an adjoining apartment, may be easily anticipated. The conquest of her heart was finally achieved, and young O'Reilly had, soon after, the happiness to be united to the beloved object of his affections.

When celebrating the praises of the descendents of the Gael, Carolan's genius appears in its brightest lustre. The O'Neills, O'Mores, and O'Connors wound him up to the highest pitch of enthusiasm. He considered himself born to " sing in their service," and nobly has he performed the duties of his fancied mission. Of this the ode before us is a splendid proof. As a poetical composition it is much and deservedly admired.

[1] "*Pride of the gay green hills of Maile.*"

The territory of Hy-Malia, an ancient district in the S. W. of the county of Mayo, comprehending the baronies of Murrisk and Carra, or at least a part of the latter. The country of the O'Malleys.

[2] "*Child of the old renowned O'More.*"

This family which holds so conspicuous a place in the annals of Ireland, sprung from *Conall Kearnach*, a Northern hero, celebrated in the famous Cualgnian war waged between Connaught and Ulster about the beginning of the first century. An old historical vellum manuscript in my possession states that, "The king of Leinster, Fitz-Patrick, being at war with the king of Munster, entered into a treaty with O'More, then settled in the North of Ireland. The latter having come with considerable force to the assistance of his ally, succeeded in defeating the Momonians, and claimed the fulfilment of the conditions entered into with him. This being refused, he seized upon the territory of Leix (Laoighes) a country now comprehending the greater part of the Queen's county, which he parcelled out amongst his followers, the O'Kelly's, O'Lalors, Devoys, or Macaboys, O'Dorans and O'Dowlins, whose descendants remain there to this day. These septs were bound on all occasions to obey O'More, to do him homage, and pay him chiefry." These transactions occurred in the tenth century. Subjoined to this account is the following entry in a modern hand—" Part of this tribute, or chiefry, continued to be paid until the year of our Lord 1753."

One of the noblest characters the world ever produced, Sir Thomas More, chancellor of England in the reign of Henry VIII., is stated to have been descended from the O'More's of Ireland.—See his Memoirs by his grandson, Thomas More, London, 1727.

Another member of this family, Roger, or Rory O'More, is rendered memorable by the prominent part which he performed in the tragic scenes of 1641. Endowed with talents of the highest order, he was esteemed the glory and protector of the Irish. His praises were sung in their poems and songs, and the national motto generally inscribed on their military ensigns was—" For God and the Virgin and Rory O'More.'

' " *For the Hawk of Erne is near us.*"
Lough Erne, in the county of Fermanagh. This is one of the most beautiful lakes in Europe. Its waters are discharged

into the sea at Ballyshannon, in the county of Dongall. At this place is the celebrated salmon leap, so well known that it needs no description here.

PHELIM O'NEILL.

[1] Time has not handed down any particulars of the Phelim O'Neill here commemorated, except that he was descended from that powerful family which so long ruled Ireland with sovereign sway. The violent commotions of the seventeenth century, struck to the dust the topmost branch of this great Milesian tree. Well may Ireland exclaim at the present day—

> " Hei mihi, qualis erat! quantum mutatus ab illo
> Hectore; qui redit exuvias indutus Achillei,
> Vel Danaum Phrygios jaculatus puppibus ignes!
> Squalentem barbam, et concretos sanguine crines,
> Vulneraque illa gerens, quæ circum plurima muros
> Accepit patrios."
> Virgil. Æneid. II. 274.

There are, however, many descendants of this celebrated family, though not bearing its ancient dignities, whose patriotic feelings and private virtues would reflect honor on their noble ancestry, even in the proudest days of its splendor. Their names I am prohibited from mentioning, and I regret the circumstance, for the cause of virtue and patriotism is ever promoted by pointing out their followers for imitation.

> Aithnighthear air thorchaibh na g-crann
> Uaisle na bh-freamh ó bh-fásaid:
> Gach geug, leir an n-géig ó b-tig,
> Ag dul leir an d-treud ó d-támig.

Aye! by the fruit the goodly tree is known;
In the proud plant the noble root is shown;
The leaves, the buds, their parent stem proclaim,
In form, in hue, in character, the same.

The translation of "Phelim O'Neill" may remind our musical readers of O'Keefe's "Rose tree in full bearing," in "The Poor Soldier." For the music—combined with Moore's beautiful words beginning, "I'd mourn the hopes that leave me," See Irish Melodies, No. 5, p. 49.

PLANXTY PEYTON.

[1] Toby Peyton was head of a respectable family of that name, in the county of Leitrim. He appears to have been a favourite with our bard, and, from the description contained in the present song, might be pronounced as possessed of kindred feelings. Carolan celebrated Miss Bridget Peyton, his friend's daughter, in a pretty poem, beginning,—

Tá inghín áenach ag Tubóid Péaton,
Do ghaib mo ghnéibh a'r mo fhláinte uaim:
Uir chársbh a céibhe 'r a porc mar fhéup ghlar,
3o g-cuirreabh rí na céubcha a' n-uárgh.

[2] *"Who has horsewhip and sword."*
So Már cloibheamh no baca 'n a lámhaibh has been translated. A Galway copy of this song reads Már piorral no baca, &c. "If pistol or cudgel, &c." After consulting some friends experienced in these matters, I am inclined to retain the former reading, as swords, in their opinion, were in use before pistols. This subject brings to mind a singular signpost, which until lately might have been seen suspended over an inn

door in that duel-loving county. It contained some ill-spelt notification now forgotten, surmounted by a huge horse-whip, and no less formidable pistol, drawn saltier. On enquiry I found that this curious specimen was " put up " subsequent to Carolan's time, in order to commemorate the well known attack made by Captain O'Kelly, of that county, on the " lying " English traveller, Twiss.—Captain O'Kelly was one of those Irish Catholics, who, in despite of penal laws, spilled their blood against Catholic France and Spain, in defence of their Protestant sovereign George III.

But to return to Toby Peyton. It is related that Carolan once praising him in the presence of a priest, the latter, for some reason, expressed his dissent, on which the bard replied, extempore—

Molann gach aén an t-é bhíbheár cráibhtheach, cóir,
Agus molann an chléir an t-é bhíbheár páirteach leó;
Dár solus na spéine is é mo ráibh go deóigh,
Go molfad gan spéis gan bhréig an t-ach mar gheobhad.

   The kind good man must all our praise command,
   Even the sage priest will bless the bounteous hand;
   And, by the blessed light that shines above,
      To this one rule I'll hold thro' good and ill—
   True to my host and to his cheer I'll prove,
      And as I find them I must praise them still.

For the air of our lively Planxty, see Irish Melodies, No. V. p. 18,—" The young May moon."

MADAM CROFTON.

[1] Madam Crofton is said to have been the lady of Sir Edward Crofton of Moate, in the county of Roscommon, baronet.

The air of these charming stanzas is sweet and simple. The English reader may recognize in the translation the metre of the well-known "One bottle more;" and our Irish friends will be reminded of their old favorite —"Cad é ṡin do'n ṫ-é ṡin naċh baineann ṡin dó."—" What's that to any one whether or no."

PEGGY CORCORAN.

¹ These elegant stanzas were addressed to the daughter of the "Hero of Limerick," to whom, as we have seen, Carolan's grateful muse had before paid a tribute. The Irish reader will immediately recognize the translation, as adapted to the sweet old air of "Ṫugamair féin an ṡamhra linn."— "We have brought the summer with us."

² "*The nobles of Spain have been seen at her side.*"
Multitudes of the exiled victims of the penal laws of Ireland, during the last century, became eminent in arts and arms throughout Europe. Many of them were conspicuous in promoting the honor and prosperity of every country except their own. In France and Spain, particularly, their virtues and valor were repeatedly crowned with the most distinguished marks of honor; and we find the politic rulers of those countries not unfrequently exalting them to the highest ranks of the nobility. Not all those honors, however, could make them forget their native land.

Deóraidhthe ṡiopa ṡan ṡġith, ṡan ṡoṡ,
Miannaid a dtíṡ, 'ṡ a n-dúthchaṡ.

Restless exiles doomed to roam,
Meet pity every where;
Yet languish for their native home,
Tho' death attends them there.

Many of these eminent individuals from time to time revisited their relatives, who, at home, dragged on a painful existence in penury and scorn, persecuted by the laws, and trampled to the dust by every official bigot who could yell loudest against Pope and Popery. Some of the visitors, in the present instance, were " The nobles of Spain," alluded to by Carolan.

JOHN JONES.

¹ John Jones was a descendant of Jeremy Jones, of Ardneglasse, and Bellaghy, in the county of Sligo, by Elizabeth, granddaughter of Sir James Ware, the celebrated Irish antiquary. We are inclined to think that the present respectable members of his name and family will be pleased to find so handsome a mark of respect to one of their ancestors amongst the Works of Carolan. Tradition has not preserved the name of the fair one described, but that she eventually gave it up for that of her admirer, may be reasonably inferred from the ardent manner in which he addresses her. We shall be disappointed, or this will become a charter song among their descendants, and follow them

" Like echo attending the voice whence it grows."

It was considered advisable to adapt the metre to Carolan's sweet air of " Young Terence M'Donogh," which will be found in Vol. I. of Bunting's collection of Irish Music.

GRACEY NUGENT.

¹ Gracey Nugent is one of the only four of Carolan's poetical compositions that have been published. It has hitherto been honoured with two versions, one in Walker's

"Memoirs of the Irish Bards," and the other by Miss Brooke in her "Reliques of Irish Poetry"; but many have thought that there was still ample room left for another. It is not to be wondered that an unfavorable opinion should have been formed of our bard's poetical talents, when judged through the medium of translations entirely destitute of the liveliness and spirit which so peculiarly mark his compositions. Here, however, must be excepted the few given by Miss Brooke, and Baron Dawson's sprightly paraphrase of "Bumper Squire Jones." I have in vain sought for the original of this excellent song, which Walker terms "one of Carolan's most brilliant effusions."

Gracey Nugent "was sister to the late John Nugent, Esq. of Castle Nugent, Culambre. She lived with her sister, Mrs. Conmee, near Balenagar, in the county of Roscommon, at the time she inspired our bard."—*Walker.*

This delightful air will be found in Bunting's collection of Irish Music, Vol. I.

In the second verse, line 5, the word ʒeɑnɑmhuıl should, in grammatical accuracy, be ʒeɑnɑmhlɑ, but the poet was obliged to adopt the former, in order to preserve the harmony of the verse.

MILD MABLE KELLY.

¹ Mable Kelly is one of the finest of Carolan's poetical pieces, and, for the reason contained in the preceding note, it has been translated for this work. This beautiful effusion, combined with others in this collection, will deservedly place Carolan in a more elevated position as a poet than he has hitherto held. The metre adapted by Miss Brooke was rather unhappily chosen. It is the same as that in which Phillips versified the celebrated Ode of Sappho, and seems to have been selected in consequence of the striking resemblance be-

tween the first line of the Greek and Irish poems. The translation of Sappho runs thus—

> Happy as a god is he,
> That fond youth, who placed by thee,
> Hears and sees thee sweetly gay,
> Talk and smile his soul away.

Carolan, as translated by Miss Brooke—

> The youth whom fav'ring Heaven's decree
> To join his fate, my fair! with thee;
> And see that lovely head of thine
> With fondness on his arm recline:
> No thought but joy can fill his mind.

Even in this translation our favorite bard need not tremble at a comparison with the beautiful relic of Grecian genius.

I hope to be pardoned for extending this note, by a few words concerning the great Irish family of which Mable Kelly was a member, though unable to ascertain, with any degree of certainty, to which branch she belonged.— The O'Kelly family was descended from Colla da Chrioch, brother to Colla Huais, king of Ireland, A. D. 327. Its chiefs were princes of Hy Maine, a Western district, comprehending the Northern parts of the county of Galway, and Southern parts of the county of Roscommon. The principal stocks were those of Aughrim, Gallagh, and Mullaghmore. From those so many branches from time to time spread over Ireland, that in the words of De Burgo, " vix enim, aut ne vix quidem pagum aut villulam reperire est, ubi Kellius aliquis non adest." Many respectable families of the name at present enjoy considerable estates in the territory of their ancestors.

A passage in this song has been adduced to contravene the assertion that Carolan remembered no impression of colours.

> Thy soft cheeks disclose,
> The mixed lilly and rose,
> ———— that soul speaking eye.

"How is it possible," says his fair encomiast, "that his description could be thus glowing without he retained the clearest recollection, and the most animated ideas of every beauty that sight can convey to the mind." many other passages, equally forcible and beautiful, occur throughout his poems, which strengthen this conclusion. The observation on the line in which he so pathetically alludes to his want of sight is just and elegant. It concludes thus—" but indeed his little pieces abound in all the riches of natural genius."

The music of Mable Kelly is published in Mr. Bunting's First Volume. Carolan composed other musical pieces for the members of the O'Kelly family.

THE CUP OF O'HARA.

[1] Kian O'Hara, Esq. of Nymphsfield, in the county of Sligo, whose descendant, Charles O'Hara, is governor of that county, and one of its Members in Parliament. This respectable gentleman is in possession of a remnant, worth some thousands annually, of those estates which have been in the possession of his ancestors for upwards of 1550 years.

One of the wisest measures which could be adopted by the British Government, after Catholic emancipation, in order to secure the pacification and consequently to promote the prosperity of Ireland, (if the latter be an object) would be to promote a few of the aboriginal families to places of honor or emolument in the several counties or districts of the country. This is advanced in perfect earnest. The veneration of the

124 NOTES.

people for the Milesian families, or even for those who can trace connexion with them, can hardly be conceived by our English brethren. To this day they weep over the political downfall of the ancient gentry of the land. " To whom, my friend, did that castle," pointing to a ruined edifice near Gort, in the county of Galway, " belong in former days?" I enquired of a poor man, who lived in a wretched cabin on the road-side : " To the O'Shauhgnessys," he replied, with a deep sigh ; " The heir is in France, he has been expected as long as I can remember, but, alas ! I am now old, and I fear he will never return." Such a people, possessed of such feelings, deserved very different treatment from that which they have experienced for ages past at the hands of England.

I will not assert that " O'Hara's full cup" is superior to Anacreon's beautifully decorated bowl, yet there is something in the former more congenial to the *taste* of an Irishman.

If a full cup was Carolan's delight, and few knew how to prize one better, it may be reasonably inferred that he was a sworn foe to an empty one. This he has shewn in the following impromptu, describing an indifferent reception which he once experienced at the house of a rich farmer :

> Ϧléuɼ tiȝhe chum ᴀ bheich buᴀn,
> beᴀn chɲuᴀϧh ᴀ'ɼ ɼeᴀɼ ȝᴀn tᴀɼt;
> Cupᴀn beᴀȝ ᴀ'ɼ ȝᴀn é lᴀn,
> 'Y ᴀ léȝeᴀnn ᴀɩɲ clᴀɲ ᴀ bh-ɼᴀϧ.

A little store they had, and it would seem
   Both had resolv'd that far that store should go ;
The dame a pinching shrew I well might deem—
   No sense of thirst the husband deign'd to show ;—
A cup, half filled, lay idle and undrain'd,
For out of reach all night that cup remain'd.

PEGGY BROWNE.

[1] The female here celebrated was daughter of George Browne, the hospitable owner of Brownstown, in the county of Mayo, an ancient and respectable family of the West of Ireland. The noble houses of Sligo and Kilmain, and the families of Castlemagarrett and Brownstown, in Mayo, and Moyne, in Galway, are now among the principal of the name.

George Browne was married to the daughter of Mac Sweeny chief of his tribe, Carolan, who never omitted testifying his respect for the aboriginal Irish, particularly addressed the lovely object of his encomiums, as "the fair and beauteous daughter of Mac Sweeney,"—ᐃl ɪnʒhín Mheɪc Ƭuíbhne, ʌ ɲuín ḃhɪl, cʌɲchʌɪʒh mé." In the Memoirs of the venerable Charles O'Conor, a curious instance of Irish hospitality is related.—" In the parish of Kilmurry, and county of Cork, the Mac Sweeney's set up a stone near Clodagh, on which they inscribed in Irish, an invitation to all passengers to repair for entertainment to the house of Mac Sweeny." The hospitality of Brownstown, however, with less ostentation, was considered more genuine. To Mac Sweeny all strangers were welcome with an invitation; to George Browne they were heartily welcome without one. Competitions of this kind are peculiar to Ireland, and honorable to its children, who are well-known, in the exercise of this virtue, often to go beyond their means. In this respect they are diametrically opposed to the wealthier and more favored natives of our sister isle. Much is it to be wished that this fine impulse were expanded into the yet nobler one of national love and friendship between the two countries; that the only competition between them would be to promote, mutually, the happiness and prosperity of each other. *Sed Diis aliter visum est.* The demon of religious discord is abroad —but we cannot trust ourselves further with this subject.

² *"Like wild fairy music they melt on the air."*

Τῐ͡ʒh-cheól, Fairy music, is sometimes heard along the delightful, but unfrequented hills and vales of our island, where these gentle beings love to reside. It is frequently mentioned in our poems and songs adapted to strains sweetly correspondent to the aerial melody which they imitate. Some of our fairy legends have been given to the world, but the tiny actors themselves yet want an historian. The most celebrated of their kings are, Finvar, whose principal residence is at Knockmagha, in Connaught; and Macaneanta, who holds his court at Scraba, in Ulster. It is not our intention here to meddle with their affairs. The reader who may be curious on the subject is referred to the elegant and entertaining account of the Fairies of Scotland, given in the "Minstrelsy of the Scottish Border," by Sir Walter Scott. Well would it have been for our Irish elves, had their destinies favored them with so noble a delineator.

Contrary to our intention we must again allude to Finvar, the fairy ruler of Knockmagha. This is a conspicuous hill in the county of Galway, and at the foot of it stands Castlehackett, the charming residence of the Kirwan family. It is very confidently believed throughout this part of the country, and that not entirely by the lower classes, that a friendly intercourse has, for time immemorial, subsisted between the heads of this family and their neighbour Finvar. According to the testimony of the domestics, the king and his elves frequently take a carouse in the wine cellar; but, in return, it is whispered that they copiously replenish the casks, which here have never been known to run dry. The principal proof of this intercourse, however, remains to be told. This family has long been noted for preserving a superior breed of racing cattle. The late respected proprietor of Castlehackett, John Kirwan, for nearly half a century took the lead at the Curragh of Kildare, where his horses were almost always victorious. This success was unequivocally attributed to his friend Finvar. The latter and his people, as the grooms solemnly averred, dressed in red jackets, took the horses out on nightly excursions, but to recompense their owner, they unfailingly endowed them with such surprizing fleetness that no racer, except one rode by a fairy jockey, could keep pace with them. Idle, indeed, would be his task who would undertake to question the truth of these relations. Many other adventures are related of Finvar, but, anticipating the full consent of the reader, they are postponed for the present.

This Fairy digression nearly caused us to omit mentioning, that " Peggy Browne" has been translated to the favorite old air of " Molly Bawn."—Mary Fair.

GEORGE BRABAZON.

¹ This lively sally of Carolan's muse was composed for one of the predecessors of Sir William John Brabazon, of Brabazon Park, in the county of Mayo, baronet, descended, with the Earls of Meath, from Sir William Brabazon, Lord Treasurer and Lord Chief Justice of Ireland, in the reign of Henry VIII. Catherine Brabazon, (surnamed boech ⱭN boꞃⱭıꞃ—" of the parting cup," from her hospitality) sprung from the ancient family of Burkes', of Glinsk, baronets, and wife of Malby Brabazon, of Ballinasloe, grandson of the Lord Treasurer, is yet remembered for her many virtues.

It has been found rather a difficult task, in the translation of this song, to preserve the peculiarity of the measure, and at the same time convey an idea of the inimitable spirit of the original. These points, however, have been in some degree attained by adapting the first four lines of each stanza to a particular measure, and the remainder to the well known humorous turns of " Paddy O'Rafferty," reversing the order of the air. This is one of the many instances in which it has been found impossible to follow Carolan's music by English words.

² "*Than Norrall and Dunmore their sports and their pleasures.*"

The former is a small town in the county of Galway, anciently the residence of the Bermingham's, barons of Athenry, one of whom, the fifteenth in descent, told Sir Henry Sidney, in the reign of Elizabeth, "that he was as poore a baron as lyveth, and yet agreed on to be the auntientest baron in this lande." — *Sidney's Letters*, I, 105. Norrall was the seat of the Mac Ranells (from whom the name Reynolds,) feudatory chiefs of Munter-Eolus, an old family of great repute, " now represented," says Charles O'Conor, " by George Mac Ranell, of Letirfian, in the county of Leitrim, Esq."

BRIDGET O'MALLEY.

¹ The versatility of Carolan's genius and the correctness of his judgment appear to us as fully established even by the few specimens contained in this volume. The reader cannot but be impressed by the difference of style, manner, and sentiment, which pervade these compositions, particularly such as are addressed to the male and female subjects of his praise. The liveliness, spirit, and expression of the former present a striking contrast to the soft, sweet, and flowing melody and tenderness of the latter. This is fully exemplified in his "George Brabazon," and "Bridget O'Malley." The latter is not inferior to any in the collection, and coupled to the sweet air "Lough Sheelin," presents a combination of music and poetry which has seldom been surpassed.

The O'Malley's are a highly respectable aboriginal family of Ireland. The celebrated "Grana Weal" (Grace O'Malley) was daughter of the chieftain of this name, in the days of Queen Elizabeth. Some curious notices of this famous heroine will be found in another part of this work. My esteemed friend, Sir Samuel O'Malley, baronet, her descendent, enjoys a large portion of the estates of his ancestors in the west of Ireland. This is perhaps one of the most ancient tenures in Europe.

SHANE GLAS.

¹ This little rural song has been long attributed to Carolan, and though not entirely satisfied as to its authenticity, yet I have admitted it, as possessing some striking features of resemblance to the general offspring of his muse. It is said to have suggested the idea of the popular English song, "The humours of Donnybrook Fair." Both are to the same Irish air, the " Plᴏ́ᴢᴀɪpe Ðubh," Englished, " Black Joke."—Shane Glas means, literally, Green Jack.

JAMES PLUNKETT.

¹ Carolan never prostituted his muse to party politics, or religious bigotry. Though attachment to the ancient faith and families of Ireland was the ruling principle of his heart, yet he could discern the virtues, and celebrate the praises, of those who dissented from the one, or claimed no connection with the other. This he has evinced in his " Planxty Payton," " John Jones," " George Brabazon," the present, and several other instances.

James Plunkett, of Bunenedin, in the County of Sligo, to whom this handsome tribute was paid, was one of the most accomplished youths of his time. At this period, the Irish language was studied as an indispensible part of the education of an Irish gentleman, and was at the same time, spoken by all classes in the west of Ireland. This explains the following passage in the first stanza—ꝼuᴀıꞃ oıdeᴀꞃ—ᴀıꞃ ᴣhᴀoıbheılᴣ bhꞃeᴀᴣh, ƚıomhchᴀ.—" He was instructed in the fine polished language of Ireland."

The "Meeting of the Waters," is the sweet air selected for the translation of "James Plunkett."

NANCY COOPER.

[1] The original answers the comparatively modern, though well known Scotch air, "The Flowers of Edinburgh." This may lead to the recovery of the air which Carolan composed for the present words. Who "Nancy Cooper" was, I have not been able to ascertain.

[2] For mhnᴀ deᴀꞃᴀ, the poet should have written bhᴀn dheᴀꞃ the genitive plural, but he was obliged to adopt the singular, in order to preserve the correspondence of the verse. The general grammatical accuracy of Carolan's compositions, considering his inability to study Irish as a written language, proves the correctness with which it was spoken in his time.

With this song, I close Carolan's lyric compositions, though in possession of several others, not inferior to most of those here given. Should the present meet with that reception, which it is, perhaps rather fondly, thought they merit, the remainder may, at some future period, be given to the world.

CAROLAN'S MONODY ON THE DEATH OF HIS WIFE, MARY MAGUIRE.

This affecting Elegy, was published in Walker's Memoirs, with a paraphrase which made some atonement to the shade of Carolan, for the versions of " Planxty Stafford" and " Gracey Nugent," given in the same publication. The Irish and English readers are now enabled to form a judgment of the relative merits of that paraphrase, and the present translation.

This Monody, and the following Elegy on Mac Cabe, are the only specimens of our bard's elegiac compositions with which I am acquainted. They present him before us, in a new character, but in such a one, as he will be found to sustain with all the genius of the true poet of nature. Simple and unadorned, they breathe the genuine language of unaffected grief. He drew from his heart, and gave expression to the anguish which he there felt, at the loss of all he held dear in this world, the wife of his bosom, and the valued friend, whom supposing dead, he so pathetically termed "the sight of his eyes." In these effusions, he appears in a more advantageous light, than, even when surrounded by an admiring auditory, in the most joyous moments of festivity, he poured forth those melodious strains, which will render his name immortal.

That Carolan was a man of irreproachable morals, and even of a religious turn, we have been already assured by the best authority. The following little prayer, or rather pious stanza, has been attributed to him; how truly I know not. It has however, been considered worth preserving.—

A írgh ná 3 cnéucht! rucír éu3 a m-bánn an chncínn,
'Ar crótbhe do chléibh do peúbadh le lámh an dáill,

Fuil do zhéuz do théacht air talamh 'na linn ;
Aip reaich do rcéiche beip féin zo paippchar finn !

Oh! king of wounds! Oh! son of heaven! who died
  Upon the cross, to save the things of clay;—
Oh! thou whose veins pour'd forth the crimson tide,
  To wash the stains of fallen man away;—
Oh! thou whose heart did feel the blind one's spear,
  While down to earth the atoning current flow'd;
Deign gracious Lord! thy creature's cry to hear!
  Shield me, and snatch me to thy bright abode.

CAROLAN'S LAMENT OVER THE GRAVE OF MAC CABE.

Carolan's friendship for Mac Cabe, and the incident which gave rise to the present instance of it, have been frequently related. The latter was a humourist, and sometimes exercised his wit in good natured sallies on his sightless friend. Once meeting him after a long absence, he disguised his voice, and "accosted Carolan as a stranger. In the course of conversation, the dissembler insinuated, that, he had come from Mac Cabe's neighbourhood; on which Carolan eagerly enquired, did he know one Charles Mac Cabe, " bhiòh aichne tpach azam aip," I, once knew him," replied Mac Cabe. " How once, what do you mean by that," says Carolan. " I mean, answered the wag, " that this day se'nnight, I was at his funeral." Carolan, shocked and moved by this melancholy news, dictated the above little Elegy, on his friend; who, soon after, assumed his proper voice, and rallied the good natured bard, on his giving such a sincere proof of his affection for one, who had so often made him the butt of his wit.—*Walker.*

The "Leabaidh be 'n chpé bhíòh cúmhang," "The narrow bed of clay," will bring Ossian's "narrow house" to the recollection of the reader. The third stanza of the above, being a play on words, could not be translated. The original of this, and the following Elegy, are given in Walker's and Miss Brooke's publications, but in a very confused and incorrect manner.

MAC CABE'S ELEGY ON THE DEATH OF CAROLAN.

Mac Cabe, afterwards lived to mourn over Carolan, and has shown himself not undeserving the friendship which he enjoyed. "The circumstances," says Miss Brooke, "which gave rise to this Elegy, are striking, and extremely affecting." Mac Cabe, had been an unusual length of time without seeing his friend, and went to pay him a visit. As he approached near the end of his journey, in passing by a church-yard, he was met by a peasant, of whom he enquired for Carolan. The peasant pointed to his grave and wept.

Mac Cabe, shocked and astonished, was for some time unable to speak; his frame shook, his knees trembled, he had just power to totter to the grave of his friend, and then sunk to the ground. A flood of tears, at last, came to his relief; and, still further to disburden his mind, he vented its anguish in the following lines. In the original, they are simple and unadorned, but pathetic to a great degree.—The conclusion of this Elegy, reminds us of Dr. Johnson's Epitaph, on Claude Phillips, the Welch Musician :—

> Sleep undisturbed within this peaceful shrine,
> Till angels wake thee with a note like thine.

The compositions of Carolan intended for this work being now concluded, it may be seen that in the few observations I thought it necessary to make, I have altogether avoided any allusion to the merits of the translations. From this pleasing part of my duty I have abstained, lest feelings of acknowledged partiality and admiration for a valued and talented friend, should lead to expressions which might give a moment's uneasiness to a mind as delicate as it is refined: but the beauties with which his translations abound are too obvious, they stood in need of no comment from me. I commit them, therefore, with confidence to the public. For myself, I shall ever esteem it a source of pride and satisfaction to have been instrumental in associating the talents of Turlogh O'Carolan and Thomas Furlong, men whose names will be remembered while taste and genius shall be respected in the land of their birth.

BACCHANALIAN ADDENDA

TO THE

REMAINS OF CAROLAN.

ADDENDA.

After the contents of the four parts which compose these volumes had been distributed, the three following articles remained undisposed of, and as they had been considered worthy of preservation, and appeared to partake somewhat of the sprightly character of Carolan's muse, it was determined to place them immediately after his " Remains." Irish compositions of the Bacchanalian class, are numerous, and many of them excellent. These given here, have been selected, not as possessing superior claims to poetical notice, but for presenting, in so many points of view, the subject which they describe with such exquisite humour. The first, is a tolerably good specimen of our jovial effusions; the second, an ingenious satire on our extra-jovial propensities; and in the third will be found a lively description of an Irish merry-making of the olden time. Taken together, they exhibit some striking features of national character.

It is well known, that, in former times, Ireland was distinguished for temperance and sobriety. At more recent periods, it became noted for some of the opposite vices. Cambrensis, Camden, who viewed the country not even " uno, oculo," and other English writers, who seldom omitted any opportunity of vilifying the Irish; in summing up their virtues and vices, have never charged them with drunkenness or intemperance. Dr. Samuel Madden, who published some Essays on Ireland, about a century ago, "and whose name," says Dr. Johnson, "Ireland ought to honour" tells us, that, "*Many men can remember*, when we were as remarkable for our sobriety, as we are now for rioting and drunkenness. Dr. Madden's political and religious prejudices, prevented him from pointing out the cause of this sudden metamorphosis. In the common cant of his day, he ascribes it to Pope and popery; but, he well knew, had he the candour to state the fact, that, it owed its baleful origin to the impoverishment of the country, to the oppressed and degraded state of the main body of the people. Wilfully passing over the cause, he takes care, however, minutely to describe the effects. "We drink," says he, "as Tacitus describes the old Germans, night and day, and though we have poisoned our bodies, and debauched our minds, though we have enriched our enemies, impoverished ourselves, *and undone our wretched country*, yet to comfort us, this may be said for our honour, that we have got the character, of bearing our national miseries with the best grace, nay, and of being the most boon companions, and the fairest drinkers of Europe," and concludes, by presenting a hideous picture of the " poverty, idleness, misfortune, and misery which too many of our people languish under," the consequences, he might have added, of English domination, and of penal laws. Not satisfied, with depriving the old proprietors of their ancient estates, or content with driving forth myriads of Ireland's noblest sons, as branded wanderers over the face of the earth, the malignancy of English laws, and English taskmasters, reduced to the situation here described, the wretched sojourners, who were declared to exist in the country, only by legal connivance.— Great is the retribution which England owes this ill-treated land. May the errors of the past be remembered as warnings for the future.

Since the relaxation of the penal laws, great and general amendment has taken place in Ireland. Habits of intemperance have gradually declined among the middle classes of society, but unfortunately, still largely prevail over the lower orders. Here also they will disappear, when, on the abolition of the impious remnant of that degrading code, security shall be increased, and property extended, the latter flowing like the blood from the heart, and revolving to its source, continually preserving and invigorating the entire system. Of this truth, a forcible illustration has been given by Mr. Coxe, an intelligent English traveller: "A Polish nobleman, Zamoiski, in 1760, emancipated six villages, in the Palatinate of Masovia. While the inhabitants were in a state of servitude, he was occasionally obliged to pay fines for disorders committed by them, for in a state of drunkenness, they would attack, and sometimes kill passengers: since their freedom, he has seldom received any complaints of this kind against them."—This fact, applied to Ireland, speaks volumes. May our "wise and enlightened" legislators profit by it, and effect on a larger scale, what the patriotic Polander so happily achieved on a smaller. If not actuated by a desire to promote the prosperity of Ireland, and consequently to secure and perpetuate the stability of the Empire; may they, at least, feel for the degradation of their species; and, by an act of legislative justice, prevent our poor countrymen, from exhibiting themselves any longer, as drunken helots to the derision of the world.

A h-Uircidhe Chroidhe na N-Anmann.

A h-Uircídhe chroídhe na n-anmann,
 Leagann tú air lár me,
Bídhim gan chéill gan aithne,
 'S é an t-eachrann do b'fheárr liom;
Bídheann mo chóta srpacaidhche,
 Agus cailim leat mo chápabhác,
A's bíodh a n-deárnair máithmhe leat,
 Acht teangmhaidh liom a márach.

An uair éisdidh tusa an t-aithfrionn,
 A's bheidh do shailm páidhte,
Déin-si ionad-coinge liom,
 A's teangmhaidh liom a d-tigh an tábhairne;
Nar a bh-feicir cairt a's cnagaire,
 A's coc a d-tóin an bharraile,
A's bíodh an lár anaice leat,
 A's pómhat-sa cuirfead fáilte.

WHY, LIQUOR OF LIFE!![1]

TRANSLATED BY JOHN D'ALTON, ESQ.

The Bard addresses Whiskey.

Why, liquor of life! do I love you so,
When in all our encounters you lay me low?
More stupid and senseless I every day grow,
    What a hint—If I'd mend by the warning!
Tattered and torn you've left my coat,
I've not a cravat—to save my throat,
Yet I pardon you all, my sparkling doat!
    If you'll cheer me again in the morning.

Whiskey replies.

When you've heard prayers on Sunday next,
With a sermon beside, or at least—the text,
Come down to the alehouse—however you're vexed,
    And though thousands of cares assault you:
You'll find tippling there—till morals mend,
A cock shall be placed in the barrel's end,
The jar shall be near you, and I'll be your friend,
    And give you a *" Kead mille faulte !"*

Och! mo rón agus mo chara tú,
   Mo shiúr agus mo bhráchair,
Mo chuirt, mo thigh, mo thalamh tú,
   Mo chruach agus mo stáca,
Mo threabhadh, mo cheucht, mo chapaill tú,
   Mo bha 'r mo chaoire geala tú,
A's thar gach nídh d'ár áirmhighear
   Do chongbhaidh me-ri páirt leat.

'S a mhuirnín mhuinte, mhargalaich,
   Is taithneamhach do phóg liom,
Na diúltuigh fós do'm chárrthannacht,
   A's gur de'n chineadh chóir me:
Leanán-sídhe leam gin a'r fium,
   Bráchair gaoil damh brén de'n t-sult,
Is cáirdeas-críost damh boul or Punch,
   A's teangmhaidh liom d'á chóruídheacht.

Is iombdha brúghin a'r eachrann
   Bhíodh eadrainn le páiche,
Acht ní fhanann brón am aigne,
   'N-uair líontar chúcam air clár tú:

The Bard resumes his address.

You're my soul, and my treasure, without and within,
My sister and cousin, and all my kin;
'Tis unlucky to wed such a prodigal sin,—
   But all other enjoyment is vain, love!
My barley-ricks all turn to you,—
My tillage—my plough—and my horses too,—
My cows and my sheep they have—bid me adieu,
   I care not while you remain, love!

Come, vein [2] of my heart! then come in haste,
You're like Ambrosia, my liquor and feast,
My forefathers all had the very same taste—
   For the genuine dew of the mountain.
Oh, Usquebaugh!—I love its kiss!—
My guardian spirit [3] I think it is,
Had my christening bowl been filled with this,
   I'd have swallowed it—were it a fountain.

Many's the quarrel and fight we've had,
And many a time you made me mad,
But while I've a heart—it can never be sad,
   When you smile at me full on the table:

Mo bheán agus mo leanbh tu,
    Mo mháthair agus m'athair tu,
Mo chóta-mór 'ſ mo ſlappeɼ tu,
    'Ṡ ní ſgaɼɼfaiḋ mé go bráṫ leat.

Táiḋ na gaolta iſ feáɼɼa agam
    Dá bh-fuil a b-talamh Eiɼeán,
Leann a'ſ bɼannda, a'ſ uiſce-beaṫa,
    Acht nach d-tagann an cláɼáeict liom;
Bronnaim ſúḋ do'n n-Eaglaiſ,
    Máɼ iſ móɼ mo ḋúil 'ſ a' m-beannuiġṫeaċt,
'Ṡ guɼ mhaiṫ leó bɼáén do bhlaiɼeaḋ ḋe,
    D' éiſ aiṫſpinn do léiġaḋ ḋúinn.

Surely you are my wife and brother—
My only child—my father and mother—
My outside coat '—I have no other!
  Oh! I'll stand by you—while I am able.

If family pride can aught avail,
I've the sprightliest kin of all the Gael—
Brandy and Usquebaugh, and ale!
  But claret untasted may pass us.
To clash with the clergy were sore amiss,
So for righteousness' sake I leave them this,
For claret the gownmen's comfort is,
  When they've saved us with matins and masses.

'Sí mo chreach! bean cheannuighe
na féile.

Air ghuth "Imbó a's Umbó."

'Sí mo chreach! bean cheannaighe na féile!
'S a mheirge mhúirneach, mo ghrádh féin tú,
Fada liom-sa táim do 'd éugmais,
'S ní fhacaidh mé o'n n-am-so n-dé chú,
Ní h-iongnadh dhamh-sa bheith gho déurach,
'S gur phós mé a g-cionn mo dhá bhliadhain déug chú,
'S nach n-deárnas riamh b'achrúghadh chéile,
Chionn mar do bhéurthá mo thoil féin damh,
'S gur rhaoíl me nach rcárrainn go h-éug leat.—

Ní h-é so amháin maith b'á n-déanfadh,
Tráth gheabhadh cách thú air clár mar phéirín;
An té bhíbheas bocht do ghníodh tú saidhbhir,

ODE TO DRUNKENNESS.[1]

BY THOMAS FURLONG.

Oh! drunkenness, spouse belov'd, where dost thou stray?
   Here in thy absence stupidly I pine;
For since we parted this time yesterday,
   Och! many a black and bitter thought was mine;
I wedded thee all freely and light hearted,
   Ere I had counted even to my twelfth year;
I lik'd thee—for each ugly care departed,
   Each big blue devil[2] flew off when thou wert near;
I vow'd all constancy, and kept my vow,
But Oh! sweet spouse, what signifies it now?

Wide is thy range, but greater still thy power,
   A worker of wild wonders sure thou art;
Strange are thy freaks in that most merry hour,
   When the full cup comes forth to warm the heart;
Oh! many a miracle thou hast effected,
Where jolly ones at table were collected.

'S an té bhiadh bruideamhuil bhiadh ré méinneamhail,
'S an té bhiadh cruadh do ghluaisfeadh féile ann,
An t-é bhiadh rantach, amrsaidh, raoghalta,
bhiadh ré greannmhar, fonnmhar, méadhrach.—

'S maith do mhúin tú dhamh a bheith tréidheach,
A d-teangain mo mháthar 's ann gach béurla,
Anoir, fárasir! gidh taoim gan aén smid!—

D'inneorainn páirt de'd thréidhibh;
Is uairle tú ioná síol Éabha,
'S do bhéurfadh buadh air fhearaibh Éirean,
An t-é bhídheas ciúin do ghníobh tú baoth é,
An t-é bhídheas óg do ghníobh tú aosda,
A's óg arís an té is léithe.—

buadh beag oile nach innsim féin ort,
Ní fhághann tu locht air leaba ná air éadach,
Ní fearr leat an doras 'ná an ghabhal-éadain.—

An tráth b'eirghid amach a n-aidhidh an fhéurta,
Siúbhlaid an oidhce go h-aigeantach aédhrach,

Chang'd by thy touch, the poor quite rich become,
  The low get lofty, and the timid bold;
Cripples get legs—speech bursts upon the dumb,
  And youth and vigour bless the weak and old;
The smile of joy steals o'er the face of trouble,
And folks, with hardly half an eye, see double.

By thee the miser's purse is open'd wide;
  The dolt, the dunderhead, thou renderest witty;
'Tis thine to lend meek lowliness to pride,
  Or melt the stony selfish heart with pity;
Even old hell-daring weather-beaten sinners,
When mov'd by thee, in grace become beginners.

How oft have I, dear spouse, inspired by thee,
  Pour'd the full tide of eloquence along;
How oft have other wights been chang'd like me,
  Now up now down, defending right or wrong;
  Subtle thou art, and valourous and strong.
'Tis thine to loose the slave, or bind the free,
  To paralize with age the limbs of youth;
  Void of all guile, with thee dwells barefac'd truth.

'As bídheann sreall chlábair air gach taebh díobh,
Luíghe agus codhla budh chumadh cá n-déansadh,
b'ionann leó an mhóin a'r lár an péidhtig,
b' ionann leo ann fheasrthainn a'r sasrach 'na n-éadan.

Ní h-iníoll a h-aithpritheár do ghaolta;
Ní raibh mac dílear ó íochdar Eirean,
Nach raibh do ghaol leis tré na chéile.—
Siúr I Dómhnaill, a's siúr I 'Néill tu,
Siúr Mac Zuidhir ó imeal na h-Eirne,
Siúr Mheic Mathghamhna na n-each léimneach,
Siúr uí Duirgthche le n-duirgthidhe déigh-ghníomh,
Siúr uí Chonchubhair o imeal na h-Erionn,
Siúr uí Fluaire agus siúr uí Flaéghallaigh,
'S an iarla bhídh fhiar gan áen locht:
Is iarla Chill'-dargha, budh gar a chéim duit,
Siúr Uí Annluain ó bharr an t-sléibhe,
Siúr Mheic Aénzura ó Chaol an éirge,
Siúr uí Chonnaill a nall ó Antruim,
Siúr uí Chatháin agus siúr Mheic Suibhne.—
Siúr gach Dochtúra, agus siúr gach liaigh tú,
Siúr gach Trúpaora agus siúr gach Saighdiúir,

BACCHANALIAN.

No friend art thou to sly hypocrisy—
Thy sway prevades each station and degree;
  Thee boor hath hail'd thee with a sleepy song—
O'er many a conquer'd conqueror hast thou smil'd,
And even the guide of realms thou turnest to a child.

Little thou heedest where thy head is laid,
  To thee the bog is as the bed of down;
Little thou mindest how thy clothes are made,
  Small thought hast thou of cloak, or cap, or gown;
For points of form thou carest not a pin,
But at the chimney would as soon come in,
Aye! just as soon as at the opening door—
The pelting rain may drench thee o'er and o'er,
The storm—the snow—the hail around may fall,
Still! still, my fearless spouse, thou smilest at them all.

To many an ancient house art thou allied,[2]
  Oh! many a lordly one thy claim must own;
The soul of valour and the heart of pride,
  Must stoop all humbly where thy face is shewn.
  Wide round the land thy relatives are known,

Siúr aoiṡ-ciúil 'ás siúr na h-eiġse,
Siúr mhór mór do lucht ḋliġhe Eireann.—
Siúr ḃan n-uasal ann uaiġneas lae thu,
Siúr ḃan n-óg gach neóin b'á ḃh-feudfaḋh,
Siúr ḃan n-díomhaoin ag luiḋhe 's ag eirġhiḋh,
Siúr ḃan síos air íochdar sléiḃhe.—

Tá páirt ṡogus agam féin leat,
Agus gaol ró mhór ag eaglais Dé leat.—

Is áirde ṡuas tú 'ná na sréurtha,
Is mó go mór tú 'ná Cnoc-Gréine,
'S biḋh tu ṡioll an lá 'ná ḋheiġh sin.—
Go fá'd thuasaim! 'ás dia do'd peiḋhteach!
A lán 's an chupán a's beiḋh me féiḋh leat.

The chiefs of might, O'Donnell and O'Neill,
  Mc. Guire, O'Rorke, Mc. Mahon, and O'Connor,
  Kildare's old earl, that pink of worth and honour,
O'Hanlons from the mountain and the vale,
Fair Antrim's chiefs, O'Connell ' and O'Keane,
And hundreds more that must unnam'd remain,
All these, though haughty, and tho' high they be,
These, darling drunkenness, are allied to thee.

Nor these alone—each doctor in the land,
  Each strutting soldier, drest in red or blue,
Each minstrel, and each poet, takes thy hand,
  Lawyers and ladies, and the clergy too.
  Knockgraney's head '—the sky so fair to view—
Than thee at moments seem not more sublime,
But low thou liest again in little time :
Fill up the cup, may victory be thine own,
Go where thou wilt—for thee I'll live alone.

Mazaiḋh laiḋir.

Seaġán O'Neaċtáin ró chán.

Ro ḃeaóiḃ sláinte Mhaʒaíḃ Láiḋir,
  Le'r mhiann ʒráḃh a críche;
A'ʃ ní ḟuil áit ó'n Slúc ʒo Máiʒh,
  Naċ bhfuil 'ʃ an t-sláinte chéaḋna!

Má mhiannaiḋ páirt an ḟial-bhalcáin
  Bhiaḋtaich, Bhráithrich, bhríoʒhmháir;
Iʃ ḋ'fuachaʃ tráċh ʒach fuar-iompáḃh,
  Air chualaċt bhfeáʒh na tíre.

Sláinte uí Néill, uí Ḋómhnaill chléiḃh,
  A'ʃ ʃlioċḋ na h-Eirne ríoʒhḋha,
A'ʃ ʒach a bh-ḟuil beó 'ʃ an Múmhain mhór
  De ʃhliochḋ an Plóiʒh mac Mhile;

MAGGY LAIDIR.[1]

BY THOMAS FURLONG.

Here's first the toast, the pride and boast,
   Our darling Maggy Laidir;
Let old and young, with ready tongue,
   And open heart applaud her;
Again prepare—here's to the fair,
   Whose smiles with joy have crown'd us;
Then drain the bowl—for each gay soul,
   That's drinking here around us.

Come friends dont fail—to toast O'Neill,
   Whose race our rights defended;
Maguire the true—O'Donnell too,
   From eastern sires descended;

Gach a bh-fuil a b-talamh aicme Mhaine,
  Slán tre sheasc do'n b-taoibh-sin.
'Sa laighean na lann, ba bríoghmhár, teann
  A maoin, a g-clann, 'sa n-díoghlabh.

Líon an mheadair do'n n-árd-easrog,
  Grábh a's sheasc na n-daoine;
Líon an mheadair do'n n-athair Peattar,
  So an teagasg fíre:
Dá chuach, trí cupáin do'n n-athair Tomás,
  Is binn a chómhrádh dílear;
Stiall a's canna do'n n-athair Ceallaich,
  Dia d'á theagasg choidhche,

Líon an tsála, so bhaoibh sláinte,
  Ultaich dána a's Muimhnich!
Sláinte laighnich, an luchd meadhrach,
  A's Chonnacht' na máighdean sgiamhach!
Líon an chata leis an tsála;
  A m-breall go h-árd air bhaoithibh,
Le'r mhiann Eire chlaoibh go h-éirgeasr,
  A Dhia, bíbh tréun le Gaedhlaibh!

Up! up again—the tribe of Maine,
   In danger never fail'd us;
With Leinster's spear for ever near,
   When foemen have assail'd us.

The madder fill² with right good will,
   There's sure no joy like drinking—
Our bishop's name—this draught must claim,
   Come let us have no shrinking;
His name is dear—and with him here,
   We'll join old Father Peter;
And as he steers thro' life's long years,
   May life to him seem sweeter.

Come mark the call—and drink to all
   Old Ireland's tribes so glorious,
Who still have stood—in fields of blood,
   Unbroken and victorious:
Long as of old, may Connaught hold
   Her boast of peerless beauty;³
And Leinster shew to friend and foe,
   Her sons all prompt for duty.

Gach neach nach ólfadh, claoidh 'sus brón air,
  Sláinte chóir na h-Éireann!
Míle grádh air, rgián 'na ghárradh,
  Pian a's plágha Éigipt!
'S gach neach nach iarrfadh an aire cheadna,
  Go rabh na piartha ag créim air!
A's é air misge ó chaol-uisge,
  A n-dólás broide a's péine!

Muc, ím, bulcán, rósh gach rolair,
  Óigfhir iomlána, Gaedhlach,
Féurta fíre chlanna Míle,
  A's féurda chroidhe na féile;
Fleadh do sháruigh, fleadh na n-árraidh,
  A's uile bhámh na n-Óiche;
Fleadh na n-uarál, 'sa mol-chualachd,
  Féurta buan Mhilésius.

Déanam gáirdeas, cosa 'n-áirde,
  Óir n-domhnach, táim-si air meisge!
Ócmhar Múimhneach, fá g-cuairt chríd linn!
  So an t-Aoibhneas clirde;

A curse for those, who dare oppose
   Our country's claim for freedom;
May none appear—the knaves to hear,
   Or none who hear 'em heed 'em:
May famine fall upon them all,
   May pests and plagues confound them,
And heartfelt care and black despair,
   Till life's last hour surround them.

May lasting joys attend the boys
   Who love the land that bore us;
Still may they share such friendly fare,
   As this that spreads before us.
May social cheer like what we've here,
   For ever stand to greet them;
And hearts as sound as those around,
   Be ready still to meet them.

Come raise the voice! rejoice, rejoice,
   Fast, fast, the dawn's advancing;
My eyes grow dim—but every limb
   Seems quite agog for dancing:

Féuch-ri Una a'r Brighitt rhúgach,
  Mór a g-clú 'r an ringce!
Fearghall, Dúnlaing, Neachtain clúiteach,
  Go raibh a rúgradh cinnte!

A Dhiarmaid gluair, 'r a Thaidhg air luar!
  Ro an rúairceár aoibhinn;—
A Chathaill mhóir, a Dhómhnaill óig,
  Ro tróft a'r pléidh, dar m'fhirinn'
Caitríona ann, go bríoghmhár, teann,
  Mór a'r Meadhbh a'r béibhionn;
Tá flór ag ringceadh, cóir 'na timcheall;
  Oil! oil! ir compán chléibh ro!

A Aengúir croídhe, a Mhághnúir bhuídhe,
  'R a Mháible bhinn, 'r a Shíle,
Le ceól a m-béul, cur ceóibh air chéud,
  Gan bhrón nó éad a n-daóine:
Seinn dhúinn rtéangcán, píob a'r tiompán,
  Ro an chómh-ghair ghleórach!
Súd ort a cháirdeár! Dia gach lá leat,
  Dar fiagh ir breágh an tróft ro!

Sweet girls begin, 'tis shame and sin,
  To see the time we're losing;
Come lads be gay—trip, trip away,
  While those who sit keep boozing.

Where's Thady Oge?—up Dan you rogue,
  Why stand you shilly shally;
There's Mora near—and Una's here,
  And yonder's sporting Sally;
Now frisk it round—aye, there's the sound
  Our sires were fond of hearing;
The harp rings clear '—hear, gossip hear!
  O sure such notes are cheering.

Your health my friend!—till life shall end,
  May no bad chance betide us;
Oh! may we still, our grief to kill,
  Have drink like this beside us;
A fig for care!—but who's that there,
  That's of a quarrel thinking?—'
Put out the clown, or knock him down,
  We're here for fun and drinking.

Ṡo oɼt a Chéiɴ, iꞅ ḃiɴɴ ḋo ḃéul,
    Tá aɴ ḃulcáɴ ḃɼeáġ, ḃɼíoġṁhaɼ,
Ḋo'ɴ ḃhalḃh ḃheiɼ ġéim, ḋo'ɴ ḃhacach léim,
    Aɴam cléiḃh, iꞅ ḃɼuiġiɴ ꞅo!
Leaġ aɴ ꞅpóiɴꞅe! ꞅóꞅ ꞅá'ɴ m-ḃóɼḋ leiꞅ!
    Ḃhuꞅ ꞅo aɴ ꞅóġhṁhaɼ ꞅíoġhḃhɼaiġh;
Iꞅ me-ꞅi ꞅéiɴ, mac ꞅiɴe ó'Ńéill,
    Ḃhá ꞅoɼ Eiɼe aġ ꞅíoġhaḋh.

Mac Caɼɼthaiġh móɼ, O'Ḃɼiaiɴ ɴa ꞅlóġh,
    Mo ġhael ġaɴ cheóiḋh, ɴa tɼéɴ-ꞅhiɼ,
Mac Aéɴġuiꞅ úɼ, Maġuiḋiɼ ɴa ɼaɴɴ,
    O miꞅ chlúɴteach Eiɼɴe;
O'Ceallaich cléiḃh, O'Conchúḃhaiɼ tɼéuɴ,
    A'ꞅ ꞅlioċt Ḃɼaɴḋuiḃh aɴ ɼuaiḋh-ꞅhléiḃhe,
O'Ḋuíɴ aɴ ꞅeaɼ, O'Móɼḃha meaɼ,
    Mo ġhael aiɼ ꞅáḋ ɴa ḋéiġh-ꞅhiɼ.

Tie up his tongue—am I not sprung
   From chiefs that all must honour;
The princely Gaël, the great O'Neill,
   O'Kelly and O'Connor;
O'Brien the strong, Maguire whose song
   Has won the praise of nations;
O'More the tough—and big Branduff,*
   These are my blood relations!!!

NOTES

TO THE

BACCHANALIAN ADDENDA.

NOTES.

WHY LIQUOR OF LIFE.

' English writers on Irish affairs, have servilely copied each other, cæci cæcos, in succession, from Girald Cambrensis to Daniel Dewar. They have had a fruitful source of invective in what they were pleased to term the demoralized state of the Irish peasantry; and this mis-statement they always took care to put forth, as a sort of excuse for the cruel treatment that devoted class received from its English task-masters. That our persecuted countrymen were remarkable beyond other people, for strict adherence to moral rules, is not pretended; but, that they were not inferior to any other, is a fact too well attested to require proof here; and when we consider the nature of the laws under which they groaned for centuries, whose general tendency it was to reduce the Irish people below the common standard of humanity, that fact, will remain an honourable testimonial in their favour to future ages.

For prowess in drinking, the Irish have been often compared to the boors of Germany and Holland, and it must be confessed, that, in this as in other pursuits when they apply themselves, they soon become distinguished proficients. This pernicious custom, as already shown, is but of late growth in

168 NOTES.

Ireland. It originated among an impoverished people, who were sunk and degraded in their own estimation, by the operation of laws founded on bigotry, and administered with partiality and injustice. The Irish are, if any people ever were, excusable for this propensity. They were driven to it by oppression, and continued it from habit.—The fascinating qualities of Irish whiskey, Peter the great's favourite wine, are well known. In the use of this enticing beverage, even our English friends, frequently become " Hibernis Hiberniores," when they visit Ireland. During the late wars, the English soldiery, when ordered hither, felt delight at the anticipated idea of cheap intoxication in Ireland; and Paddy, with characteristic hospitality, always took care to soften down their prejudices by copious libations of his " liquor of life," which too often proved to them liquor of death, by too frequent potations. Even royalty itself, has owned its potency. One of our " staunch" protestant ascendancy aldermen, thought he could not evince his zeal in a stronger manner, than by presenting his sovereign with a few hogsheads, as a sample of Irish loyalty. As for poor Paddy, his " good nature" for the " native" always overpowers him. Like Boniface in the play, he eats, drinks, and sleeps on his whiskey. It is often his only breakfast, dinner, supper, and, in the words of our song, his " outside coat." Saving, he never thinks of, and accumulation is out of the question. He generally sings:—

Copóinn ápiámh ná ṫeilliṅn
Mı ḋheápnáıḋh me ḋhe chpuımneáṫ,
Áċt léıʒeánn ḋo ṫılleáḋh
Máp ḋhpuchḋ áıp án bhṫéup.

Or, with Anacreon:—

Ὅτί 'γὼ πίω τὸν οἶνον
Τόδε μοι μόνον τὸ κέρδος.

Hence the immediate cause of his poverty and wretchedness, but our wise legislators seem determined that he shall be indulged in his career, at the cheapest rate; not, of course, with any sordid view to paltry revenue, but to increase Pat's comforts: and while potatoes continue to be the necessaries, and whiskey the luxury of his life, surely it would be cruel to tax them; besides, the trifle he pays for leave to lose his reason by whiskey, is applied to save his soul by bibles. Kind and compassionate legislators, continue to supply him with both; thus you will at once consult his temporal and eternal welfare, leave to the world a monument of your superior wisdom, and by thus promoting the prosperity of Ireland, and placing her above temptation, deter America from audaciously, perhaps successfully, making love to her on some future occasion.

Under such auspices, is it surprising that Paddy should *praise* his whiskey, as in the humourous effusion before us, and in numerous others interspersed throughout the country. The present appears to be the production of some repentant rake, whose praises are intermingled with keen satirical touches, which seem the result of poignant reflection. It may be necessary here to remind the reader, that after the destruction of the old Irish families by Cromwell, Charles II. and William III. of England, there were thrown in a state of utter destitution on the world, a vast number of younger sons, cousins, nephews, &c. all gentlemen, with abundance of family pride, but a proportionate lack of worldly means. Their ancient estates being possessed by English adventurers, several of those deprived individuals, who were too proud to remain paupers in their native land, entered into the service of foreign states. Of those who remained at home, many were long after known by the name of "roving blades;" while others of more ardent dispositions, under the appellations of Tories and Rapparees, became the terror of various districts. The latter class is extinct. The former has been thus described by a modern writer:—" A race of gentlemen, as they call themselves, who, too poor to support themselves, are, however, much above any commercial or manufacturing profession. I have known some of them without home, wander for months together from house to house, without the ceremony of an invitation. They ate and drank freely every where, and it would be deemed a great infraction of hospitality, to shew them by any indication that they were not welcome." To this roving fraternity, many of whose members are still remembered under the appellation of "Bucks," belonged the hero of our song, who seems, like most of his countrymen to have been gifted with more wit than prudence. The composition is a finished picture of such an Irish character.

² The original does not quite warrant this epithet, but we believe our tour d'expression is national.—T.

³ I am no enemy to puns, they sometimes operate like the little gods of laughter, that Lycurgus set up in every Spartan home, yet I must assure the reader, that if this word presents such a quibble of wit, it is not a child of mine. In the original, the line is " Gin and rum are my fetch, my familiar spirit," (leẛnẛn,) I will not presume to say that the conclusion of this stanza is so literal ; but, without some few liberties, it were quite impossible to humour the genius of the one language, and maintain the structure of the other.—T.

⁴ This singularly arch address may remind the Bacchanalian student of Cicero's celebrated encomium on study; but, while I write these lines where that orator's countrymen were once triumphantly encamped amidst all the sublimities of St. Vincent's rocks, I have no opportunity, and I confess, but an equal quantity of willingness, to employ time in identifying the illustration. Verbum sat.—T.

NOTES. 171

This species of Irish poetry, is replete with wit. The original humour of the following lively passage, in the well known song, *Cailin deas chruidhte na m-bo*, will be felt by every Irish reader.—

ḣᴀcᴀ ḃ-cɼí ʒ-coc ᴀ m-bɪᴀḃh ʀcɪúɪɼ ᴀɪɼ,
Aʒuʀ mᴀɪʒ ᴀɪɼ ᴀ núnn 'cum cíʒhe ᴀn óɪL.

The lover of Irish whiskey can best supply the comment on the following lines, in the concluding stanza of the same composition.—

Ḃo bhɪḃh me-ɼɪ Lᴀʒ, mᴀɼbh, ɼínce,
Ƴ ʒᴀn bɼíʒh ᴀnn mo choɪʀ nᴀ ᴀ'm Lᴀɪmh.

ODE TO DRUNKENNESS.

[1] The original of this ode, is much, and deservedly admired. It was composed by some unknown bard, or in Irish phrase ꝼɪLe eɪʒɪn, in the latter part of the seventeenth century, when the practise it describes so well, was beginning to spread among the broken down and oppressed Irish. In the year 1792, a translation was published by Charles Wilson, a youth of promising genius, who, afterwards repaired to the great theatre of Irish talent, and Irish disappointment, London; where, in essaying

————" To climb
The steep where Fame's proud temple shines afar,"

he sunk, like most of his countrymen, unnoticed and unknown. The following passage in his translation, has been often praised :—

"At twelve years old I felt thy charms,
Thy very name my bosom warms;
Wed to thy sweets, I cannot rove,
And age thy beauties will improve.
Oh! with thee blest beneath the shade,
In vain dull cares my breast invade;
When win'try storms would freeze my blood,
You add new vigour to the flood:
The purple flood that swells my veins,
Or else when summer clothes the plains,
I seek the shelter of the shade,
If blest with thee, dear melting maid:
O never from my bosom part,
In thy soft durance hold my heart;
In vain without thee friends would smile,
And song the ling'ring hours beguile.
In vain the morn her sweets would shed,
And pleasure spread her downy bed;
In vain the rose her tints unfold,
Or lilly spread her summer cold.
For thee, what would I not endure?
Deprived of thee, the rich are poor;
And who is poor of thee possest,
Thou dearest soother of the breast?
The covetous, once touched by thee,
Grows generous to the last degree;
The dumb, thou can'st with words inspire,
The brave, grow bolder from thy fire;
The song without thee now grows weak,
Transparent as the silver lake,
Oh! quickly on the board appear,
And all my drooping spirits cheer.
Thy joys my ravish'd sense confound,
Soft leaping through thy crystal mound;
What nymph with thee, say, can compare?
Thy stream, the ringlet of her hair;
Thy crystal ray, what eye so bright?
Transparent azure ting'd with light."

The "versicle" of the poem, which has not been translated for this work, is here subjoined with Mr. Wilson's version:—

Ʉ mheᵹe chꝑéᵹcheᴀch, bhéuᵳᴀch, mhᴀᵳᴇᴀch, ᵳhᴀmh,
Ⅰᵳ clıᵳ̇ɓe, ᵴᵳéᴀnmhᴀꝑ, mᴀéᵳɓhᴀ, meᴀᵳɓᴀ ᴀ ᵹ-cᴀıl;—
Me-ꝑı, ᴀ chéıle, bheıch ᴀm ᴀonᴀꝑ uᴀıᴛ-ꝑı lᴀ,
Ⅰᵳ ɓᴀóıᵳ céılle ᴀ'ᵳ céuᵳᴀɓh buᴀn ᴀn ɓᴀıl.

> How often on thy sweets I've hung
> Thy charms shall oft employ my tongue;
> Still let thy sweets my verse employ,
> Without thee, what is human joy?

However smooth Mr. Wilson's translation may be, it wants the spirit and humour of the author; but, in Mr. Furlong's, the English reader has the same advantage in these respects, that the Irish reader possesses in the original. Our talented translator has here succeeded with his usual felicity.

¹ "*Each big blue devil flew off when thou wert near.*"
This line is not literally warranted by the text, but the nature of the stanza, will, it is hoped, excuse it.

² "*To many an ancient house art thou allied.*"
This allusion to the ancient Irish families, was conceived in the spirit of genuine satire. At the period when the ode was written, the habit of drinking, was becoming general among them, from the causes already stated. They were, at the time, considerably reduced from their former state of opulence and dignity; or, according to my learned friend, Counsellor Matthew O'Conor, in his History of the Irish Catholics, they "were involved in one promiscuous ruin. Henceforth," continues he, " they disappear from Irish history. Their descendants had continued long known and revered, under a cloud of poverty. A century of adversity, depression, or exile,

obliterated every trace of them." The last sentence must, however, be taken in a qualified sense, perhaps, in a political one. The ingenious Historian's own respectable family, is, at present, one out of many distinguished exceptions.

' *" Fair Antrim's chiefs, O'Connell and O'Keane."*

In some copies which I have seen, the original reads, " Ṫiúp ui Chonnaill Anall ó bpeancpíbhe"—O'Connell of Breantrye, in the County of Clare. The line, however, as it stands in the text, is the true reading. The family of Mac Donnell of Antrim was originally Mac Connall or O'Connell. The following curious extract, relating to the first of the name, in the North of Ireland, I have taken from the original Irish Privy-Council Book of Queen Elizabeth, preserved in Dublin Castle.—

" Articles entered into, at the Campe near Dunluce in Ulster, the 18th September, 1584, between Sir John Perrott, lord deputy and the rest of the council there, and Donell Gorme Mac Connell of the Glynnes in Ulster, reciting that humble sute had byn made by the ladie Agnes Cambell wife to Turloghe Lenoghe O'Neile, mother to said Donell Gorme, and also by said Donell himselfe, that in respecte of his humble submission, and protestinge by his oathe his loyaltie and fidelitie to her Majestie, the council would vouchsafe to accept of hym, and not onelie to graunt unto hym to become a free denizen of this realme, but alsoe that he might hold so much of the Glynnes, as were the lands of Mysset alias Bysset."— By the articles these demands were granted, " provided that the said Donell or his heirs, or any of his followers or servants, shall not serve any forraine prince or potentate within this realme; nor kepe any Scottes, *but such as be natives of Irelande*, without lycense; shall serve with a rising-out, of fower skore footemen within Ulster; shall not unlawfullie intermeddle with any of the borderers of Ulster—shall paie a yearlie rent of three skore good and lardge fatt beoves at the

Nurie (Newry); shall always serve against Saverlie Bwoy and any other forraine Scott; shall preserve to the governor of the realme, for the tyme beinge, all the hawkes, which shall be breede in the Glynnes; shall not drawe to him any of the followers of Clandeboy, the Rowte or the Ardes; and shall in all things behave himselfe as a good and faithfull subjecte—Signed DONELL GORME MC. CONALD."—Such was the origin of that great family, in the County of Antrim.

⁵ Knockgreany—Cnoc Ṡṕéine, the hill of the sun, in the County of Limerick, from which Ꝏloy Ṡṕéine, the small County Barony, in that County.

MAGGY LAIDIR.

¹ This inimitable description of an Irish feast, was written in the seventeenth century, by John O'Neachtan, author of several poetical compositions in his native language, and is now printed from a transcript made in the year 1706. It is supposed to be delivered by the chairman, or president of the meeting, and of such a personage the reader may be enabled to form a tolerable idea, from a curious account of an individual of the ancient family of O'Leary, given by Mr. Townsend, author of the Statistical Survey of the County of Cork. O'Leary long lived, and lately died at Millstreet, a small town in the County of Cork, and he took a pride in being one of the last of his countrymen representing old families, who maintained the ancient hospitable way of living. "He was known," writes Mr. Townsend, "only by the name of O'Leary. He lived in a small house, the lower part consisting of little more than a parlour and kitchen, the former of which, properly supplied with every article of good cheer, was open to every guest, and at every season; and, what will more surprise, this profusion was accompanied with perfect cleanliness and

decorum. His cellar, well stocked with good liquors, never knew the protection of a lock and key; for, as he said himself, nobody had any occasion to steal what any one might have for asking. It derived security, however, from other causes; from deference to his sway and respect for his person, both of which were universally felt and acknowledged within the circle of his influence. He was also a justice of peace for the County. The appearance of O'Leary, was always sufficient to maintain order in fairs and meetings, and to suppress any spirit of disturbance, without the aid of soldier or constable. He possessed, indeed, some admirable requisites for a maintainer of the peace; for he was a very athletic man, and always carried a long pole, of which the unruly knew him to be no churl. To these good qualities, O'Leary added an inexhaustible fund of original humour and good natured cheerfulness; and being very fond of the bottle himself, it was impossible to be long in his company sad or sober."—In many respects, O'Leary may be fairly taken as a genuine representative of the chairman of our Irish feast.

In point of composition, Maggy Laidir, is superior to O'Rorke's Feast, so humourously translated by Dean Swift. Here the chairman only speaks throughout. His first toast is, old Ireland, under the name of Maggy Laidir.—then the beauteous daughters of Erin—the ancient families of the four provinces, Leinster, Munster, Ulster, Connaught—the clergy, who have been always dear to the Irish—and finally, he wishes disappointment to the foes, and success to the friends of the Country.—After these libations, he becomes a little gay, and must have music. He calls on the harpers to strike up. As the glass circulates, conversation and noise increase. Finally, a quarrel, *more Thracùm*, ensues, which our elevated chairman, in the true Irish stile of commanding peace, orders to be quelled, by knocking down the combatants, and he concludes by alluding to his noble ancestry and kindred, to enforce his claim to respect and obedience.

The air as well as the words of Maggy Laidir, though long naturalized in North Britain, is Irish. When our Scottish kinsmen were detected appropriating the ancient saints of Ireland, (would that they rid us of some modern ones,) they took a fancy to its music. Not satisfied with borrowing the art, they despoiled us of some of our sweetest airs, and amongst others, that of *Maggy Laidir*. This name signifies in the original, strong or powerful Maggy, and by it was meant Ireland also, designated by our bards, under the names of *Sheela na Guira, Grauna Weale, Roisin Dubh,* &c. By an easy change, the adjective *laidir*, strong, was converted into Lauder, the patronymic of a Scotch family, and the air was employed to celebrate a famous courtezan of Crail.

Although Ireland was always famous for sanctity and music, and could spare liberally of both, yet our countrymen ever felt indignant at the unacknowledged appropriation of many of their favorite saints and airs by their northern relatives. Now and then, some dauntless hagiographer ventured to vindicate, and succeeded in restoring a few purloined ascetics; but, until lately, the Irish had other things, more material than music to defend; and, it was not until Mr. Bunting appeared, that any effectual effort was made to rescue our national melodies from Scotland, and oblivion. The Irish origin of Scotch music has been admitted by the best informed writers on the subject. Mr. Ritson, however, merely thinks it "by no means improbable." Thompson, the correspondent and friend of Robert Burns, in the preface to his "Select Melodies of Scotland," says, "Some airs are claimed by both countries, but, by means of the harpers, or pipers, who used to wander through the two, particular airs might become so common to both, as to make it questionable, which of the countries gave them birth."* The inspired bard

---

* Mr. Thompson records some curious anecdotes of Scotch music worth laying before the reader. "The 'Banks and Braes of Bonny Doon,' was composed by a gentleman of Edinburgh, who had been jocularly told, that a

himself, in a letter to Thompson, in 1793, mentions the
"wandering minstrels, harpers, and pipers, who used to go
frequently errant through the wilds, both of Scotland and
Ireland, and so some favorite airs might be common to
both." Thus far only are the modern writers of Scotland
inclined to admit. If space allowed, I could here show the
Irish origin of several airs, claimed even by the respectable
names just quoted, but the fact may appear in the succeeding notes to the original words of the airs alluded to.

Among the many wandering minstrels to whom Scotland is
acknowledged to be indebted for the importation of Irish
music, may be enumerated, in modern times, O'Kane, the
"famous Irish harper," as he has been termed by Boswell, in
his Journal of a Tour through the Hebrides, and Laurence,
brother of Thomas O'Conellan, a celebrated Irish composer.
The latter was born at Cloonamahon in the County of Sligo,
early in the seventeenth century, and died at Loughgur in the
county of Limerick, some time previous to the year 1700. After
his death, his brother Laurence went to Scotland, bringing with
him several of the deceased bard's compositions. Of these,

Scottish air could be produced by merely running the fingers over the black keys of a piano-forte, which gave precisely the progression of the national scale.—The much admired song, set to the Flowers of the Forest, beginning, 'Ive heard o' lilting,' written on the battle of Flodden, though it has been supposed a production of that remote period, is said to have been written about the year 1755, by a sister of Sir Gilbert Elliot, of Minto.—A short time before the Teatable Miscellany, in 1724, it had become very much the fashion in London, to write and compose songs and tunes in the Scottish style. Some of these were adopted by Ramsey; and, by this means, have obtained a place among our popular airs, though they possess very little of the Scottish cha- racter. The composers of those airs, from Doctor Green down to Doctor Arne, seem to have adopted a kind of conventional style, which they chose to call Scottish; and, a good many of their airs having found their way into Scotland, have become naturalized among us."—*Preface*. Had this ingenious collector candidly made the latter admission, as to our Irish Melodies, he would, indeed, have proved himself entitled to the character of a "sturdy moralist."

two, from their celebrity, deserve particular notice, viz. "Planxty Davis," since well known as the "Battle of Killicranky," and a prelude to the "breach" of Aughrim, universally admired under the name of "Farewell to Lochaber." According to tradition, O'Conellan composed upwards of seven hundred airs, which he played on the harp; but of these comparatively few have been preserved. His character, as a performer, may be ascertained from the following little ode, said to have been addressed to him by a cotemporary bard, whose name has not survived.

Oıð ðo'ꞃ ᴄ-ꞅᴀoı ᴄoıꞃðeᴀıbһᴀꞃ.

A Ṁıoᴣһᴀıðһe, ꞃuᴣ ꞅıoꞃ-ᴣһnᴀoıðһ
   Ꞃᴀ ꞅóðlᴀ ᴀıꞃ ꞅᴀð,
A'ꞅ ꞅuᴀıꞃ ᴀóın-ᴛ-ꞅlıᴣһ ꞅһıoꞃ-ᴄһꞃoıðһe
   Ꞃᴀ ᴄᴄeól ᴀmᴀᴄһ,
Iꞅ ðıomһᴀóın Ṁıᴀnꞅᴀıðһe
   Ꞃᴀ һ-Eóꞃpᴀ ᴄһᴀꞃᴛ,
Ð' éıꞅ ᴄһımᴄһıðһe mһᴀoꞃðһᴀıðһe
   Ðo mһeóꞃ lᴀᴣ, m-bꞃᴀꞅ.

Ꞃı'l mıᴀnn-ᴄһꞃoıðһe ᴀᴣ ꞃıoᴣһꞃᴀıðһe
   Ꞃᴀ һ-Eóꞃpᴀ ᴀıꞃ ꞅᴀð,
Ꞃᴀᴄһ mınıᴣһᴛᴄһeᴀꞃ le mᴀéᴛһ-ꞅᴄꞃıb
   Ðo mһeóꞃ ᴣo pꞃᴀb,
Ðo ᴄһlᴀéᴄһlóıðһıꞅ ꞃe ꞅᴀéᴛһıomһ,
   Ꞃe ᴣeóın ðo ᴣһlᴀᴄ,
A Ṁıoᴣһᴀıðһe, ꞃınne ꞅoᴣһbһꞃuıᴣһe
   Ꞃᴀ ꞅóðlᴀ ꞅһlᴀð.

A chaoin-tí, re maothuízhear
   Chum deór zach deare,
A'r le bh-fraoírizheann clí-phían
   Zach breóbh-chorp lag;
Ní'l aen t-raoí nach claen bíbh
   'S an n-órd air rad,
A líonaíbhe, re d' fhíozhaíbheacht
   bhaineas ceóbh de rearir.

ODE TO O'CONELLAN, THE IRISH MINSTREL.

TRANSLATED BY JOHN D'ALTON, ESQ.

    Spirit of Minstrelsy!
  Supreme o'er Erin's bards thy sway.
To thee the silvery sounds belong,
The thrilling sympathies of song,
The warblings of an angel sphere,
That Europe's minstrels when they hear,
    O'erpowered—enchanted—pine away—
      And yield the palm to thee!

      In vain do mighty kings
   Invite the world to bardic feats;
To try the mastery of thy art,
To fire the soul or melt the heart;
Immortal one! thy glowing hand
The wilder music of the land
    Hath silenced.—Echo but repeats
      The magic of thy strings.

> And they—the gentle ones,
> The fairy spirits of the hill,
> That used to breathe so softly round
> Our midnight dreams—ecstatic sound!
> Are silent all; for only thou
> Canst wring the tear, or smooth the brow,
> And charm the heart's pulse with the skill
> Of more than mortal notes!

That this vivid description of O'Conellan's performance on the Irish harp is not altogether the result of poetic fancy, may be easily shown. Not to tire the reader with many testimonies of the power of this ancient instrument, I shall be content with one only, and that, perhaps, the latest, but certainly not liable to any suspicion of prejudice or partiality. Mr. Gunn, of Edinburgh, in his " Historical Enquiry respecting the performance of the Harp, in the Highlands of Scotland," printed in 1807, says, " I have frequently heard it related of O'Kane the celebrated Irish harper, that he very commonly drew tears from his auditors. During my residence at Cambridge, Manini, our first violin, often spoke of the performance of O'Kane with great rapture; assuring me that, together with an astonishing variety of other things, he could, although blind, play with great accuracy and fine effect, the first treble and bass of many of Corelli's concertos, in concert with the other instruments."—The strains of Patrick Quin, an old Irish harper, who performed publicly in Dublin in 1809, are still remembered with delight.

> ² " *The madder fill with right good will.*"

The madder was a wooden drinking cup, formerly much used in Ireland, but at present to be found only in the western districts.

³ "*Long as of old may Connaught hold
Her boast of peerless beauty.*"

Connacht na maighdean sgiamhach — Connaught of beauteous maidens.—This province has been long celebrated for female beauty. Limerick stands similarly distinguished. It has been remarked by a witty French traveller, that the "women of Limerick are more celebrated for their beauty, than the men for their understanding," but of him it has been observed, that however qualified he might have been to appreciate the former, he was too superficial to be able to form a judgment of the latter. Very different is the description of the men of Limerick given by my excellent friend Mr. Mc. Gregor, in his History of that city and county.

⁴ "*The harp rings clear.*"

"Among the Celtic nations, the harp was in the highest esteem. The great Theban harp in, and even before, the time of Sesostris, was possessed of power that has made even modern musicians doubt the authenticity of its history. But in no country has the harp been in greater estimation than in the British Isles. It has been the national instrument of these countries. The Saxons were passionately fond of it—Doomsday Book mentions it—Bede is lavish in its praise. In Wales, it is delivered down to us, that it was so requisite that every gentleman should play the harp, that it was sent round after supper to each person in the company, and that one who could not execute on the instrument, slunk away from the banquet ashamed of being unacquainted with the accomplishments of a gentleman. In *Ireland, the true land of the harp*, its entire history presents such an endless variety of anecdote, both of the instrument and the bards, its masters, that it is unnecessary to trace its antiquity amongst that people; indeed one of the first mentions of it, speaks of the two brothers, the leaders of the Milesian Colonists, disputing which should have the harper, and which the poet." — *Literary Register*, October 26, 1822.

Mr. Gunn, in the treatise before referred to, states "that from the middle of the sixth until the end of the twelfth century, singing to the harp was considered an indispensible part of the education of the upper ranks of society; and at their festivals it was customary for the harp to be handed round, and each of the company in his turn to sing to it—This custom was introduced from Asia with the harp itself. It was probably during this period that the separation of poet and musician in the same person, at least, that the separate profession of a minstrel, or merely instrumental performer, took place in Ireland."

The harp continued in general use in this island until the middle of the seventeenth century. In an unpublished History of Ireland, written about the year 1636, now remaining in manuscript in the Library of the Royal Irish Academy, Dublin, we are told that, " the Irish are much addicted to musick generally, and you shall find but very few of their gentry, either man or woman, but can play on the harp; alsoe you shall not find a house of any account, without one or two of those instruments, and they always keep a harper to play for them at their meales, and all other times, as often as they have a desire to recreate themselves, or others which comes to their houses, therewith." — During the troubles after 1641, when a war of destruction was waged against every thing Irish, Lynch, in his Cambrensis Eversus, informs us that the harp was broken by soldiers wherever it could be found, and adds, " the memory of its form and materials will be unknown and lost to our immediate posterity." The war of 1688, which completed the downfal of the ancient Irish families, also silenced their national instrument. A solitary harp might occasionally be heard emitting mournful sounds over the fallen fortunes of the country, but it was no longer in general use. It seems to have been destined not to survive its masters. It is not, perhaps, going too far to say that, but for the patriotic exertions of Mr. Bunting and the gentlemen of Belfast, in 1792, and of the talented but eccentric John Bernard Trotter, in Dublin, in 1809, the Irish harp would now be numbered with the things that were, and "the memory of its form and materials" preserved only by the antiquary or historian.

⁵ In the "feast of O'Rorke," translated by Dean Swift, a similar passage occurs :—

Atcháip ná n-ʒpápá ce be chipeáṫ án ʒhápnáiṫ,
Iáp lionáṫ á cecpoicne, ir á lápáṫ ján ól.

Good Lord, what a sight! after all their good cheer,
For people to fight in the midst of their beer!

From this admitted propensity of the Irish, (although it is well known to be one of the many evils resulting from their political degradation,) an English antiquary, well skilled, as may be supposed, in the matter, employed many words and some learning, to prove us descended from the ancient Thracians. For this purpose he adduced the excellent lucubrations of that admirable essayist, Doctor Ledwich, in *his* antiquities of Ireland, and the equally good authority of Horace:—

>Natis in usum lætitiæ scyphis
>Pugnare, Thracum est.

But leaving this important point in the hands of such able investigators, we choose rather to address our fellow countrymen in the succeeding words of the same poet:—

>Tollite barbarum
>Morem, verecundumque Bacchum
>Sanguineis prohibete rixis.

6 "*O'More the tough, and big Branduff,
These are my blood relations.*"

The ancestorial pride and inflammable composition of the old Milesians, are humorously described in this poem. The following fragment, by Hugh M'Curtin, containing a similar description, is intended for the Irish reader:—

An tán théidhid rin le céim 'n a ttuaine ag ól,
Ní réidir a n-eirteacht le ruaim a n-zeón;—
An tán théithrid a m-beula a g-cuachaibh teóth,
Beidh a n-gáel le gach aén de'n n-uairle ir mó.

Deársár an brádebáire ir buaidheárthá de'n g-cóir;—
" Ir mé féin á'r mo chéile ir uairle air bórd;
Ir ó Eibhir, mac Eibhric do zhluair mo phór,
A'r tá gáel ag ua Néill, dár Duach! le Mór."

Beárráibheár an t-éitheach gan ruarádh dhó;
A'r beidh tréice ag gach aén aca ruar 'n a dhóid;
Pléurgráid a chéile le tuárgádh trróic,
'T ir bog, réubthá bhídheár béul aca, cluará á'r trón.

Branduff, *(Brandubh,)* was a victorious king of Leinster, who flourished about the close of the sixth century. From him descended the O'Byrnes of Wicklow, who, during centuries, were the terror of the colonists of Dublin. For a detailed account of the spoliation of this ancient family, see Carte's Life of Ormond. This English writer, notwithstanding all his prejudice, admits that, " This case contains in it such a scene of iniquity and cruelty, that, considered in all its circumstances, is scarce to be paralleled in the history of any age or country." The respectable family of Cabinteely, in the county of Wicklow, now represents this ancient house.

Tradition, and an old manuscript in my possession, state,

that the chairman of the feast in *Maggy Laidir*, was intended to represent a member of the O'Kelly family, whose ancestors formerly enjoyed considerable possessions in Leix, (see p. 115.) where many of the name still remain. To this ancient family the narrative which follows, principally relates. As it is esteemed curious, and has never before been published, it is hoped that it may not prove altogether irrelevant or uninteresting.*

In the year 1579, Fergus O'Kelly of Leix, married the daughter of O'Byrne of Glenmalure, in the county of Wicklow. The young lady remained at her father's until a suitable *stone-wall house* should be built by her husband for her reception, there being but few stone buildings at that time in the Queen's county. For this purpose O'Kelly set a number of his tenantry to work. The building was commenced on a Monday morning in spring, it was completed the Saturday following, and the bride was soon after brought home with great rejoicings. This house was then called the week house, and its ruins are now known by the name of the old stone.

It happened that on the following Michaelmas-eve, O'Kelly's lackey, Mac Leod, was from home. On his return he found that *none of the goose* had been reserved for him. Of this he complained to his master, who desired him to settle the matter with the cook, or go to the yard and kill a goose for himself, but not to trouble him with such trifles. Mac Leod, disappointed and dissatisfied with this answer, departed, resolving

---

* This narrative is taken with very little alteration in words, and none whatever in substance, from a manuscript lately found after the death of Garret Byrne, a worthy old Milesian, who resided at Fallybeg, in the Barony of Ballyadams, the scene of the principal transactions which it relates. The paper was indorsed—"A traditional, tho' certain, account of the transactions which happened in and about Logacurren and the rest of O'Kelly's ground in that neighbourhood, beginning in the 22nd of Queen Elizabeth's reign, as told by boddered Catherine Mc. James (who served seven years apprenticeship in O'Kelly's house,) to old Edmund Cowen, and by him to me; the rest by people who recollected it themselves, and I myself remember what happened from the year 1720 to this year 1780.—GARRET BYRNE."

to seek revenge. He immediately repaired to the Earl of Kildare's * castle of Kilkea, where he remained until Christmas-eve, and then told the earl that his master, O'Kelly, had sent to invite his lordship to spend the Christmas with him. The invitation was accepted, and the earl set out with a numerous retinue for O'Kelly's residence. When they came to the top of Tullyhill, near the house, Mac Leod gave three loud calls or signals, as was customary with lackeys in those times. His master hearing them said, that wherever Mac Leod had been since Michaelmas, that was his voice, if he was alive. He soon after arrived and announced the earl's coming, who was received with due honor and attention. His lordship about twelfth day began to prepare for his departure, and expressed the greatest satisfaction at his kind reception, and the friendship of O'Kelly, whose hospitality, and particularly the profusion of his table, he highly praised. O'Kelly observed that it should be more plentiful had he been aware of his lordship's intention to visit him. The earl, surprised, asked if he had not sent to invite him. O'Kelly replied not, but that, notwithstanding, his lordship was welcome; and added that, as he had been pleased to remain until twelfth day on his lackey's invitation, he hoped he would honor him by remaining until candlemas on his own. To this the earl assented, but requested that, as he had so many attendants, he might be at liberty to send occasionally to Kilkea for provisions. O'Kelly answered that as soon as his lordship should find the supplies beginning

---

* This was Gerald the eleventh Earl of Kildare, to whom in October 1579, the custody of the north borders of the English pale was committed. The year following he was suspected of favoring the Irish, and was sent in custody to London, where he was imprisoned in the Tower; but having acquitted himself before the queen and council, he was restored to all his estates. Then it was that he presented to the Royal Herodias of England, the head of O'Kelly.

The castle of Kilkea was situate on the river Greece, in the barony of Kilkea and Moone, county Kildare. For a view and description of this castle, see Anthologia Hibernica, iv. 241.

to fail, he might do so, but not before. Accordingly the fare increased, and the banquets became more sumptuous than ever. When candlemas arrived, his lordship departed with many professions of gratitude, having particularly requested that he might have the honor of standing sponsor for O'Kelly's first child, in order more closely to cement the friendship that subsisted between them. Mrs. O'Kelly was soon after delivered of a son, and his lordship attended the christening, which was celebrated with great pomp and rejoicings. The house was filled with guests, and resounded with music and merriment; but the morning after the earl's arrival, the poor young lady and her infant were both found dead. This melancholy catastrophe was attributed to the boisterous revelry and noise with which they were surrounded. O'Kelly's joy was turned into sorrow, but even this was only a prelude to still greater misfortunes.

Kildare remained for some time to console his friend, whom he invited to Kilkea until he should recover from the effects of his grief, offering him, at the same time, his sister in marriage, and profering his service in any other way which might be most agreeable or acceptable. Unfortunately for O'Kelly he accepted the invitation, and fell, an unsuspecting victim, into the snare which had been insidiously laid for him. A few days after his arrival at Kilkea, the earl took him to the top of the castle under pretence of viewing the surrounding scenery; and with the assistance of some ruffians, whom he had placed there for the purpose, he cut off O'Kelly's head. This atrocious and treacherous murder was soon communicated to the queen, as a meritorious proof of Kildare's loyalty in beheading an Irish rebel; and her majesty was so well pleased, that she directed a grant to be forthwith passed to the earl, of all O'Kelly's estates. The earl being of English descent, an Irish bard applied the following verse to this perfidious transaction:—

Ná béán cománn le peáp Ʒallbá
Ná ʒhníbhip ní peippbe bhuic
beibh chóibhche áip cí bo mheállcá
Aʒ pin cománn án phip Ʒhallbhá piot.

With one of English race all friendship shun,
For if you don't you'll surely be undone;
He'll lie in wait to ruin thee when he can,
Such is the friendship of an English man.

And such have been the aggressions which so long contributed to keep the people of these islands in a state of disunion and enmity. In former times, practices similar to that related were but too frequent in Ireland; and dreadful, though just, were the reprisals made by the natives, on the English settlers.—But to conclude—The earl of Kildare soon after demised his ill-acquired possessions in O'Kelly's lands, to his illegitimate son, Garrett Fitzgerald, at a nominal rent.* This Garrett had a son named Gerald, who was afterwards known by the name of Old Gerald, and long remembered for his atrocious cruelties. He possessed the estates for a long time, and was a great improver. He built where the old orchard now stands at Logacurren, and planted many trees, the last of which were cut down in 1740. He also made several roads, one leading to Rahinahowle, another called the Long-lane, to Timogue, and another through Barrowhouse, being part of O'Kelly's estates, and he planted many ornamental trees in each place. When making these roads he yoked a plough of bullocks, drew a strong chain round some poor widows' cabins which stood in the way, and pulled them down. He surrounded Logacurren with a broad double ditch, and planted quicks on both sides; on these works he employed Ulstermen, whom he paid in cattle, with which they

---

* This demise is mentioned in Lodge's Peerage of Ireland, Vol i. p. 97.

departed for home, and remained the first night at Portnahinch. Gerald pursued them with an armed force, under pretence of robbery, and the unfortunate men, having made some resistance, were slain, and the cattle brought back. Soon after this, he had a dispute respecting some incroachments which he had made on a neighbouring gentleman. It took place on the high road, and after some altercation, Gerald proposed to leave the matter to the decision of the next passenger, who he knew would be his own cow-herd. The poor man was accordingly required to determine the point, and he immediately decided, according to justice, against his master. This so enraged Gerald, that he took the cow-herd and his son, and locked them up in a stable in order to hang them. The cow-herd's wife hearing the danger in which they were placed, came crying for mercy, offering all she was possessed of for their ransom. Gerald told her if she brought him her twelve cows and her bull, they should be released. The poor woman hastened home overjoyed for the purpose, but on her return found her husband and son executed. Gerald, however, kept the cattle for permitting her to take away the dead bodies, over which she mourned in a doleful manner, mixing her wailings with bitter imprecations against Gerald, as follows, in Irish:—

" A ġeaṙaılt ġeaıpp an ġáıpe ġonta—Ḟáraċ ʒo táıpreaċ do ġeata—Oıreoʒ aʒuṛ a dá ċeann ıṛ an b-talman—loċ uaıċne aıp uaċdáp do h-alla.—Neaḋ an t-ṛeaḃáıc a b-poll an deataıċ—Aʒuṛ cac na n-ʒaḃáp ann áıt do leaḃċán—Máp do ḃuaın tú ḋíom an Mac.'ṛ an t-Atċáıp—ḃuaın tú ḋíom an dá ḃó ḃéuʒ 'ṛ an tapbh—Aʒuṛ oıʒhpeaċt náp ṛhaʒh d' oıʒhpeaḋa-re, a Ġeaṙaılt."

" Oh! Gerald of stinted growth and laugh of guile—may desolation reach the threshold of thy door—a bramble with its two ends in the earth—a green lake overflow the surface of thy hall—the hawk's nest in the chimney of thy mansion—and the dung of goats in the place of thy bed—because thou didst bereave me of the son and father—thou took'st from me the twelve cows and bull—an inheritance may your heirs never find."—

All which, as will appear, were speedily fulfilled. Gerald continued his career with impunity, for a considerable time, until at length he fell foul of the Earl of Kildare's agents, when they came to demand the trifling chief rent payable out of O'Kelly's lands. After this his lordship declared against Gerald, and had the estate advertised and sold. It was purchased by one Daniel Byrne, well known by the name of "Daniel the tailor." Gerald was finally dispossessed, his dwelling laid waste, and the possession of the entire lordship delivered to the purchaser. Then it was that the imprecations of the cow-herd's wife were fulfilled; for Gerald losing the inheritance, destitute of friends, and execrated by his neighbours, was obliged to build a little shed in Clopook, and was glad to become keeper of *a sodwall pond.* Here he had no support but the milk of two goats, and these animals frequently lay and dunged in the straw on which he slept, as was prayed for long before by the cow-herd's wife.

Several other particulars relative to the Byrne family and the Fitzgerald's are contained in the manuscript alluded to, but although they might by many be esteemed curious, they are here omitted to make room for other matter more appropriate for the present work. The Irish reader will, no doubt, be satisfied to find their place supplied by the following popular drinking song, by Andrew Magrath, a bard of the last century, well known in Munster by the name of the *Mangaire Sugach.*

OL-ÓAN.

Aindrias M'Craith ró chán.

Nuair théidhim go tigh an tábhairne,
Budh ghnách liom fuireach oidhche ann
Agus buidhean shultmhar fárta,
Ag ól sláinte am thímchioll.—
Mar budh mhiann liom an t-árthach,
Bheith lán gan áen chinnteachcht,
Agus gárraidh bhreágh, ghrádhmhar
Ná'r ghnáchach a bheith cinnte.—
Súd ort féin 'r an g-ceárpt,
A púim-ghil súidh le m'ais,
Bídh rúgach a's ól do dhram,
A'r an ceárpúrgá-ro go fras,
Go n-diúgaim é go cneás,
Go n-glaodhaim tuilleadh a fteach,
As a thréin-fhir na tréig me.

Glór pibe agus bheidhlin,
A'r ceól cruite gan áimhreás,
Níor mhór liom a bheith am thímchioll,
Ag ól Punch go meadhrac,
No beóir maith agus Cíder,
Is iad do dhiúgadh le h-íntinn,

'S go m-budh leór liom már rhaíobhbhreás,
Iad do púrgadh le h-adhmad,
Már do'b fhonn rin már acht,
Gach n-aon ag ól a bhrám,
Go rúghantach cóipach, ceápr,
'S an cpúrga tár air
Ag tnuth le tuilleadh théacht
Go n-diugamaóir ár g-can
       Ag ól planteadha chéile.

A chuideachta bhreágh, bhéurach,
A tá taobh liom 'r a g-cuibhreann,
Ní ngárrram le chéile,
Go n-glaobham tuilleadh fíona;
Ag ro plainte gach trén-fhir
Do'b fhéile, a'r budh ráíche,
'S na'r churr a d-tairge d'a ghaolta
Gach ár rhaothruigh ré le crionacht.
Már mheáram beárt gach éin neach
Do cháith a choróinn 'r a péul gheal
'S a liacht ngrámaire gan chéil
Do mealladh rir an t-raoghal,
A tá noir ag dreoghadh 'r an ccré,
Fir ag a mnáibh d'a n-déir,
       'S iad gan phreab fá líocc 'r an teampoll.

Here, on taking leave of our Bacchanalian Compositions, I consider it but due to my country to observe, that a single English writer, Walter Mapes, Chaplain to Henry II. has left behind him more licentious and irreligious verses, than the utmost misapplied industry could collect throughout the whole range of ancient Irish Literature.—*See Camden's Remains.*— Even Martin Luther the great Apostle of the Reformation, as a profane *bon vivant*, has excelled the best of us. Witness his own description of himself. " Possum jocari, potare, sum facetus convivator, sæpiusque bene bonum haustum cerevisiæ facio *in Dei gloriam.*"—*Coll. Francof. f.* 445.

From among the many sprightly songs which once were favorites with the roving fraternity mentioned in page 170, the two following are selected for the Irish reader. The first is named from the town of Moat or Moatagrenoge, Co. Westmeath, and was generally sung to the well known, lively, and comical air of that name. The other is the original " Twisting of the Rope."

MOCU ZhƞUIɳɳℯ OIZ.

Shiúbhail me-ʃi Cipɼ ʃa bhó,

U'ʃ Móca Zhƞainne óiz az ʃilleabh bhamh;

longnabh ní ʃheacaʃ ba mhó

'ɳa buachaill na m-bó zan zimléact.

    ʃill! ʃill! a ʃúin! O!

    ʃill, a ʃúin O! U'ʃ zaipim chu.

    ʃill! ʃill aʃuin O!

    Azuʃ zheabhaibh cu an zhlóiʃ ma chuilleann

      cu.

bhídh mé a d-tigh Sgolóige a péin,
ba chóip a 'y ba yhéimh an duine yin
bhídh díy de na cailíneadhaibh óga
Y ay tyuagh gan mé poyta ag duine aca
Fill! pill, a pún O!
Fill a pún O! a'y gaipim thu
Fill! pill apún O!
Agur gheadbhaidh tu an ghlóip ma chuilleann tu.

CAYADH AN T-YUGAIY.

Nach é an each mapbh chay ann na h-áite-yi mé,
'Y a liacht cailín deay d' fhagay-ya ay mo dhéigh,
Tháinic me yteach 'y an teach paibh gpádh geal mo chleibh,
'Y chuip an chailleach amach, aip chapadh an t-yúgain mé.

Ma bhidheann tu liom bídh liom do ló a'y d'óidhche,
Ma bhidheann tu liom bídh liom óy comhaip an t-yaóighil,
Ma bhidheann tu liom bídh liom gach ópblach ann do chpóidhe,
Y é mo léun nach liom tpathnóna tú map mhnaói.

A'r síos a Sligeach chuir mé eolus air mo shrábh,
A'r shuas a n-Gaillibh d'ól me léi mo shárth,
Ar brígh mo bhará muná léigfidh bhámh-ra mar a táim.
Déansaidh me cleas a bhainfeas tiubhál ar na mnáibh.

The foregoing are given only as specimens of a class of song formerly fashionable with the "Ranting Irishman," a character somewhat resembling the "Drunken Barnaby" of our English neighbours, but now rather rare in Ireland.

PART II.

SENTIMENTAL SONG.

" Leurs compositions sont d'une grace, d'une mollesse, d'un raffinement, soit d'expression, soit de sentiment, dont n'approche aucun peuple ancien ou moderne. La langue qu'ils parlent dans ce monde à leur maitresse semble être celle qu'ils parleront dans l'autre à leurs houris. C'est une espece de musique si touchante & si fine; c'est un murmure si doux; ce sont des comparaisons si riantes & si fraîches : je dirois presque que leur poésie est parfumée comme leur contrée. Ce qu'est l'honneur dans les mœurs de nos Paladins, les imitations de la nature le sont dans les poëmes Arabes. Là c'est une quintessence de virtu ; ici, c'est une quintessence de volupté.

Raynal—Hist. Philosophique, &c. Suppl. Tom ii.

SENTIMENTAL SONG.

The glowing description of Arabian Poetry given by the elegant and philosophic historian of the Indies, may with truth and propriety be applied to the Sentimental Song of Ireland. The resemblance between them indicates the same origin. The grace, softness, and refinement in expression and sentiment, which distinguish the voluptuous compositions of the East, are found, even to exuberance, in the passionate effusions of the Irish. The rich and varied descriptions of beauty and natural objects, with which this divine art abounds in both countries, will be sought in vain in the national poetry of any European people. "The Irish poems," says the venerable Vallancey, "have none of that wild barbarous fire of the Northerns; all that I have seen are moral, replete with oriental imagery."*—But the affinity

---

* He compares an Irish poem with the Arabic poem of Old Zoheir, translated by Sir William Jones, and declares that nine words in ten are pure Chaldaic and Arabic.—*See Specimen of a Dictionary, &c.*

between the language of Ireland and that of Arabia, is, even still more remarkable. Those best capable of forming an opinion on the subject, have not hesitated to pronounce them to have been anciently the same. These are circumstances which can be accounted for only by the Eastern descent of the ancient Irish, as related in their early annals.

Until of late years the beauties of oriental poetry were but imperfectly known to Europeans. The learned labors of Sir William Jones, and of Professor Carlyle of Cambridge, first enabled the English reader to enjoy the sweets of the " perfumed" compositions of Arabia; but the recent translation of the poem of Antar, from the language of that country, published under the title of a Bedouin Romance, is the most valuable addition that has as yet appeared to this class of literature. With these specimens an opportunity is now afforded of comparing some of the relics of Irish song. That our national muse will answer the description already given, or at least, that it it will not materially suffer by the comparison, is rather confidently anticipated.

The aptitude of the Irish language for lyric poetry has been often observed. The number of consonants, rendered quiescent by elision and aspiration, preserves its harmony and cadence. The broad and slender vowel sounds are capable of being disposed with such variety and effect, that, as has been already observed by my ingenious predecessor Miss Brooke, the poetry of many of our songs is indeed already music without the aid of a tune. Some of these qualities in the Scottish dialect of the English tongue have flung peculiar charms round the rural poetry of Scotland. The soft and sweet language of the Italians has been deservedly celebrated for imparting those essential qualities to their admired productions; but in all the graces peculiarly requisite for lyrical composition, these languages will still be found to fall short of the Irish. In this assertion I disclaim all national prejudice, but the proofs in support of it are now before the public, and will be critically examined by many infinitely more capable of judging than I can pretend to be. One pervading feature in all our songs cannot fail of attracting attention, namely, the exquisite choice and position of words which give full tone and effect to the principal notes of the melodies with which they are associated. The Irish singer will immediately feel the force and assent to the truth of this observation.

Amidst all the misfortunes of Ireland, and it has had its share, the iron hand of oppression through a long series of years has never been able to erase from the land the more tender sympathies of the heart. The devotion and affection for the fair which have ever characterised our youth, are still fondly cherished by them with chivalrous enthusiasm. Sentiments of virtuous love were never more delicately or fervently expressed than in the ancient relics of the pastoral muse of Ireland. The language in which they are conveyed is chaste, elegant, and pure, and the imagery which they present, is a faithful delineation of the most captivating features of natural scenery and rural beauty. The blossom bloom and fragrance of the flowery ornaments of the garden and field—the charming verdure of our island of green—the murmur of the waterfall—the sparkling of the dew—the plumage of the swan, and the mildness of the dove—the sweet notes of the cuckoo, the black-bird, and the thrush, and the liquid gold of the bee, perpetually occur, and continue to heighten the rich descriptions of female beauty contained in these rural effusions.

In the present part of this work will be found some of the most popular songs of Ireland; the original words of those charming melodies which have raised the character of our native music beyond that of almost any other country. These combinations of sweet melting sounds, refined sentiments, and ardency of expression, addressed to the tender virgin, the adored object of virtuous affection were irresistable. They seldom failed to reward the happy swain with the heart and hand of his beloved. To the fascinating influence, of these songs have been attributed many of the early marriages, and much of the "superabundant" population of our country. This, no doubt, will be deemed a new discovery in the science of political economy, and as such, is respectfully offered to the grave consideration of the Malthuses and Hortons of our day. Although I may incur the censure of these wise depopulators, for contributing to increase this national evil, by circulating such alarming marriage-making ballads as *Eileen a Roon*—*Cean dubh dileas*—*Molly a store*—*Coolin*—*Mary of Meelick*, and many other soul breathing ditties to be found in this collection; yet under such censure I shall feel quite at ease, if my humble labors prove successful in rescuing even a small portion of the neglected poetry of my native land from oblivion.

It may be necessary to observe, that, as far as I could discover, one only of the following originals, namely, *Emon a Knock*, has been hitherto printed. Translations, or rather imitations, of a few, are current among the people; but these attempts are of so mean a description, as to be wholly undeserving of consideration.

bpiġhoin paḋuic.

Ní'l báṛún tréan ná áṛb-ḟlaich,
  Do ḋeaṛṛṡaḋ bṛiġḋín páḋuic,
Naċ d-tiobhṛaḋ ṛeaṛc a'ṛ ġṛáḋ ḋi
  Tháṛ mhnáiḃ ḋeaṛa an t-ṛaoġhail;—
A ṛúile aṛ ġlaiṛe ḋeallṛaḋ
  Ná'n dṛúcḋ aiṛ mhaidin t-ṛámhṛaiḋ,
Iṛ ciúin, bṛeaġh, deaṛ é a ġáiṛe,
  'Ṡ í iṛ áilne aiṛ biṫ meinn.

Cá'ṛ bh'ionġnaḋ ṛeaṛa ḟáil
  ḃeiṫ claoiḋte ṛeal a nġṛáḋ léi,
Tráṫ ċiḋhim an ḟaoileann áluinn
  Ġo ṛeannṛúiġheann ṛí me,
'Ṡ a ċioċa caile táṛṛaingṫe,
  Máṛ ṛeṛiobhṛaiḋhe a b-pṛionnḋa ṗáṛiṛ,
'Ṡ a ṗíob maṛ eala aiṛ lán-mhuiṛ,
  'Ṡ í bháṛúiġheann ġaċ aén.

BRIDGET FERGUS,[1]

BY JOHN D'ALTON, ESQ.

What chief of Erin's isle with coldness could regard,
 When wandering o'er
 Our western shore
The flower of Rahard![2]
 Her eyes so blue,
 Like glistening dew
On summer rosebuds seen;
 Her smiles so bright;
 Her heart so light,—
Her majesty of mien!

What wonder Erin's sons should be spell bound in her
  gaze,
 For when I chance
 To catch her glance,
I startle in amaze.
 A swanlike grace
 Her neck displays;
Her eye what witchery tells!

Do'n ḟlàth-àṗḃ tinn má ṫéiḋheann tú,
  Aġ ḋeaṗcaḋh mhnáói na méuṗ láġ,
Ḃṗiġḃín ḃheaṡ na n-àol-chṗoḃh,
  Ṅí ḃaéġhal ḃuit-ṡe an ḃáṡ:—
'Ṡ í an mhúinte, mhaiṡeach, mhaoṗḃha,
  Ṅa ġ-cṗaoḃ-ṡholt m-búclach, b-ṗéuṗlach
Ġo ḃlúth aġ téacht le chéile
  'Ṡ aġ claonaḋh ann a m-báṗṗ.

Iṡ míliṡe blaṡ a béil taiṡ,
  'Ṅá mil aġ ṡilleaḋh aṡ chéiṗ ḃheach,
A ṗíġh na ḃh-ṡeaṗt! ġuṗ éuloiġh
  An ṡġéimh léi thaṗ mhnáiḃh;—
A ṗíoġam ḃheaṡ, a ġhéuṗ-ṡhlaḋ
  Le'ḋ ġhnaóiḋh, le'ḋ ġheán ġach éan ṡheaṗ,
Ġuṗ ṡamháil ḃuit-ṡe ṗéult maiḋne
  Aġ éiṗġhíḋh ġach lá

O chṗuthúġhaḋh an ḋomháin ġo ḃ-tíġh ṡo,
  Ṅí'ṗ ṡhiúḃháil an talamh naóimhtha,
A ṡámháil ṡúḋ ḋe mhnaói aiṗ ḃith,
  Ann áilne 'ṡ a ġ-cáil;

Her budding breast,
But half confest,
Like living marble swells.

Should sickness weigh your frame or sorrow cloud your mirth,
Once look upon,
This lovely one,
This paradise on earth;
Her winning air—
Her tender care
Will put e'en death to flight;
For though her eyes
Beam witcheries,
Her angel soul's more bright.

Her lips more sweet than honey a pouting freshness warms,
While all must own
That beauty's throne
Is centred in her charms;
Though thousands prove
The force of love
Deep cherished in her sight,
A morning star
She shines afar
On all with equal light.

Tá lasadh glan na g-caóin-chon
  'Na leaca geala míne,
A's boladh cúmhra an time,
  Air phóigín mo ghrádh.

Mo chreach! gan mé 's an stuaire,
  le na chéile ag gluaiseacht,
Fó choim, fó choillte a's chuantaibh
  'S gan ar d-tuairisg le fághail
D'fhearr liom 'ná ór na ríogachta,
  Go m-béidhinn-si léithi sínte,
Ann uaigneas seal ós íriol,
  'S ní chreigfinn í go brách.

Since the birthday of creation this sacred earth ne'er
bore
A heavenly mind
So fairly shrined,
As her's whom I adore:
Just like the rose
The blush that glows
O'er all her kindling cheeks,
The dewy thyme
In all its prime
Seems breathing where she speaks.

Oh! that my fair and I were in some lonely place,
Whose woods and groves
Might hide our loves,
And none our wanderings trace :—
That bliss untold,
Beyond the gold
Of nations, would I prize;
For ever there
Her love to share,
And triumph in her eyes!

Eibhlín a Rúin.

Och! le grádh dhuit ní'l rádhapc a'm chionn,
A Eibhlín a rúin!
Bheith trachtadh ort is aoibhneas liom,
A Eibhlín a rúin!
Mo mhórbháil pó-ghrínn is tú,
Rólás an t-saoíghil-n tú,
Mo ghreann a's mo mheadhair is tú,
A Eibhlín a rúin!

Mo bhruinneall-sa go deimhin is tú,
Mo cholúr b'á bh-fuil 'sa' g-coill is tú,
'S air mo chroídhe-sa ní'l laighead gan tú,
A Eibhlín a rúin!

Le cúirtéis agus clú bheathúghadh,
A Eibhlín a rúin!
Dúbhrais bréag nó's liom féin tú,
A Eibhlín a rúin!

EILEEN A ROON.

BY JOHN D'ALTON.

Blind to all else but thee,
    Eileen a Roon!
My eyes only ache to see
    Eileen a Roon!
My ears banquet on thy praise,
Pride and pleasure of my days!
Source of all my happiness!
    Eileen a Roon!

My dove of all the grove thou art,
Without thee sickness wastes my heart;
Who can alone the cure impart?
    Eileen a Roon!

Break not for king or throne,
    Eileen a Roon!
The vows that made thee mine alone;
    Eileen a Roon!

Is breaghdha 'ná bhénus tu,
Is áilne 'ná Pléiteann tu,
Mo Hélen gan bhéim is tú,
　　　　　　　A Eibhlín a rúin!

Mo rós, mo lil, mo chaer is tú,
Mo stór a bh-fuil 'san t-saoghal-so tú,
Plúr mo chroidhe 's mo chleibh is tú,
　　　　　　　A Eibhlín a rúin!

Pachfainn tar sáile leat
　　　　　　　A Eibhlín a rúin!
'S go deóigh, deóigh ní phágfainn tu,
　　　　　　　A Eibhlín a rúin!
Le stárthaibh do bhréugfainn thú,
Do bhlasfainn do bhéul go dlúth
A's rinnsinn go réimh le'd chúm,
　　　　　　　A Eibhlín a rúin!

Thabhairfinn aedhruidheacht duit chois amhán,
Faoi gheugaibh glasa crann,
Ceól na n-éan ann ós ár cceionn,
　　　　　　　A Eibhlín a rúin!

Venus of my ev'ry vow,
Brightest star on heaven's brow!
My Helen—without stain art thou,
   Eileen a Roon!
My rose—my lily—both confest,—
My treasure—all I wish possest;—
The hearted secret of my breast,
   Eileen a Roon!

With thee o'er seas I'd sport my way,
   Eileen a Roon!
Never—never from thee stray,
   Eileen a Roon!
I'd wander o'er thy honied lip,
With love-tales charm thee on the deep,
Then lull thee on my breast to sleep,
   Eileen a Roon!
To vallies green I'd stray with thee
By murmuring rill and whispering tree—
The birds will our wild minstrels be,
   Eileen a Roon!

Le díograis tar bheatha dhuit,

   A Eibhlín a rúin!

Do luídhfinn air leaba leat,

   A Eibhlín a rúin!

D' fhairgfinn a'm ghéugaibh tu,
Coimgeóchainn go féunmhar tu,
Ghrádhfainn thar aén-neach tú,

   A Eibhlín a rúin!

A péiltionn mhaiseach mhodhamhuil,
Sul a m-beidhinn duit bun-os-cionn,
Och! Eugadh budh thuirge liom,

   A Eibhlín a rúin!

With more than human passion warms,
   Eileen a Roon!
I'd fold thee in these 'raptured arms,
   Eileen a Roon!
Press thee—kiss thy bosom's snow,—
Round thee all my fondness throw;—
Joys that only lovers know,
   Eileen a Roon!
Heaven beams in all thine eye,
Spotless star of modesty!
Ere I deceive thee—may I die,
   Eileen a Roon!

Pairtín Fionn.

Grádh le m'anam mo Pháirtín Fionn!
A croidhe 's a h-aigne ag gáireadh liom!
A ciocha geala mar bhláth na n-úbhall
'S a píob mar eala lá Márta!

   A's óró bog liom-sa! bog liom-sa! bog liom-sa!
   A's óró bog liom-sa! a chailín bheas, dhonn!
   A's óró bhoghrainn, dá m-bogfadh-sa liom,
   A b-tús an phluide go sásta.

Cara mo chroidhe mo Pháirtín Fionn,
Bh-fuil a dá ghruadh air lasadh mar bhláth na ccrann!
Tá me-si saor air mo Pháirtín fionn,
Acht amháin gur ólas a sláinte.

   A's óró bog liom-sa, &c.

PAISTHEEN FION.

BY JOHN D'ALTON.

Oh! deep in my soul is my Paistheen Fion,
A love-light for ever this bosom within,
Like the apple's young blossom her breast it is fair,
And her neck with the March swan's can more than compare.
  Then, Vourneen! fly with me—fly with me—fly with me—
  With thy nut-brown ringlets so artlessly curled;
  Here is the one that will live and will die with thee,
  Thy guard and thy guide through the wilds of the world.

Oh! my Paistheen Fion is my heart's repose,
The blush of her cheek's like the opening rose;
These lips that would stain one so earthlessly bright,
Can but drink her a blessing from morning to night.
  Then, Vourneen! fly, &c.

Dá m-béidhinn-ri ann-ra' m-baile m-biadh rúgradh a'r greann,
No idir dhá bharraíle lán de leann;
Mo rhiúirín a m'aici 'r mo lámh raoi n-a ceann,
Ir rúgach do ólrainn a rláinte.
            A'r óró bog liom-ra, &c.

Bhidh me naoi n-oidhche a'm luidhe go bocht,
O bheith rinte raoi an bilinn idir dhá chor;
A chomainn mo chroidhe rtigh! 'r mé ag rmuainneadh ort,
'R na' raghainn-ri le read 'na le glaodh thú!
            A'r óró bog liom-ra, &c.

Tréigreadh mo charaid 'r mo cháirde gaoil,
A'r tréigrid mé a maireann de mhnáibh a' t-raoighil;
Ní thréigreadh le'm mharchainn tú, ghradh mo chroidhe!
Go rinreár a g-cómhra raoi chlár me.
            A'r óró bog liom-ra, &c.

With what rapture I'd quaff it, were I in the hall
Where feasting—and pledging—and music recall
Proud days of my country! while she on my breast
Would recline, my heart's twin one! and hallow the feast.
   Then, Vourneen! fly, &c.

Remember the feverish hours I have pined,
And for thee have I braved them—the storms and the wind—
The night-groves were dropping their dews on my frame,
Yet I sought thee—I wooed thee—I whispered thy name.
   Then, Vourneen! fly, &c.

The friends of my youth and the kin of my birth,
The fair ones I once thought—stray angels on earth;
I'll forsake them for ever, but thee, thee alone
Will I cherish—till life and its memories are gone.
   Then, Vourneen! fly, &c.

Síle bheag ní Chonnalbháin.

A Shíle bhán na b-péurlaíbhe,
 A chéad-shearc ná'r fhulláing snuaim,
D'fág tú m'intinn baortha,
 A'r a'b dhéigh-ri ní bheidh mé buan;
Muna b-tigidh tú do'm fhéuchain,
 A'r éulóghadh liom fá ghleanntaíbh cuain,
Beidh cúmhaíbh a'r tuirse a'b dhéigh orm,
 A'r beidh mé chómh dubh le gual.

Tugthar chugainn na fíonta,
 Agus líontar dúinn an gláine is fearr,
Muna bh-fághad féin cead rince,
 Le mín-chneis an bhfollaich bháin,
A Phlúir is gile 's is míne
 'Ná an fíoda 's ná chlúmh na n-éan,
Is buaidheartha tuirseach bhídhim-se
 'N-uair smuainighim bheith sgarramhuin léi,

LITTLE CELIA CONNELLAN.

BY JOHN D'ALTON.

My Celia! smiling gladness,
   My first love!—my pearly dear!—
My days must set in sadness,
   If long you leave me lonely here.
Oh, should you still so doom me,
   Through sighing glens unblest to rove;
Despair shall soon consume me,
   And leave my heart in ruins, love!

In wine—in wine—to drown care—
   In wine I'll plunge—a maddening tide,
If heaven refuse my one prayer,
   To lie my snowy fair beside.
Far softer to your lover
   You seem than down or silks so gay;
Oh! words can ne'er discover
   My loneliness when you're away.

Dá m-béidhinn-si féin a's mín-chneas
 Chaoimheas, an bhfollaich bhreágh,
A ngleanntán aoibhinn éanach
 O thuitim oidhche go n-éirgheóchadh lá,
Gan neach a bheith d'ár g-cóimhdeacht,
 Acht ceárca-fraoich no'n coileach feadha,
'S go m-biadh greann gan cham am chroidhe stigh,
 Do Shíle beag ní Chonnbeálbháin.

How blithe the breezes gambol
    Through yonder valley wild and free;
Oh! were my love to ramble
    From dawn to sunset there with me;
Where none should see our blisses,
    But heath birds or the cooing dove;
Nor mortal count my kisses,
    With Celia Connellan—my little love!

STUAIRIN NA M-BACHALL M-BREAGH REIDH.

Táid na péultá 'ná reárábh áir án rpéir,
An ghréin á'r án gheálách ná luíbhe,
Tá án pháirge tráighte gán bráén,
'S ní'l péim ág án eálá már bhíobh ;—
Tá án chuáichín á m-báppábháibh ná n-géug,
Ó'á ríor-ráobh gur eálóighir uáinn,
A stuáirín ná m-báchall m-bréágh, réibh,
Ó' fáig Eire fáoi fhábchuirr chruáibh.

Trí níobh' do chíbhim trér án n-gráobh
An reácábh, án bár á'r án prán ;
Agus m'intinn dá' inrin gách lá bhámh,
M'áigne gur chrábh rí le ciách ;—
A mháighdeán, do mhill tú á'm lár mé,
Agus m'impíbhe ó'm láimh chúghát-rá n-iár,
Mé leighár ó ná ráighiobáibh-ri á'm lár,
S go bh-fághaibh tú ná gráró ó Dhiá.

THE LASS OF FAIR FLOWING TRESSES.

BY JOHN D'ALTON.

Each cold star glooms motionless o'er ye,
    No heaven light plays in its eye;
The sun and the moon lack their glory,
    The springs of the deep are run dry.
The drooping swan feels all our sadness,
    The cuckoo responds our despair;—
She is gone who made every thing gladness,
    The maid with the sunny bright hair.

The various emotions that sway me,
    A lover alone can impart;
The heavy forebodings that weigh me,
    The anguish that tortures my heart.
Relieve me, my love! I implore thee,
    From pangs thou alone couldst excite;
And oh! may the heavens shed o'er thee
    An Eden of smiles and delight.

Is binne í 'ná an bheidhlinn 'ṡ ná an liúit,
  'S ná ceileabhar na ccéirṡeach thá ciarr,
Is deallraíche í 'ná an féur trés an n-drúcht,
  'S is fíor-ḃeas gach alt ann a cliaḃ ;—
Tá píob mar an eala air an tsráiġ,
  'S dóiġ liom gur breaġḋa í 'ná 'n ġrian,
'S é mo ċumhaiḋ ġéur mar do ċuġ mé ḋi ġráḋ,
  'S go m-b'ḟearr liom nach b-ḟeicfinn í riamh.

Her voice with more melody flowing,
    Than lute—blackbird—or violin too;
She's brighter than morning grass glowing,
    Empearled with sunbeams and dew.
Her beauties on earth not excelled are,
    Nor the sun shines more glorious above;—
Alas! that I ever beheld her,
    Alas! that I ever should love.

Tiġearna Mhaiġeó.

Dáibhíd O'Murchaḋh ró chan.

Is miann liom feasḋa gluaiseachḋ
 Go cuan ceart an ḟíona ól,
Agus comairc an t-é tá ṡuas ort,
 A Ṫiġearna Mhaiġeó;
A ḟíp-ṡmip scoiṫ 'na nġruaġach,
 Fuair buaḋ agus clú ann gach gleóiḋ,
Tá mé teacht an uair-so,
 Faoi ḋíbeán do ṡlóġ:
Me-ṡi féin bhur n-dall bocht,
 Tá pilleaḋ orraibh annsacht,
Ag ar éirġioḋ failliġhe mhall ḋamh,
 Le blaġḋain mhór faoi cheóiḋ.

A n-geall air an t-é tá láthair,
 Agus áen-mhac Dé na nġrás,
'Nocht óiḋche noḋlacc claóiḋhteár cogaiḋ
 Ṫiġearna Mhaiġeó;

LORD MAYO.[1]

BY THOMAS FURLONG.

Here I rest! my wanderings ending—
   Here the generous wine we quaff;
Here! where sunny smiles are blending,
   With the song, and jest, and laugh.
May the powers above presiding,
   On our host each bliss bestow;
Evermore his footstep guiding,
   Far from guilt and free from woe.
Famed in many a field is he,
The high born boast of chivalry;
Higher and happier may he be,
       My own! my lov'd Mayo.

The blind bard once more returning,
   Seeks thy cheering smile to gain;
Nights and days have found him mourning,
   Doom'd to darkness, grief, and pain.

Feárdá ná cuir ruár díom,
A chraobh na fola is uaisle,
Dár a bh-fuil de mhór-chloig
  Ha naomh ann ran flóimh,
Ni bheidh mé an fad ud uait-re,
  A chraobh na bh-fipéun m-buacach,
Go d-teidh cré na h-uire 'nuar
  Air mo fhean-chorp chaoch faoi fhód.

'S í an bhaintigheanna Máire,
  Thar mhnáibh fuair an chraobh a g-clódh,
A méinn, a b-peárraínn fhárta,
  'S ann gach cáitibheacht mar is cóir;
Geal-ghrian í air gach banntracht,
  A g-ceannraacht 's a g-céill ró mhór,
Fá rhiochcháin d'fhághail damh 's an am-ro,
  Uait fein agus ó'b leómhán :
'S é Tubóid óg de búrc,
  An chraobh chúmhra tá éireachdach mór,
Faoi chomairc Dé na n-dúl do,
  'S go m-budh buan do bheidh ré beódh.

On this eve of eves most holy,
    Let not anger on thee grow;
Gentle thoughts should touch thee solely,
    Pity in thy soul should glow.
Branch of the old and stately tree,
With favouring eyes thy minstrel see,
And let him chaunt all loud and free,
              The praises of Mayo.

Spurn him not, in thee confiding,
    Chide him not, but hear him swear
By each saint in Rome residing,
    By each blessed bell that's there—[2]
Hear him, vow that faithful ever
    In thy step his steps shall go;
Turning, failing, flinching never,
    Until death has laid him low.
Until all his toils are done,
Until life's last sands are run,
The theme his heart must dwell upon,
              Shall be his lov'd Mayo.

'S í Siobhán dheas na cciúin-portz,
 Is múinte 's is féile glór,
Agus bíoh fá ímpíohe dhamh-sa,
 Um péidhteach fházháil o'm león :
Trzíoh feasda, a chúizeasp,
 Chuirfeadh maise air chlannaibh cóize,
A's canaibh caint fá ohúthrachd,
 Ann mo dháil mar is cóir :
Rízh na ffann d'bhur ccumhdach,
 Zo m-budh raozhlách, slán an cúizeasp,
Mar tá Hébíoh, Nellíoh, Tom a's Betíoh,
 Agus Péupla an chúil óir.

Loveliest! gentlest Lady Mary,
  Fairest form of earthly mould;
Bards might praise thee until weary,
  And leave beauties yet untold.
Speak! oh speak, thy lord shall hear thee,
  Speak, and sooth the wanderer's woe;
Let young Theobald be near thee,
  Future dread of every foe.
Plead for me ye blooming train,
Plead ye may not plead in vain,
And let me sing in glee again,
            The praises of Mayo.

bpoigeaŋaŋ boŋŋ.

Ir bóich le céud ḟeaṛ ʒuṛ leó ḟéin me 'n-uaiṛ a luiʒheaṛr
  baṁh mionn,
'Ϝ ʒo b-téibheann bá ttṛian ṗóg bíom, tṛáth ṛmuaiṁʒhim
  aiṛ a chómhṛább liom ;
béilin meala, ʒṛuabh aiṛ laṛabh tá aiṛ ṛhliabh ua
  ḟloinn,
'Ϝ ʒo bhḟuil mo ʒhṛábh-ṛa maṛ bhláth na n-aiṛníbhe aiṛ
  an bṛóiʒhneaṛ bonn.

Ṁi'l acht cluanaíbhe bhe bhuachaill bo'm mheallabh
  ʒach lá,
Ṁí ʒhlacḟaíbh le bean aiṛ bith ʒo bh-ḟáʒh ṛé mé,
Ʒibh ʒuṛ leaṁh é, nioṛ bhṛeachnuiʒh ṛé ʒo ḟóil mo mhéinn,
Tuilleabh tubaiṛte aiṛ, ir ṛaíbheach bo ʒhuilḟeabh ṛé an
  tṛáth Ṗóṛṛaṛ mé.

THE BROWN THORN.[1]

BY THOMAS FURLONG.

Tho' some deem me won if I wear a smile,
As their oaths of fond passion are pour'd forth the while;
When I think, but for once, of my own lov'd swain,
Then the tales they have told me are told in vain.

What hoards of rich sweetness his lips disclose?
How fair are the tints that his cheek still shews!
Oh! when near him, all others must be seen in scorn,
For he is bright as the blossom on the gay brown thorn!

Let the clowns who still seek me, their cares resign,
They can touch not, or move not, a heart like mine;
O'er their woes I shall smile, tho' they droop forlorn,
When home by my true love as his bride I'm borne.

Ni bean búclaidhe na h-údaidhe do b-fhearr dhuit féin,
Na tsapuidhe dhe chaitín bheag óg gan chéill;
Acht ainfhir chaoin na ngeal-chioch gan phóint gan
spréidh;
Ta cúmhaidh agam a nóidigh mo mhuirnín a's ní nár
liom é.

Ní'l acht peidín beag, buighdeach d'fear ann sa' n-áit,
bh-fuil a chuilín 'na dhualaidhe 'sus é fighte go bárr;
Ní'l crann caorthan b'a aoirde nach bídheann searbh ann
a bhárr,
'Sgo bh-fasann smeara agus subha craobh air an ngéig
is ísle bláth.

'Nuair éirghim-se air maidin agus an drúchd 'na luidhe,
Deasraim air an m-baile m-bídheann grádh mo chroidhe;
Nior labhair me le'm mhuirnín gidh tám do'm chnaoi-
dheadh,
'S a cheád-shearc! nach bochd nach bh-féudaim do
chúmhaidh do chlaoidheadh?

SENTIMENTAL SONG.

'Tis not a vain girl deck'd in gems of pride,
That my dearest should choose as his destined bride;
'Tis one whose firm fondness with her years has grown,
Who can bless him, and caress him, and be all his own.

Tho' lowly in stature my lov'd youth may be,
Yet not lowly does he seem when he smiles on me;
In the garden there are plants that grow straight and tall,
But the shrub richly laden will outweigh them all.

When I rise in the morning ere the dews are past,
To the home of my sweetest my first glance is cast;
To that dear one I have spoken but by looks alone!
For thus, and thus only, shall my love be known.

Caisiol Mumhan.

Phógfainn thú gan bha gan púint 'r gan mórán sppéidh,
A'r phógfainn thú maidin drúchta le bánadh an lae;
Mo ghalar dúbhach gan mé a'r tú, a dhian-ghrádh mo chléibh!
A g-Caisiol Múmhan, 'r gan de leabaidh fúinn ann, acht clár bog deal.

A chaoin-bhean! an cuimhin leat-ra sliabh na m-ban fionn?
Nó an cuimhneadh leat n'uair do bhídhinn-si 'r mé fiadhach 'fa'n ngleann?
'Nois ó chaith an aois mé a'r gur liath mo cheann,'
Ni cubhaidh dhuit mé dhíbirt, a'r tá'n bhliadhain-so gann.

CASHEL OF MUNSTER, OR THE "CLAR BOG DEAL."

BY THOMAS FURLONG.

I would wed thee my dear girl without herds or land,
Let me claim as a portion but thy own white hand;
On each soft dewy morn shall I bless thy charms,
And clasp thee all fondly in my anxious arms.

It grieves me, my fairest, still here to stay,
To the south, to the south love! let us haste away;
There plainly, but fondly, shall thy couch be spread,
And this breast be as a pillow to support thy head.

Bethink thee my sweet maid of old *Slieve-na-mon*,
And the vales where I sported in the days long gone;
Tho' my locks now look grey, and my blood runs chill,
The fond heart that then lov'd thee can love thee still.

Ní saoil-si gur b'iriioll a'r nach uarsal mé,
A'r na saoil-si gur 'sa 'n-diz do ruaireadh mé;
Sin ríos leam real míorsa agus cuarruigh mé,
Agus gheabhair sgríobhtha ann mo chaoibh bear gur
    b'uarsal mé.

Ní'l ór buidhe ann mo phócaíbhe ná airgiod geal,
Ná mo bólacht le seoladh tráthnóna air fad,
Ní'l óig-bhean do thóigfeadh mé follamh gan bhóibh,
Nach b-tógfainn air mo sheolta go contae-thíre-Tóghain.

A chailín, is maith-aithním go bh-fuil buaidhreadh ort,
Agus, a chailín, is maith aithním go bh-fuair tú guth;
Caitin mé fuair iompadh fasí ghradh sir,
A'r fior mo leath-tróim, ná raibh ag mnáibh an t-saé-
    ghail uile.

SENTIMENTAL SONG.

Oh! turn not upon me that cold glance of scorn,
Nor deem me as a mean one, or one basely born;
Nay, take me to thy arms love! and thou shalt see,
That the gentlest of the gentle I can prove to thee.

Not from wealth closely hoarded can I claim delight,
Not with herds or fair flocks can I tempt thy sight;
Nay! these gifts of frail fortune midst the crowd may fall,
But the soul fraught with fondness is beyond them all.

On thy young brow my sweet one, a cold gloom appears,
And thy glance of mild brightness seems dim'd with tears;
The world, dear, may slight thee, but when friends are gone,
This heart ever constant shall thro' life love on.

Máire Chuirle.

A Mháire Chuirle! a bhláth na finne,
　Ghéig an oinich n-iar ó'n Máir,
Béul is binne ná 'n chuach air bile,
　D'fág tú me-si a' n-argnóbh báis;
Ní léir damh coingeal, clár na fuireann,
　Uradh do mheirge, a ré bheag mná;
Stáid-bhean mhaireach, mhéadurgh ar máirg,
　Och! gan d'fallaing liom go lá!

Thiúbhal me Arbach, a's go Cionntsáile,
　Go Droichead-áithe, a's air ais a rís,
Go ceathairlach agus go Dun-Pátruicc,
　Samhuil Mháire ní fhacaidh mé:
Cóistídhe árda air eachraibh bána,
　Marcshluagh gallda troid fá'n mnaoi;
Má d'imthigh tú, Mháire, go bh-filldh tú slán,
'S go n-déanfadh do ghráile solus gan ghruain.

MOLLY A STORE.[1]

BY THOMAS FURLONG.

Oh! Mary dear! bright peerless flower,
   Pride of the plains of Nair,
Behold me droop through each dull hour,
   In soul-consuming care.
In friends—in wine—where joy was found—
   No joy I now can see;
But still while pleasure reigns around,
   I sigh—and think of thee.

The cuckoo's notes I love to hear,
   When summer warms the skies;
When fresh the banks and brakes appear,
   And flowers around us rise:
That blithe bird sings her song so clear,
   And she sings where the sun-beams shine—
Her voice is sweet—but Mary dear,
   Not half so sweet as thine.

'S í Máire go deimhin, an planndá breágh leinbh,
Is réimhíbhe 'sis deise d'á bh-fuil le fághail;
A píob már an lile, a rúil már an g-criostál,
A gruadh is deirge 'ná rós d'á bhreághacht:
Dochtúifíbhe na cruinne, a's a g-cruinniughadh uile,
Níá'r mhór an cumás a g-cur air fághail,
Ní laighearrádh an appáing, acá dul tríom tarsna,
Acht póigín mheala ó'd bheilín tais, tláith.

SENTIMENTAL SONG.

From town to town I've idly stray'd,
    I've wander'd many a mile;
I've met with many a blooming maid,
    And own'd her charms the while:
I've gaz'd on some that then seem'd fair,
    But when thy looks I see,
I find there's none that can compare,
    My Mary, dear, with thee!

Caitlíġ Tippiall.

Is miann liom tráchtaḋ air gach níḋ le tucaim,
  Agus is mhithiḋ liom tráchtaḋ air Chitíḋ na
    g-cuach
'Sí an plannda breáġ leinbh tá saoitheamhuil suairc,
  A's a samhuil ní ḟacas a m-bailtibh na dtuaich:
'S é mo chreach mhaiḋne, nár ḟágbhaḋ mé,
  Air bhruach locha Eirrill le fáinne an lae!
Mar ṡúil go bh-faġainn amharc air Chitíḋ na
    g-craébh,
  Mar do chualaiḋ mé teastás bhpeaġḋḣachta a
    sgéimh'.

'S é mo léunġuirt! mar chonairc mé dúbhach na peann,
  Ná do chul breáġh, triopallach, fáinneach, fionn;
Dá d-tóigeaḋ an tiġearna easboig-si lámh ós mo chionn,
  bhéurfainn Citíḋ an stáid-bhean tar sáile liom:

CATHARINE TYRRELL.

BY THOMAS FURLONG.

Sweet girls 'tis mine to frame each tender ditty,
   Or touch the heart with many a thrilling air;
And now my theme shall be my blooming Kitty,
   The first, the fairest, seen amidst the fair.
Young bud of beauty, all bright and peerless,
   Long have I lov'd thee—and must yet love on;
Thy smile is cheering, when life looks cheerless;
   Thy glance gives hope, when all hope seems gone.

Oh! might I wander down by bright Loch Errol,
   There should I linger at the dawn of day;
To gaze in rapture on my own dear girl,
   As thro' the green fields she bends her way—

Is gile í 'ná'n eala, 's is deirge í 'ná 'n ghrian,
   Is binne í 'ná g-cuaclaidh mé de cheoltaibh ariamh,
Ní'l aén teach leanna fearca fá an t-sraid so shiar,
   Nach n-ólfaidh mé sláinte Cháitilín T'riall.

Is truaigh nach bh-fuil me-si agus Citidh dheas, chaoin,
   Fá chúl an toim chuilinn go n-ólfamaois braon,
Mar shúil le Dia dílear go d-tógfainn a croidhe,
A's go d-tiúbhrainn a bhaile ó na máthair liom í :—
Léigh mé do litir a muich air an t-sliabh ;
   Budh bhinne í 'ná iomad de cheólcaibh fíghe
Páirt mhór de'm chruadhtan, gur leat chaill mé mo
       chiall
   Is mór a n-aghaidh d'anama é, a Cháitilín T'riall.

Oh! sweetest! dearest! had I never met thee,
　　Calm nights and days I might still have known;
But who that sees thee, can e'er forget thee?
　　Thine image fades but with life alone.

Oh! that we were in holy bonds united,
　　How sweet, how sacred, would that moment be;
The sails should flutter as with hearts delighted,
　　I and my lov'd one would cross the sea:
Or by some holly bush, in greenness blooming,
　　Our languid limbs we at noon might lay;
In love's dear dalliance the time consuming,
　　Scarce heeding seasons as they wore away.

An Chuil-fhionn.

Dá bh-feicfeá-rá an chúilfhion agus i ag siubhal air na bóithribh,

Ag ionnsaidhe na h-úr-choille á'r an drúcht air a bróga,

'Sí mo sheárc í 'sí mo rún í, a'r ní'l tnúth aici le h-óige,

Agus nag sí báinn áilne air mhnáibh breághtha na fódhla.

A m-béal-áth-na-gár a tá an scaid-bhean bhreágh mhódhamhuil,

Bh-fuil a gnuadh mar na cáor-chon agus sgeimh ann a clódh geal,

Budh bhinne guth a béil-sin 'ná 'n chéirseach 's ná 'n smólach,

'Sná an lonn-dubh air na coilltibh le soillse an tráthnona.

Eirgidh ad shuidhe, a bhuachaill, agus gléus damh mo gheárrán,

Go go leansaidh me an stuaidh-bhean úd shuas air na cnócáin,

Tá sí dá sior-luadhadh liom ó bhidh sí 'na leanbán,

'S go m-budh bhinne liom naoi n-uaire í 'ná 'n chuach 's na orgáin.

THE COOLIN.[1]

BY THOMAS FURLONG.

Had you seen my sweet Coolin at the day's early dawn,
When she moves thro' the wild wood, or the wide dewy lawn;
There is joy—there is bliss in her soul-cheering smile,
She's the fairest of the flowers of our green bosom'd isle.

In Belanagar[2] dwells the bright blooming maid,
Retired like the primrose that blows in the shade;
Still dear to the eye that fair primrose may be,
But dearer and sweeter is my Coolin to me.

Then boy, rouse you up! go and bring me my steed,
Till I cross the green vales and the mountains with speed;
Let me hasten far forward, my lov'd one to find,
And hear that she's constant, and feel that she's kind.

Má thug mo chroíbhe grádh bhuit 'r gur tú áilne gach
    rolair,
'S gan mo mhuintir fár-fhárda leat, a ghrádh bhil na
    g-comann,
Páirt mhór be'm chruadhtán a'r mé ag cruadh-ghul go
    dainzean,
Fáoí 'm leanán bréagh uarál do luadhadh liom a'm
    leanbh.

A stóir bhil mo chroíbhe! bíoh bíleas agus dainzean
    damh,
Ná tréig rún do chléibh a ngeall air é bheith dealbh,
Dhéurfainn duit-ri an bíobla a bh-fuil fáoí agus tháipir.
Go b-tiúbhradh Dia bíleas ar fáith bhúnn le caitheamh.

An cuimhin leat-ra an oíbhche bhíoh tu-ra agus me-ri,
Fá bhun an chrainn chaortháinn a'r an oíbhche ag cur
    chuirneadh
Ní raibh foreach ó'n ngaoith aguinn ná bídean ó'n
    bh-fearthainn,
Acht mo chóta chur fúinn agus do ghúna chur thárainn,

Oh! dearest, thy love from thy childhood was mine,
Oh! sweetest, this heart from life's opening was thine;
And tho' coldness by kindred or friends may be shewn,
Still! still, my sweet Coolin, that heart is thine own.

Thou light of all beauty be true still to me,
Forsake not thy swain, love, tho' poor he may be;
For rich in affection, in constancy tried,
We may look down on wealth in its pomp and its pride.

Remember the night, love! when safe in the shade,
We marked the wild havoc the wild wind has made;
Think! think how I sheltered thee—watched thee with
    care,
Oh! think of the words, love, that fell from us there.

Póiṟíṅ Duḃ.

A Ṗóiṙín, ná bíoḋ brón orṫ fá'r eiriġioḃ ḋuiṫ !
Tá na bráiṫre teaċṫ ṫar ráile, as iad aġ ṫriall air
    muir,
Tioċfaiḋ do ṗárdún ó'n b-Pápa, a'r ó'n Róiṁh a n-oir,
A'r ná sparáil fíon Spáinneaċ air mo Ṗóiṙín Duḃ.

Is fada an féim do léig me léi ó n-dé ġo b-tíġh a n-diu,
Táirrná sléiḃte ġo n-deaċaṫar léiṫi, fáoi ṡeóltá' air
    muir,
An Eirne a'r ċáiṫ me léim í, ciḋ mór an ṫruiṫ,
'S ḃíoḋ ceol téud air ġaċ taéḃ ḋiom a's mo Ṗóiṙín
    Duḃ.

Ṁarḃ tú mé ḃrídeóiġ, a's ná'r buḋ fearr-de ḋuiṫ,
'S ġo bh-fuil m'anam a rtiġh a n-ġeán ort, 's ní a n-dé ná
    n-diu
D'fág tú laġ anḃfann mé, a n-ġnéiḋ 's a ġ-cruṫ,
Ná feall orm a's mé anġeán ort, a Ṗóiṙín Duḃ.

ROISIN DUBH.[1]

BY THOMAS FURLONG.

Oh! my sweet little rose, cease to pine for the past,
For the friends that come eastward shall see thee at last;
They bring blessings—they bring favors which the past never knew,
To pour forth in gladness on my Roisin Dubh.

Long, long with my dearest, thro' strange scenes I've gone,
O'er mountains and broad valleys I have still toil'd on;
O'er the Erne I have sail'd as the rough gales blew,
While the harp pour'd its music for my Roisin Dubh.

Tho' wearied oh! my fair one! do not slight my song,
For my heart dearly loves thee, and hath lov'd thee long;
In sadness and in sorrow I shall still be true,
And cling with wild fondness round my Roisin Dubh.

Thiúbhailfinn féin an drúcht leat agus fársaich soirc,
Mar shúil go bh-fághainn pún uait, no páirt de'm thoil,
Chraoibhín chúmhra, ghealtais domh-sa, go raibh grádh
   agat damh,
'S gur b'í fíor-scoich na Múmhan í mo Phóifín Dubh.

A Phóifín mhín, mhódhamhail, na m-bán-chíoch ccruinn,
Is tú d'fág míle arraing a g-ceart-lár mo chroídhe :
Éaloigh liom, a chéadh-shearc, agus fág an tír,
A's dá bh-féudfainn nach 'n-déansainn-si bainríoghain
   dhíot, a Phóifín Dubh.

Dá m-biadh seispeach agam do threabhfainn a n-aghaidh
   na g-cnoc,
A's dhéansainn soiscéal ann lár an aithfrinn do'm
   Phóifín Dubh,
Bhéurfainn póg do'n g-cailín n-óg do bheurfadh a h-órge
   dhamh,
A's dhéansainn cleas air chúl an leasa le'm Phóifín Dubh.

Tá an Eirne na tuilte tréana, agus péubraidhear cnoic,
A's tá'n fhairge 'na tonnaibh dearga, a's dóirtfear fuil,
Beidh gach gleann sléibhe air fuid Eirean a's móinte air
   chroich,
Lá éigin sul a n-éagraidh mo Phóifín Dubh.

There's no flower that e'er bloom'd can my rose excel,
There's no tongue that e'er moved half my love can tell;
Had I strength, had I skill the wide world to subdue,
Oh! the queen of that wide world should be Roisin Dubh.

Had I power, oh! my lov'd one, but to plead thy right,
I should speak out in boldness for my heart's delight;
I would tell to all around me how my fondness grew,
And bid them bless the beauty of my Roisin Dubh.

The mountains, high and misty, thro' the moors must go,
The rivers shall run backward, and the lakes overflow;
And the wild waves of old ocean wear a crimson hue,
Ere the world sees the ruin of my Roisin Dubh.

Uileacán Dubh O!

Dá d-tiocfá-rsa liom-sa go cúntaé Liachtroim,
    A Uileacáin Dhuibh O!
Bheadsannn-ri mil bheach agus meadh mar bhiadh dhuit,
    A Uileacáin Dhuibh O!
Béarfad aer na long na seól 's na m-bád duit,
Fáoi bharradhaibh na d-tom a's rinn ag filleadh ó'n
  d-tráigh,
'S ní léigfinn-ri áen bhrón cóidhchedo'd dháil,
    'S gur tú m'Uileacán dhuh O!

Ní ráchradh me-ri leat, a's ní'l maith dhuit do'm
  iarradh,
    A Uileacáin Dhuibh O!
Mar nach g-coingeóchadh do ghlórtha beódh gan bhiadh
  me
    A Uileacáin Dhuibh O!
Míle céad fearr liom bheith cóidhche gan fear,
'Ná bheith ag rúbhal an drúchda 'r na bh-fársach leat,
'Sior chug mo chroídhe dhuit grádh na gean,
    'S ní tú m' Uileacán Dubh O!

UILEACAN DUBH O!

BY THOMAS FURLONG.

If to Leitrim's green fields thou wilt wander with me
                Sweet Uileacan Dubh O!
Thy cup shall be sweetened with the honey of the bee,
                My Uileacan Dubh O!
There the trees rich and shady shall wave o'er thy head,
There the barks shall glide by with their sails gaily spread,
There each day as it flies some new blessing shall shed
                On my Uileacan Dubh O!

Oh! what says my dearest! and can she deny me,
                Sweet Uileacan Dubh O!
My words may not win her—but why will she fly me,
                Sweet Uileacan Dubh O!
Oh! think not sweet maiden through life to be free,
While in each that beholds thee a slave thou canst see;
Oh turn not—oh look not thus coldly on me
                My Uileacan Dubh O!

Chonairc mé ag teacht chugam í tré lár an t-sléibhe,
    Mar péilton thríd an g-ceóbh;
Bhídh mé ag cáint a's ag comhrádh léi,
    Go n-deachamair go Páirc na m-bó:
Shuidheamair-ne síos ann lúib an fháil,
Go d-tug mé dhi scríobhthcha sgaoi mo lámh,
Nach b-fuil coir d'á n-déanadh sí nach n-íocfainn a cáin
    A Uileacán Dhuibh O!

Mo chreach a's mo chrádh gan mé fáigzche síos léi,
    Uileacán Dubh O!
Air leaba chaol, ard nó air chárnn tuíbhe,
    A Uileacán Dhubh O!
Gan duine air bich ann Eirinn bheith lámh linn 'sa
    'n-oídhche,
Acht ag sugradh agus ag gáiread féin mar budh
    mhiánn linn,
A Dhia! nach cruadh an cás é, muna bh-fághaidh mé
    mo mhiánn
        Air an Uileacán Dubh O!

I saw the fair damsel round the hill slowly bending,
     My Uileacan Dubh O!
Like a joy-giving star thro' the grey mist ascending,
     Sweet Uileacan Dubh O!
I spoke to her gently—I spoke of my pain,
I vow'd—I protested again and again;
But my vows of affection were pour'd out in vain
     My Uileacan Dubh O!

Oh were I beside thee in rapture reclining,
     My Uileacan Dubh O!
On some soft rushy couch with the moon o'er us shining,
     Sweet Uileacan Dubh O!
How blest might I be in the arms of my dear,
Where no shape or no sound to disturb us came near;
But she waits not—she deigns not my story to hear,
     Sweet Uileacan Dubh O!

ceann oubh oileay.

A cheann dhuibh dhílis, dhílis, dhílis!
  Cuir do lámh mhín-gheal thorm a nall!
A bhéilín mheala, bh-fuil boladh na tíme air,
  Is duine gan chroidhe nach d-tiubhradh duit grádh.—

Tá cáilíneadha air an m-baile-so air builleadh 'r air
buaidhreadh,

Ag tarraing a n-gruaige 's dá léigeann le gaoith,
Air mo shon-sa, an fear is fearr ann san tuaithe,
Acht do threigfinn an méid sin air rún dhil mo chroídhe.

A's cuir do cheann dílleas, dílleas, dílleas!
  Cuir do cheann dílleas tharm anall!
A bhéilín mheala, a bh-fuil boladh na tíme air,
  Is duine gan chroidhe nach d-tiubhradh duit grádh!

CEAN DUBH DEELISH.

BY THOMAS FURLONG.

Oh! sweetest and dearest of maidens behold me,
  All lowly before thee thy victim must fall;
Oh! let thy white arms in fondness enfold me,
  Oh! let thy lov'd lips my lost spirit recall.
There are maidens around that too partially view me,
  Aye, girls whose gay glances enchant and enthrall;
But idly they watch me, and vainly they woo me,
  For thee *Cean Dubh Deelish* I'll fly from them all.

Then dearest and sweetest come let me caress thee,
  Come lay thy lov'd cheek on the breast of thy slave;
Where is he who could see and not seek to possess thee,
  Oh such must be, heartless and cold as the grave.

Eibhlín a Rúin.

Thiúbhairfinn féin a g-cómhnuidhe leat,
  A Eibhlín a rúin!
Thiúbhairfinn féin a g-cómhnuidhe leat,
  A Eibhlín a rúin!
Thiubhairfinn féin a g-cómhnuidhe leat,
Síos go Tír-Amhalgaidh leat,
Mar shúil go m-béidhinn a g-cleamhnas leat,
  A Eibhlín a rúin!

D' ólfainn féin bó leat-sa,
  A Eibhlín a rúin!
'S d'ólfainn dhá bhó leat-sa,
  A Eibhlín a rúin!
Thiúbhairfinn an ráoghal mór leat,
Acht cleamhnas d'fághail ó'm stór,
'S ní searrfainn go deóigh leat,
  A Eibhlín a rúin!

EILEEN A ROON.

BY THOMAS FURLONG.

I'll love thee evermore,
    Eileen a Roon!
I'll bless thee o'er and o'er,
    Eileen a Roon!
Oh! for thy sake I'll tread,
Where the plains of Mayo spread;
By hope still fondly led,
    Eileen a Roon!

Oh! how may I gain thee?
    Eileen a Roon!
Shall feasting entertain thee?
    Eileen a Roon!
I would range the world wide,
With love alone to guide,
To win thee for my bride,
    Eileen a Roon!

An d-tiocfaidh tú no'n bh-fanfaidh tú,
> A Eibhlín a rúin!
D-tiocfaidh tú no'n b-fanfaidh tú,
> Chuid de'n t-saoigheal 'sa stóp!

Tiocfaidh mé, 's ní fhanfaidh mé,
Tiocfaidh mé, 's ní fhanfaidh mé,
'S tiocfaidh mé, 's ní fhanfaidh me,
> 'Sealóghaidh mé le'm stór.

Céud míle fáilte rómhat,
> A Eibhlín a rúin!
Céud mile fáilte rómhat,
> A Eibhlín a rúin!
Céud míle fáilte rómhat,
Ngói g-céud míle fáilte rómhat,
Och! fáilte agus fichche rómhat,
> A Eibhlín a rúin!

Then wilt thou come away?
>Eileen a Roon!
Oh! wilt thou come or stay?
>Eileen a Roon!
Oh yes! oh yes! with thee
I will wander far and free,
And thy only love shall be,
>Eileen a Roon!

A hundred thousand welcomes,
>Eileen a Roon!
A hundred thousand welcomes,
>Eileen a Roon!
Oh! welcome evermore,
With welcomes yet in store,
Till love and life are o'er,
>Eileen a Roon!

Eḋmoṅḋ aṅ Cnoic.

A chúil áluinn ḋeas, na bh-painneaḋ́a g-cas,
 Is breáġ ġus is glas do ṡúile,
'S dá bh-paġḟainn ó cheart, ceaḋ sineaḋ leat,
 Is eaḋtrom, tápaiḋ ṡiúḃáilḟinn :—
Siúḃáilḟinn leat an Mhúmhan air ḟaḋ,
 Dá d-trian agus leath na h-Eireann,
'S go sinḟinn ort, mo chroiḋe 'gus mo chorp,
 A ṡiod́a na m-ban gan aén locht.

A cháilín óig, ṡéimh, an d-tuigeann tu féin,
 Gur duine mé atá air buaiḋḟreaḋ,
'S go bh-ḟuil mo cháirde go léir, a bh-ḟeirg liom féin,
 Chionn tú ḃeith a'ḋ luaḋaḋ liom :—
Air ṡaiḋḃhreas an t-saeġail, a leinbh ḋil mo chléiḃ,
 Ní chreidḟinn-ṡi sgéulta fuara ort ;
'S gur biaḋ iomaḋ na m-breág, do chuir ṡinn araen,
 A bh-ḟaḋ ó n-a chéile i n-uaigneas.

EMON A KNOCK.

BY THOMAS FURLONG.

Oh! maiden more than fair,
Whose ringlets rich and rare,
  Are o'er thy white shoulders flowing;
Whose eye of winning hue,
  Large, languishing, and blue,
With love's own wild light is glowing:
  How happy should I be,
  If blest my girl with thee,
But fairest, thou art too cruel;
  I'll range the nations o'er,
  I'll wander evermore,
Or win thee, my dearest jewel.

Dear blooming gentle maid,
Thy smile comes not to aid
  The weak one who droops in anguish;
Tho' friends and kinsmen jeer,
  And taunt me when they hear,
That thus for thy love I languish.

A Chailín óig, sheimh, an b-cuigeann tú féin,
  Gur duine mé tá air slighe dóchchuir,
Munab iondon a's an t-é ud, bhidh aithnid agat féin,
  Agus b'fáig faoi ghnéidh bróin tu:—
Tá do shúil mar an sméar, do ghruadh mar an cnop,
  Is breagh í do bhéid-si, a óig-bhean,
'S gur b'é gáire geal do bhéil, thug bás do na céudaibh,
  Mo ghrádh 'gus mo mhíle stór tu!

A ghrádh 'gus a chuid, ná déan féin rud,
  Acht tréig-si do bhaile dúthchais,
A's tarr 's an n-áit-si 'na bh-fuil na gartha ag an lon,
  Agus abhla ann air chois 'na g-cúpladhaibh;—
Tá an t-éan ann is binne, an féur ann is gláise,
  Tá an chuaichín air bhárr an iuir ghlain;
'S go lá an bhrácth ní thiocfaidh an bás air ar ngáire,
  Air lár na coille ag fúgradh!

Imcheamaoid anois, gan mhaill air bith,
  Faoi lár na coille craobhaíche;
Is fuar agus is fluch, an uain so thá 'gainn,
  Agus gluaiseamaóid le n-a chéile;—

SENTIMENTAL SONG.

Vain are the taunts they throw,
For all that earth can shew,
I would not—nay dare not doubt thee—
Whate'er of joy I've known,
Hath sprung from thee alone,
There's love, life, and bliss about thee.

Oh! damsel ever dear,
Speak, speak, and let me hear,
If vainly this hope I cherish;
Say, must I drop like him,
Whose star set dark and dim,
Who left thee in gloom to perish?
The stars may brightly shine,
But still those eyes of thine,
Seem brighter when bent upon me;
And then, that careless smile,
Fraught with each witching wile,
Oh! sweetest, that smile has undone me.

Come, lov'd one, turn to me,
Come, leave thy home, and see
The scenes that spread here before thee;
Here streamlets brightly play,
Here the green fields look gay,
And fresh flowers shall hang clustering o'er thee.

'N uair do chualaibh si-si, fuaim na coille.
    Ag bualadh air fuid a chéile,
S é mo bhuaidhreadh, air si-si, an chuach a bheith air
    gur,
'S gan an lon a bheith teacht d'á feuchain!

A chuid agus a ghrádh! an ag cur ruag díom a táir,
    'Snach me-si do pháirt cheile,
Nach fear mar a táim, do'b fheappa leat do phághail
    Acht malairt ar ait éigin,
Thógradh an srad, agus pómharpadh an bán,
    'S beidheadh go cumarach lá an chéuchda?
A ainfhir chiúin, tláich, na bh-rad-fholt m-buidhe,
    m-breagh,
Mo bheannacht-sa go lá'n éug' leat!

Here sweet, and loud, and long,
  The cuckoo sings her song;
Here danger can ne'er invade us;
  Here thro' the leafy grove,
  From morn to eve we'll rove,
Till darkness descends to shade us.

  Then dearest, come away,
  Come! thro' these woods we'll stray,
Tho' dull seems the path we've taken;
  The whistling winds blow shrill,
  And the small birds sit still,
Nor venture one note to waken.
  Oh! deign, dear maid, to stay,
  Why turn thy looks away?
Oh! are we thus doom'd to sever?—
  If there's a youth more dear,
  Then be our parting here,
Adieu! my sweet girl for ever.

Aṅṅ ʀa m-baile-ʀo cha aṅ Chuilḟionn.

Aɼ n ʀa m-baile ʀo cha an Chúilḟionn, a'ɼ an maɼiġɼe bɼeaġ, múinte,
'Ɽ í an buinneán iɼ úiɼe í, ḋ'a bh-ḟeicim iḋiɼ mhnáibh,—
Ɽ í mo ṗeaɼc í, 'ɼ í mo ɼún í, 'ɼ í annɼaċt mo ṡúl í,
'Ɽ í mo ṗámhɼa ann ɼa' bh-ḟuaċt i, iḋiɼ noḋhlaiġ a'ɼ cáiɼg.

A Chiuɼpiḋ mhilir, chluanaich, tá lán ḋe'ḋ chuiḋ ċɼuaiḋhḃheaɼt,
A'ɼ ġo bh-ḟuil mo chɼoiḋhe aiɼ ḃuaiḋhɼeaḋh, le h-iomaɼcaiḋh ġɼáḋh;
Ma'ɼ ḋe'n m-buiḋheann tú ġhlac ṫɼuaiġh ḋhomh, taḃhaiɼ ɼceula ġo luaṫ ḋhamh,
Cia aca iɼ ḟoġha leat mé ṡuaɼġlaḋh, nó mé léiġeann chum báiɼ?

IN THIS CALM SHELTERED VILLA.

BY THOMAS FURLONG.

In this calm shelter'd villa my fair one remains,
The flower of all flow'rets, the pride of the plains;
She's my heart's hoarded treasure, my soul's sole delight,
In winter she's my summer, and my sunshine at night.

Oh! love, cruel love, thou hast led me astray,
My heart sinks within me, and my strength wastes away;
Speak, speak, dearest maiden, to my passion reply,
Or breathe all I dread, and then leave me to die.

Oh! thou my soul's darling! most lovely, most dear,
There's nought can bring pleasure if thou art not near;
Our trust through the future in kind heaven shall be,
I'll long not for wealth love! if bless'd but with thee.

’S a mhaighdean bhreágh, mhaordha, d’á d-tugar-sa m’aon-toil,

Ná tuig-si go bh-fuil éireacht ann raidhbreas gan grádh,

’S an t-é chum de’n g-cré sinn, is uaidh gheabhamaoid ár n-daochain

’S air bólacht ní thréigfinn tú, ’s táim céusda ag do ghrádh.

A mhúirnín a’s a annsacht, gan mhailís gan chlampar,

D’á d-tug mo chroidhe geán duit, tár a bh-feacas de mhnáibh,—

Ní féidir liom gan rann a bheith, leis an t-é bh-fuil mo ghreann air,

A’s má iompóighir-si cam damh béidh m’anam a’d láimh.

Is buachaill gan cheill tú, a’s a’d ghlópchaibh ní’l éireacht,

Tabhair aire dhuit fein, a’s ná léig ort an bás;

Ní’l maoin mhór, ní’l spreidh ’gad, priomh-cháirde ná gaolta;

’S mo chlíochán ni tháebhfear leat, le m’aen-toil go bráth.

Then smile my beloved—let this coldness depart,
Oh! come till I press thee in bliss to this heart;
Nay! nay—then I'm doom'd for thy loss to repine,
I die, dearest maiden, and the blame shall be thine.

Nay, call me not senseless—nay, deem me not vain,
Nor think that of pangs all unfelt I complain;
Tho' lowly my kindred, and scanty my store,
Oh! why wilt thou tell me to love thee no more.

beile ṅ-i Chiarabháiṅ.

Taréis mo réime ro chríochaibh Fáil,
'S mo léirmheadsa 'nn-Eirinn tar aoibhne cháich,
Thug mé, is féuchtar an críona an ósail,
M'aen-shearc do bhéile n-í Chiarabháin.

An fhéach-bhruinne bhéul-tana, mhín tais, bhláith,
Shaer-ghasda, fheughain-ghlic, shítheach, shamh,
Ġeug-shada, bhéud-chailte, chíoch-chruinn m-bán,
Do léir-chuir mé a ngéibheann 's a g-cuíbhreach gráidh.

'S air fhéuchain a péidh-shorg mar líg a g-ráth,
'S a crsébh-fholta beagh-dhaichte síos go sáil,
A dhé neimhe, is baéghal sur ab níph gan áirb,
Ṅach léur dam air éunchor nach óibhche an lá.

Is céud binne b'ason a bheith claóibhte, tláith,
Ag éisteacht le séis-ghuth a gníos-ghoib shamh,
Ioná an mhéid is féidir le saóithibh b'fásháil,
De shaor-phortaibh Eirean a's Chaoimh-Ṡioclán.

ELEANOR O'KIRWAN.

BY EDWARD LAWSON, ESQ.

All around the green isle of my birth,
Too long I've delighted to rove;
And was I not happiest on earth,
To fix on dear Ellen my love?

Kind, generous, gentle, and coy,
Her white bosom's unconscious of guile;
Her mouth, a rich casket of joy,
Enchanted my heart with a smile.

But her eyes' irresistible rays,
Like diamonds, so dazzle my sight;
(Oh God!) that I scarce, in amaze,
Can distinguish the day from the night.

Dár mo bhréithir ní h-éidir nach fíor arádh,
Go n-geillfeadh Bhénus nó Minerbhá,
'S dá n-eirghidheadh Déirdre le áothamh árd,
Do'n rgéimh sin bhéile n-í Charabháin.

Yet thus overwhelmed and confounded,

Tis a thousand times sweeter to hear

Her voice, than loud anthems resounded,

And organs that ring to the sphere.

Fiadhaidhe bheara.

'Sé an fiadhaidhe úd bheara an fear fial bhí ag beallaigh,
A's ní'r bh'iadhta é fá'n teach-ro, le luidhe ann am nóin :
Sa mhaighdean bhreagh, bhárramhail, ná'r chuir freis
  riamh a bh-fearaibh,
Cum gléigheal mar shneachta, 's i Cairrín mghín t-Seóm.

Tá na céudcha d'á macaibhe, dul ann éugcruth d'á fearc-
  sion,
Port réidh, glan, chluain meallabh, béul tana mar rós,—
Cearbúncail a m-bíodh breas ann, bhíbh iolrabh gach
  dathá ann,
Gach céibh bhreagh mar shneachta, a's iad ag táirdioll,
  'na deóigh,

Tá ar bh'iongnabh do'n régiún, ag ar gairreabh fiúbh
  bhénur,
Mar do bhíbh Conchubhar fá Dhéirdre, dul a b-piantaibh
  d'á grábh ;—

THE HUNTER OF BEARHAVEN.

BY EDWARD LAWSON.

'Twas young Bearhaven's hunter pursuing his game,
At noon to this roof—not to banquet—he came;
On fair Catherine, whose thoughts never wandered on man,
Pure and spendid as snow, thus his extacy ran.

What hundreds of swains woo this innocent dove,
And languish desponding disputing her love!
Oh! her clear azure eye it bewitches each heart,
Her lips, like twin rose buds, deliciously part.

Down her ivory limbs flow her bright flaxen locks,
Like light wreaths of snow over Parian rocks;
Admired by the learned and adored by the gay,
The worship of Venus to her's would give way.

A péulc eoluir na h-eiʒrí, aip chópúʒhabh na ʒréine,
'S í mo roʒhabh chap mnáibh Eipean í a méinn a'r a ceáil.

Déud-chonpabh aip mhnáibh a cineabh í, 'r i pialmhaich
  an oinich í,
Ʒach reóid bhear b'á bponnabh 'r óá rcáipeabh aip luchc
  ceóil,
'S i múipne chlanna Muipeabh í, 'r í pó-ʒhpábh na bh-pile í,
Pléulc-eólair Shléibhe-Ʒuilinn í, 'r í Caitrín inʒhín
  c-Seóin.

'S í rcáchán ʒach bpoinʒil, chuʒ bhénur di uppáim,
Tá deallpabh o'n n-ʒile innci 'r a cúl ciuʒh map an c-óp;
Eala ʒhléʒheal locha Ʒlinne í, 'ra caébh map an lilí,
Chuaidh do mhop-chlú ó Dhaipe do Chéidh Dhúm-na-lónʒ.

Most brilliant of gems—fairest daughter of Eve,
To the sons of sweet song still delighting to give;
The beloved of Clanmurray, the bard's darling care,
Slieu Gullin's bright pole-star is Catherine the fair.

The mirror of maidens in homage who bow,
Her locks to the sunbeams new lustre bestow;
A white lilly perfuming the amorous gales,
Like the swan of Loughglin fair and stately she sails.

TA SAIZHEADA AGUS CNEAD AG DUBAILT AM SHLAD.

Tá ṡaiġheada aġus cneaḋ, aġ ḋubáilt am ṡlaḋ,
  O chṙéuchḋaiḃh choilġ ġhaṫháiḃh Chiúpiḋ,
Ḋo ġhéuṙ-ġoin ġo beaċt, mo chṙoiḋhe áṙtiġh aṙ ḟáḋ,
  A'ṡ do léiṙ-chuṙ mé, aṙ eaṙbáiḋh ṙúḃháchaiṡ :
A ṗéiltionn 'ṡ a ṡheáṙc, ó ṫhéuṙnoiġh do ḃhṙeách,
  Iṡ ġléiḋhe 'ná ṡneaċta aṙ ḃúḃh-chnoic,
A'm ḃionta, mho chṙeách ! ní áoiḃhinn mo ḃháil,
  A'ṡ táim cláóiḋhte do'ḋ ġheán a lionn-ḋuḃh !

D'éaḋán iṡ ġile, 'ná Ṗhoéḃuṡ aṙ miṙe,
  'Ṡ ná bláiṫh, ó ! ná ṡéiṫhleánn cúmhṙa ;
Do ṗíġhin-ṙoṡġ úṙ, iṡ ġláiṡe 'ná ḋṙúchḋ,
  A'ṡ 'ná ṗéuṙla iṡ ġláine lonnṙa ;
Do chláon-ṗhoilt ṡinne, 'n-a ġ-cláon-ḃheaṡta' aġ ṡilleaḋh,
  A'ṡ aġ téuṙnóġhaḋh ġo mullách ġlún oṙt ;
Do ġhṙuáiḋh maṙ an lil, do ḃhéul maṙ an mhil,
  'Ṡ do ċháéḃh maṙ an eála aṙ chiúin-t-ṡṙuiṫh.

WOUNDED BY CUPID'S BURNING DART.

BY EDWARD LAWSON.

Wounded by Cupid's burning dart,
Increasing sighs and groans betray
The anguish of my bleeding heart,
Which wastes with sure though slow decay.

Enchantress! since my dazzled sight
Beheld those limbs like mountain snow,
Ting'd by Aurora's roseate light,
I droop, forlorn, and drowned in woe.

As gilding beauty's vernal bower
Emerging fresh from ocean's breast,
Thro' curling woodbines odorous flower,
Shines out the sun and all is blest.

Táid do ǵhéugaibh go h-uile, le chéile ag iomádh,
'G a ḟéuchain ciá aca is cúmṫa;
Bhénus dá b-tigeadh, a's na Dé-mhná eile,
Helen, Minerbhá a's Iúnó;—
Gan phléidhreacht 's agád-sa, a chéud-ḟheárc 's a chomáinn,
Ṫabhairfidís uile an t-ubhall duit,
Is tráochta tá me-si a'd éiliúghadh gan mhisneach
Le glé chomann duit-si, a chúil-ḟionn!

So through your long wreathed locks appear
Your vermeil cheek, your honied lip;
Your full mild eyes like dew drops clear,
That from the young green herbage trip.

Your limbs in fair proportion vie,
As rivalled by themselves alone;
Alas! exhausted I must die,
Unless you bid me cease to moan.

Deirdre Dheagh-ghnúigheach.

Do chártár tár áen án Deirdre bheágh-ghnúigreách,
Mhárgálách, mháoróbhá, bhéib-gheál, ghlár-rhuíleách,
Chámárrách, áobhbhá, rháor-ghlán, rheárc-chnúchách,
Cháthránnách, chéilíbhe, bhéurách, bhrágháib-púnách.

Ir ámárrách eláén, 'r ir cráobhách, cráth-úrlách,
Táirchneámhách, téubách, ráon-chár, reác-ghlúnách,
Leábháir-cheárc, láobách, rláodách, rráth-lúbách,
Á báchált-rhoilc cháomh-ghlán, ghéugách, rhádchúrrách.

Á mámá gán mhéib, á'r é gán bhleáchtúghábh b'rhior,
Do bhálláibh ir péult á peábháibh ámúrálách,
Ir cáilce 'r ir cáol á táebh 'r ir cneár-ch'ímhrá,
'R ní mheárám gur réibir-téimheál rhámhlúghábh leir.

BLOOMING DEIRDRE.[1]

BY EDWARD LAWSON.

Sweet Deirdre 'bove all else I prize;
Such pearly teeth! such azure eyes!
O'er which dispersed by zephyr's play,
Dark-shining, twining, tendrils stray,
In full luxurient wreaths descending,
Those small soft-heaving orbs defending;
Whose vestal snow no touch profane,
Of man, has ever dared to stain.

Like orient Venus, when she presses
The brine from her ambrosial tresses,
That down her sleek side glittering flows,
Like dew-stars on the milk-white rose;

Fanaid na h-éirg le rgeímh a flat-chúil chair,
A'r canaid na h-éin a réir ag beannúghadh dhi,
Gabhaid na deithe leithi gan athchúmdar,
'S a n-deachaidh tar bhénuy breagrraidh an bhean úd
  rin.

Do ghabhay-ra léi mar rgeith do'm cheart-chúmhdach,
Gidh reary mo ghnéidh mar naomh a nglar-uaimh cnoic,
Ir mairg do'n n-éug nach ngléuyann dárt chúgham-ra
Do chaithyeadh mo rae go péidh gan mhartyúghadh
  m-broid.

Do chealg, do chréucht-ghoin mé go lag-thuirreach,
D'athpuigh mo ghnéidh mar aey-fhear an-tyúgach,
Fhéary ní léughaim nó téct ó ghlan-úghdar,
London duinn é ní ghéillfidh an bhean úd damh.

De ghearraibh na géige ir glé-ghlan, geanamhuil cruth
Mo cheangal a ngéibhionn dáer go deacamhlach,³
Budh cneardha dá céimibh téacht ag cnearúghadh an loit
Do dearyadh léi le éigceart athúmhalta.

SENTIMENTAL SONG.

The gleamy tenants of the tide,
With wond'ring gaze forget to glide;
Suspended in the liquid sky,
The plumy warblers cease to fly;
Choiring her praise to heaven above,
Where she'd depose the witching queen of love

Her tutelary power I hail;
Though like a cavern'd hermit, ' pale,
Hopeless, I pine; accusing death,
Whose barbarous shafts still spare my breath.
A martyr to protracted anguish,
Like joyless, sapless age I languish;
Nor read a line, nor tune an air,
To all indifferent—whelm'd in deep despair.

The facinating white arm'd maid,
By some enchantment has betray'd
My hopeless bosom, which remains
Wrapt in inextricable chains.
In charity she ought to heal,
The tortures that from her I feel.

Ceangal.

Is maith an mháire ann ainnṡir chneasda a géug-ḃlaoiḃ cham,

A beara glara, a máma geala, a geur-chíocha gann',

A bara taise, lága, leabhaire, a h-ael-phíob pamhar;

Crosaim feasda air fhearaibh ḃhreasáinn, gaoḃal í a's gall.

COMBINATION.[4]

My blue-eyed, pearl-teethed, blooming fair,
With heaving breasts and curling hair;
Whose dusky-flowing wreaths effuse,
Down her white limbs the pearly dews;
I claim for mine, and here defy,
The whole wide world my title to deny.

Maire Ruin.

A Mháire rúin, is tú bláth na n-úbhall,
  Ha meallabh Muimhneach thú, a ghrábh,
Do chuirreabh se a g-céill duit, le briathraibh béil,
  Chuig chéud bréag ann bhá uair de lá :—
B'fearr liom féin tu, bheith choibhche a g-céin,
  Mar bhidheas na céuchta bán is fearr,
Ha bheith pósta ag péic tu, do shiubhal an ráoghal,
  Ag déanabh bréag 's ag meallabh mná.

Do shaoil me rcóirín, mar do bhidh tu óg, deas,
  Go n-déanfabh deónabh air eulóghabh liom,
'S nach bh-fuil tráthnóna ná oidhche dómhnaich,
  Hach tura an t-reóid, bhiodh air an m-bealach romham:
Shiubhailfinn bóithre agus coillte cnóbh leat,
  Choibhche a's go deórgh, ní bhiabh orrainn brón,
D'á m-beidhinn do'm phósabh leat, a mhíle rcóirín,
  'S mo lámh go móbhmhair a'b bhrollach bhán.

MARY A ROON.[1]

BY EDWARD LAWSON.

My sweet apple blossom, dear Mary, beware,
Lest the Munster man's flattery² your heart should ensnare;
His tongue is so oily, so roguish his eyes,
In one hour they would tell you whole hundreds of lies.

Much rather I'd see you for ever a maid,
A pale rose of the wilderness, languish and fade;
Than espous'd to a rover, whose profligate arts,
Seduce simple virgins and break their poor hearts.

How fondly I fancied that blooming in youth,
You'd be led by my voice, and inspired by my truth;
Each fair sunny morn when all nature look'd gay,
You shone the clear gem that illumined my way.

An cuimhneach leat an oidhche ud, um fhéile Brighde,
  A rabhamair thíos air an Mullach mór,
Is duit-se, a phaoileann, thug me gean le díogracas,
  Mar a bhíodh tú aoíbhinn, deas, álainn, óg;
Is tú go cinnte, do mharbh m'intinn,
  Agus leágh na Múmhan ní bheanfadh mé slán
'S go bh-fuil mo chroidhe stigh na mhíle piosa,
  'N uair nach bh-fághaim céad rince le'm mhúirnín
    bhán.

A péilcionn mhín taís, na tréig me chóibhche,
  'S a liachd codla oidhche do chaill me leat,
Tá fuil mo chroidhe stigh, 'na bradám chnionn,
  Le gean do'b ghnáoí, a's do'b cháil, a phearsc;
M'uch ó'n óch! a's mo mhíle brón ghuirt!
  Gan an oidhche rómham 'r ine bheith pósta leat!
Acht 'nois ó's eol damh, go brách nach geabhair liom,
  Mo mhíle stóirín, mo bheannacht leat!

With you the wild nut-groves delighted I'd range,
Immersed in soft raptures and fearless of change;
Oh! treasure of treasures, were you my reward,
With the soft hand of love your fair bosom I'd guard.

Last feast of Saint Bridget, ah! can you forget,
When on Mullamore's* summit transported we met;
But now you have plunged me in sorrowful gloom,
And hopeless of healing I sink to the tomb.

Sore, sore is my heart, it is rent to the core,
Beside Murneen Bawn⁴ I must never lean more;
Thou star of mild lustre, my prayer do not slight,
By day all my thoughts, all my visions by night.

Admiring, adoring, imploring thy ray,
My heart's blood grows congealed, and I wither away;
But alas, you disdain me!—then break, oh my heart!
My treasure of treasures for ever to part.

Nóra an Chuil Omraich.

A Nóra an chúil omraich,
   'S é mo bhron-sa nach bhféudaim,
Lámh do chur fáoi'd cheann-sa,
   No a m-brollach do léine;
Is tú d'fág mo cheann-sa
   Gan únsa air bith céille,
A's go n-éalóchainn tar tóinn leat,
   A rúin-sheárc dá bh-féudfainn.

A bhaill íntinne mo chróidhe stigh,
   Ná déan-si liom bréag,
A's gur gheall tú mo phósadh,
   Gan feóirling 's an t-saoghal,
Thiúbhairfinn-se air an n-drúchd leat,
   A's ní bhfúighfinn leat an féur,
A's a Nóra an chúil omraich,
   Is deas a phógfainn do bhéul.

HONOR OF THE AMBER LOCKS.

BY EDWARD LAWSON.

Sweet Honor of the amber locks,
   'Tis to my sorrow, beauty's blossom;
My hand can't prop your lovely head,
   Nor touch your gently swelling bosom.
'Tis none but you my darling maid,
   Of reason that has quite bereft me;
With you I'd traverse oceans wide,
   For you forget all else that's left me.

Most precious treasure of my heart,
   With broken vows do not deride me;
How oft you promised to be mine,
   Though worldly wealth was still denied me.
With you I'd trip the dewy lawn,
   Nor bruise the green luxuriant grasses;
And still more tenderly I'd kiss,
   Those pouting lips, my best of lasses.

Taobh chall be'n Mhárgh
  Tá rór geal mo chroíbhe,
A cúl tiugh mar an t-ómar
  Le'r chaill mé mo ghnaoibh;
Guidhim-si Rígh an Domhnaich,
  Go d-tionntóighe an ghaoith,
A'r go bh-feicibh me mo bhólacht
  Ag gabháil bóithre bhaile-ách-buíbhe.

Beyond that verdant flowery field,
  The darling of my heart reposes;
Whose amber locks profusely curled,
  Have dimmed my cheeks that bloomed like roses.
O King of mercy change the scene,
  And let me, for her sake, recover;
And see my lowing herds again,
  Wind round their native hills of clover.

Aisling an Oig-fhir.

Aisling ghéur do dhearcas féin
  Go fábhar go fann reallad a'm luidhe,
Faoi gheugaibh crann choir amhan a'm aonar,
  Mar a m-biodh dér agus spóirt a' t-saoghil;
Bhidh ceileabhar eun ann; a ngcaiseabhaibh ngéura,
  Bidh gleacaidheacht éisc ann le feistin tridh,
Monbhar beach agus mil 'na slaodaibh
  le fághail ag gach aon neach d'á ngeabhadh an t-slízh.

Rinn me scad tamall ag éisteacht
  Le ceileabhar éin bhidh a m-bárr na craoibh',
Ag rior-chur nótaidhe a g-cóir a chéile,
  A's dhearc mé sbéir-bhean mhin, dhear le'm thaoibh,
A gruadh ag lasadh air dhath na g-caer-chon,
  A rosc mar péult ghlan seaca bhidh,
A ruadh-pholt ómrach fighte go bróg léi,
  S le cúmhaidh na deóigh rud ní mhairfeadh mí.

THE YOUNG MAN'S DREAM.

BY EDWARD LAWSON.

In a dream of delusion, methought I was laid,
By a brook overarched with a fluttering shade;
A delicious recess, where silver-tongued rills,
And far cataracts deep roar echoed round from the hills:
Gleaming fish in clear waters were wontonly playing,
And hoarse murmuring bees o'er wild flow'rets were straying;
While sweet honey distilled from old oaks to regale,
The young and the fair in that odorous vale.

A beautiful bird on a blossomy spray,
Was warbling a varied and rapturous lay;
As I listened entranced in delightful surprise,
A lovely enchantress astonished my eyes;

Do bhíodhg, do phreab an ainfhir mhaordha
  A's labhair go féimh be chómhrádh chaoin;
"A thogha na bh-feár mo grádh ná béun-ri
  " 'S gur máighdeán mé cárádh a'd líon,
" Ná bídh-si ciontach le cám le claon-bheart
  " O táoim a'm aonar air mo chlíu bhuain díom,
" Oir gheabhainn-si bás tríbh náire an tseil sin
  " Nó'm gheilt do bhéidhinn-si air feádh mo shaoghil."

A thogha na mbán, ná tuig-si féin,
  Do shlad go n-déanfainn air aon t-slighe,
Le cám, le cleas, ná le beartaibh claona,
  Oir tá mac Dé aguinn ós cionn ag t-saoighil;
Cuirim-si m'impídhe chum Rígh na gréine
  A's chum gach Náomh eile ghabhann le Criost,
Tu-sa agus me-si bheith ag a chéile,
  A mháighdion mhaordha, air feádh ar saoighil.

A phlúir na m-bán—a bheallrádh na rcéimhe,
  Ní fhásfáidh féur glas tré chalamh a níos,
Ní bhiadh teas ann ná neart na gréine,
  Agus ní bhiadh péulta ann a d-tosach oídhch',—

Her cheeks like the quicken's rich clusters were glowing,
Her amber silk locks to her white ancles flowing;
Like a keen freezing star gleamed each sparkling blue
     eye,
Alas! in one month, for her loss, I must die.

When first she descried me, she startled, alarmed,
And with coy supplication my sympathy charmed:
" Oh favoured of men! do not ruin a maid,
By fate to your power unprotected betrayed;
For with sorrow and shame broken hearted I'd die,
Or for life thro' wild desarts a lunatic fly."—

" Oh, peerless perfection! how canst thou believe,
That I could such innocence hurt or deceive?
I implore the Great Fountain of glory and love,
And all the blessed saints in their synod above;
That connubial affections our souls may combine,
And the pearl of her sex be immutably mine.

The green grass shall not grow, nor the sun shed his
     light,
Nor the fair moon and stars gem the forehead of night;

Ní bhéanfaidh an ghealach solus d'ein-neach,
    'S ní bheidh eirg ann air muir nó air tír,
Beidh aghaidh gach sruthán a g-coinne na sléibhte
    Trath bheidheadh-sa claon duit, a ghrádh mo chroidhe!

Tareis gach geallabh d'á d-tugas féin di,
    Phog mé a béilín go bláith áluin,
Leag mé lámh air a bráighaid bhreagh, ghléigeal,
    A's rugas am ghéagaibh air rún mo chroidhe;—
'N-uair d'úmhluigh sí gábhail liom mar chéile,
    Bhídh mo chroidhe mar éun ag dul le gáoith;
Trí lár mo shúgradh do mhúsgail mé,
    'S mo chumhaibh nír bh' áen fead acht aisling í.

The streams shall flow upward, the fish quit the sea,
Ere I shall prove faithless, dear angel to thee."
Her ripe lip and soft bosom then gently I prest,
And clasped her half-blushing consent to my breast;
My heart fluttered light as a bird on the spray,—
But I woke, and alas, the vain dream fled away.

A ġraḋh aġus a ṗuiṁ ḋil.

A ġráḋh aġus a ṗúin ḋil, an tinn nó an dúḃaċ leat,
  Me-ṗi ḃeiṫ aġ ṗúil leat a'm aonar?
Is cráiḋte me a ċúilḟionn, a'm ċoblá aġus a'm
  ḋúiseaċt,
Aġ maċtnaḋ air do ġnúis ḃrpeaġh, ġléġheal;—
Is mór an t-ionġnaḋ liom-ṗa, tu ḃeiṫ bun-ós-cionn
  ḋámh,
'S mé lán de ḟonn a ḃeiṫ péiḋ leat,
Eiṗġiḋh, a ġrém-ġil, taḃair solus an lae leat
Aġus scaip-ṗi ġo léir mo néullta.

M' uċ ó'n óċ! ṗé mo ċroíḋhe tá marḃh,
  Is truaġh mar puġaḋ riamh mé!
M'intinn aéḋhraċ aġ ġealaḋ leat-ṗa,
  A ṗúin aġus a ċuiḋ ná tréiġ mé!

MARY OF MEELICK.[1]

BY HENRY GRATTAN CURRAN, ESQ.

Long in lonely despair have I worship'd the dream,
   That brightens my heart with the glow of thy form;
Let my slumber's vision, my day's hallowed beam,
   Let it shine, my soul's treasure, to brighten and warm.
How can thy bosom be cold to the swell,
   Of the faith, the devotion, that's nurtured in mine;
Nay, my own love, let thy kindness dispel
   The clouds, and bid morning around me to shine.

In the sorrow, the anguish, that tortures my breast,
   I weep for the hour that endued it with life;
In thy sight alone, I have rapture and rest,
   Look down, my soul's love, on my spirits dark strife.
Fly from the world, from its coldness, its guile,
   Oh fly to the breast, whose rich promise thou art;
Let not distrust ever shadow the smile,
   Chill the love that united us once heart to heart.

Seachain seasta, na bealaich cama,

Agus fill a bhaile air mo chomhairle,

Milleann an míochomann, an gnádh buan daingeann,

Och! is ré bhíodh eadrainn a ccómhnuíbhe!

Air an leacht-so shiar roilltigheann an ghrian

Maidin aoibhinn t-samhra;—

Tá an t-iasc air linn, a't é teacht ann san tsoinn,

'S na coinneadha ann sna gleanntaibh;

Tá an chnodh air an t-srair, 's an t-éan air a nead,

'S é seinneadh ceóil air an am sin,

S an t-é bhéanpadh a leas, do pachadh sé air bheas,

Go Mileach ag déanadh cleamhnais.

A'm chroíbhe taigh tá ramhail, aoibhinn mo chara,

Tá a Cúilín carsa, craobhach,

A béilín measla, a's a gruadh air lasadh,

S a píob mar shneachta réidheach;—

A chomainn mo chroíbhe! na'r shona bho'n t-í

Do chaithfeadh an oidhche b'á bréagadh,

'S e a gnádh do chlaoidh me, a't chradh fí m'intinn

Agus d'fhág mé air bith mór céille.

SENTIMENTAL SONG.

O'er the monument brightens the midsummer dawn,
    Where it looks from the west on the gush of the morn;
Through the wave bright forms wanton radiantly on,
    And the warren's grey flock the green valley's adorn.
The nuts thickly cluster; the bird to the day
    His shrill matin pours while it streams thro' his bower;
Blest is his lot, doomed in Meelick to stray,
    And to call thee his own, the bright vale's brightest flower.

Deeply shrined in my soul is thy image, dear maid,
    Thy lip's honied store—and thy cheeks summer glow;
And the tendril play of thy brow's sunny braid,
    And the sheen of thy neck like the sparkling of snow.
Light of my soul! what a transport for him,
    Through whose bosom can tremble each motion of thine;
My soul is enslaved—and my sight becomes dim,
    As I gaze on the riches my love must resign.

In yon bright distant isle,' with my Mary to rove,
    To gaze on the amber of each glowing tress;

Mo chreach ghéur bhrónach! gan me a's mo rtóirín,
    'S an oileán ruar, aébhrach, aoibhinn!
Máire an chúil ómrach agus Aobh bán a bheith pórda,
    'S gan cuir aei a cómhairle do chaoineadh:—
Ní'l b'ár n-doich, agus ní bheidh go deóigh,
    Muna bh-róirribh orm an óig-bhean mhíonla,
'S ó táim-re gan rógjhnadh, déantar mo chómhra,
    Agus fáigtheár mé a g-Ceillmháin rínte.

With each vow fulfilled and recorded above,
 Grant me this, fate hath nought that beyond it may bless.
Alas! cruel fair one—she heeds not my tears,
 And the truth I have cherished consumes me in vain;
Sorrow hath brought me the whiteness of years,
 The cold grave brings repose—let me rest in Killmain.'

NOTES
TO
SENTIMENTAL SONG.

NOTES.

BRIDGET FERGUS.

'Throughout our lovely island, in the most sequestered vales and by the loneliest mountains, may be heard numerous charming melodies, linked to sweet stanzas in our native language, which form an unrivalled combination of music and poetry. Several of these airs have been collected and published, and have called forth general admiration; but the words to which they were originally "married,' and which it may now be seen, had some claim to attention, lay universally neglected. This can be attributed only to their being wrapped up in a dialect but little known to literary men, for their merits have been testified by many distinguished names. James Mac Pherson, author, or, as our Scotch friends insist, translator! of " Poems of Ossian," in his preface to that work, declares, that the Irish love sonnets and elegies "abound with beautiful simplicity of sentiment, and wild harmony of numbers." A much higher poetical authority, Edmund Spenser,* describes

---

* The admirers of this celebrated English Poet may be gratified by a few particulars concerning him and his family, (extracted from original documents,) which may serve to correct some errors of his biographers, or supply information which they do not appear to have possessed. On 12th of August, 1580, Arthur, Lord Grey, accompanied by Edmund Spenser, as his secretary, arrived in

Irish poems as, "sprinkled with some pretty flowers, which give good grace and comeliness unto them." Other testimonies

---

Dublin, and on the 7th of September following, was sworn lord deputy of Ireland. On the 22nd of March following, Spenser was appointed clerk of the decrees and recognizances of chancery, and his patent was given "free from the seal in respect he is secretary to the Right Honorable the Lord D." In this department he was succeeded on the 22nd of June, 1588, by Arland Usher, kinsman of the celebrated archbishop of that name, and Spenser was appointed clerk of the council of Munster, an office afterwards filled by Richard Boyle, first earl of Cork. On the plantation of that province, queen Elizabeth, by letters patent, dated 26th of October, 1591, granted him the manor and castle of Kylcolman, with other lands, containing 3028 acres, in the barony of Fermoy, county Cork, also chief rents "forfeited by the late lord of Thetmore, and the late traitor, Sir John of Desmond."—*Orig. Fiant, Rolls office, Dublin.*

Here on the banks of the Awbeg, the poet's "gentle Mulla," was written the Faery Queen. But Spenser was not so devoted to the muses, as to neglect his newly acquired possessions; on the contrary he stands charged with having unjustly attempted to add to them. His encroachments on the Mac Carthy's are well known, but he did not confine himself to these alone. In 1593, Maurice, lord Roche, viscount Fermoy, petitioned the lord chancellor of Ireland, stating, " wheare one Edmond Spenser, gentleman, hath lately exhibited suit against your suppliant, for three plowe lands, parcell of Shanballymore, (your suppliant's inheritance,) before the vice president and councell of Munster, which land hath bene heretofore decreed for your suppliant against the said Spenser and others under whom he conveied; and neverthelesse for that the said Spenser being clark of the councill in the said province, and did assyne his office unto one Nicholas Curtey's, among other agreements, with covenaunt that during his lief, he should be free in the said office for his cawses, by occacon of which imunity he doeth multiply suits against your suppliant, in the said province, uppon pretended title of others."—*Orig. Rolls office.*—At the same time, lord Roche presented another petition against Joan Ny Callaghan, whom he states to be his opponent, "by supportation and mayntenaunce of Edmond Spenser, gentleman, a heavy adversary unto your suppliant."—*Orig.*—He again exhibited another plaint, "that Edmond Spenser, of Kilcolman, gentleman, hath entered into three plough land, parcell of Ballingerath, and disseised your suppliant thereof and continueth by countenaunce and greatnes the possession thereof and maketh great waste of the wood of the said lande, and converteth a great deale of corne growinge thereuppon to his proper use, to the damage of the complainant of two hundred pounds sterling. Whereunto the said Edmond Spenser appearenge in person had several dayes prefixed unto hime peremptorilie to answere which he neglected to do; therefore after a daye of grace given," on 12th of February, 1594, Lord Roche was decreed his possession.—*Orig. Decree.*—

might be produced, but the originals, or those contained in these volumes, and now, for the first time, collected, preclude the

---

When Spenser—the poetic, the gentle Spenser, was guilty of these oppressive and unjust proceedings, the reader may easily guess at the conduct of his more ignorant and brutal fellow planters, by whom the country was converted into a desert. For these, and other aggressions on the unfortunate natives, the poet soon afterwards felt the full weight of their vengeance. Ben Jonson informed Drummond of Hawthornden, that Spenser's house was burned, and a little child of his consumed in the flames; that he and his wife narrowly escaped, and that he afterwards died in King Street, Dublin, in absolute want of bread. His name is still remembered in the vicinity of Kilcolman, but the people entertain no sentiments of respect or affection for his memory.—*See Trotter's Walks in Ireland.*

That Spenser died in London has been asserted by some of his biographers; but Ben Jonson's information seems corroborated by a record lately found in the Rolls office, Dublin. He left two sons, Sylvanus and Peregrine. In 1603, the former petitioned the chancellor of Ireland, stating, "where your petitioner's father Edmund Spenser was seized in his demesne, as of fee, of Kyllcollman and divers other lands and tenements in the county of Corke, which descended to your petitioner by the death of his said father—so it is right honorable, the evidences of the sayd inheritance did after the decease of petitioner's father cum to the hands of Roger Seckerstone, and petitioner's mouther, which they uniustly detayneth, which evidences for as much as your petitioner can have no accion at comon lawe, he not knowing theire dates and certainty, he is dryven to sue in consideracon byfore your Honourable Lordship, and avereth that the said Roger Seckerstone, his mouther's now husband, uniustly detayneth the said evidences to your petitioner's damage of one hundred pounds, wherein he prays remedy."—*Orig. Petition.*

Sylvanus had two sons, Edmund and William. On 18th of February, 1638, Charles I. by letters patent, confirmatory, granted to Edmund the manor, castle, &c. of Kilcoleman, and other lands in the barony of Fermoy.—*Patent Inrolled.* William survived his brother. The following letter, dated White-hall, 27th of March, 1657, appears in the Irish privy council book, A. 28, p. 118, preserved in Dublin Castle.—" To our right trustie and right wel beloved our councel in Ireland. A peticon hath been exhibited unto us by *William Spenser*, setting forth that being but seaven years old, att the beginning of the rebellion in Ireland, he repaired with his mother (his father being then dead) to the Citty of Corke, and dureing the rebellion continued in the English quarters. That hee never bore armes or acted against ye comon wealth of England. That his grandfather *Edmund Spenser* and his father were both protestants, from whome an estate of lands in the barony of Fermoy, in the county of Corke, descended on him, which dureing ye rebellion yeilded him little or nothing towards his releife.

necessity of so doing, by enabling every reader to form his own opinion on the subject.

That ye said estate hath been lately given out to the soulders in satisfaccon of their arrears onely upon the accompt of his professing the popish religion, which since his comeing to years of discretion hee hath, as hee professes, utterly renounced. That his grandfather was that Spenser, whoe by his writings touching ye reduccon of ye Irish to civilitie, brought on him the odium of that nacon, and for those workes and his other good services, queene Elizabeth conferred on him ye estate which ye said William Spenser now claims. Wee have alsoe been informed that ye gentleman is of civill conversacon, and that ye extremitie his wants have brought him to, have not prevailed over him to put him upon indirect or evill practices for a livelyhood. And if upon enquiry you shall finde his case to be such, wee judge it just and reasonable, and doe therefore desire and authorize you that hee be forthwith restored to his estate, and that reprisall lands be given to ye soulders elswhere; in ye doeing whereof our satisfaccon will be greater by ye continuaccon of that estate to ye yssue of his grandfather, for whose eminent deserts and services to ye comon wealth that estate was first given him. We rest your loving freind. OLIVER, P."—This letter so creditable to Cromwell, proved highly serviceable to the object of his consideration. Though Kilcolman and the other lands were passed under the act of settlement to lord Kingston, sir Peter Courthop, Robert Foulke, and other adventurers, yet they were afterwards restored to William Spenser, and he had moreover, a grant dated 31st of July, 1678, of Caltrahard, and other lands in the county of Galway, and Ballynasloe, Tullrush, and others in county Roscommon, containing nearly two thousand acres.—*Patent Inrolled* 29° *Charles II.*—This William, by his wife Barbara, left a son Nathaniel.

The poet's second son Peregrine, died in 1641, seized of the lands of Rinney, near Kilcolman. Hugolin his eldest son and heir succeeded to those lands. Being a Roman catholic, he attached himself to the cause of James II. and was outlawed. By letters patent, dated 14th of June, 1697, the forfeited estate of Hugolin Spenser, in Rinney, three hundred and thirty-two acres, &c. were granted to Nathaniel, son of William Spenser, esq. the next protestant heir of said Hugolin.—*Inrolled* 9° *William III.*—On 24th of November following, William and Nathaniel Spenser, for £2,100, mortgaged all their estates in Cork, Galway, and Roscommon, to Robert Peppard. On 26th of February, 1716, they sold the lands of Ballinasloe, with the fairs and markets there, to Frederick Trench, ancestor of the present earl of Clancarty. These fairs afterwards became the most noted in the British empire. On 14th of October, 1718, Nathaniel Spenser made his will, (proved in 1734, in the court of Prerogative, Dublin,) wherein he names Edmund his eldest, Nathaniel his second, and John his third son: he devises to Barbara his daughter, a remainder in his estate, her husband taking the name of Spenser. He also names his sister Susannah, and

"Bridget Fergus," is, in the original, *Brighdin Padruic*, Bridget, the daughter of Patrick. It was formerly usual in Ireland, where in many places it is yet customary, for a female until married, to be called by the christian name, and after marriage, by the surname of her father. This is a Mayo song, and has always been a favorite. The description of beauty which it contains, is as heightened as in any composition of the East. The allusion to the star may remind the reader of Edmund Burke's* celebrated description of the Queen of the unfortunate Lewis XVI. of France, "Surely never lighted on this orb, which she hardly seemed to touch, a more delightful vision. I saw her just above the horizon, decorating and cheering the elevated sphere she just began to move in, glittering like the morning star, full of life and splendour."

In this beautiful passage, the force of early impressions is clearly shown. Beauty in our native lyrics, is frequently compared to a star :—

Chonċipc me aʒ ceaċċ chuʒam í cpe lap an c-pléibh,
Mar péulca chmó an ʒ-ceoóh.

I saw the fair damsel round the hill slowly bending,
Like a joy-giving star through the grey mist ascending.

Uilecan Dubh O!

'S é ɼhaoilim ɼéin ʒuɼ b'í ɼeulc na maiòne.

O'More's Fair Daughter.

---

his wife Rosamond. Soon after this the rest of the property passed away from the poet's name and family. The latter has long since become extinct, but his name will last as long as the language in which he has left such an imperishable monument of his genius.

* The partiality of our immortal Countryman, Burke, for his native literature and its ancient remains, is well known. Through his interference, the Seabright Irish manuscripts were sent to Trinity College, Dublin. He considered he had thus restored them to Ireland, but the boon has hitherto proved fruitless. These venerable national documents have been transferred from the gloom of the convent to the tomb of the capulets. They have ever since slumbered undisturbed on the almost inaccessible shelves of our college.

² *The flower of Rahard!*

The language of Bridget Fergus, and indeed of most of the articles contained in these volumes, is of the purest dialect of the Irish. The present part of the work proves the superiority of our language for lyrical composition. In these amatory effusions, no indelicate sentiment or allusion can be found; nothing which may alarm the modest and virtuous character of maiden innocence. As to the fair object of the present song, tradition relates, that she lived about the middle of the seventeenth century, and was the most beautiful female in Connaught. Her father resided at Rahard, near Ballinrobe, in Mayo. The song was the joint composition of two contemporary bards, Mac Nally and Fergus, the latter having composed the third and fourth stanzas. It has been taken from the recital of Hugh King, an old man, who stated, that his Grandfather had often seen *Breednine Padruic*, as he called her, and used to speak in rapturous terms of her beauty. This lyrical remnant is often sung, and some commence with the third stanza. The first line of the first, as dictated by another person, ran, Ṡil mac Ṫiʒh na Aipóylaich, and the first of the fourth, Iṛ millṛe blaṛ a beilin, both, I think, better than those given in our text. The acumen and taste of the Irish when delivering their opinions on the poetical productions current amongst them, have often been matter of surprise. Many a remark have we heard from uneducated villagers, on the sentiments and poetical expressions contained in their old songs, which would not disparage the pages of modern criticism. In this respect, they far excel Englishmen of the same class, but this may be easily accounted for. From infancy they are accustomed to hear these compositions repeated and sung. The words and sentiments are imperceptibly imprinted on their minds, and thus, a taste is formed of which the possessors are generally unconscious. The Irishman, through every vicissitude retains the impress of those early feelings, which so powerfully sway the human heart, and to this source may be traced much of the formation of our national character.

ᴛ ᴀ píob mᴀp eᴀlᴀ—
A swan-like grace her neck displays.

Second Stanza.

The swan, a bird with which Ireland formerly abounded, is an object of frequent allusion in Irish and Oriental poetry. So Lord Byron in his poem, " The Giaour," an Eastern Tale :—

> " The cygnet nobly walks the water ;
> So moves on earth Circassia's daughter,
> The loveliest bird of Franguestan ;
> As rears her crest the ruffled swan,
> And spurns the waves with wings of pride,
> When pass the steps of stranger man."

The beautiful simile of the swan in " *O'More's Fair Daughter,*" p. 35, may here recur to the recollection of the reader. Our Irish poets, like the Arabians, have delighted in description of female hair. Thus, Lord Byron in the same poem :—

> " Her hair in hyacinthine flow,
> When left to roll its folds below ;
> As midst her handmaids in the hall,
> She stood superior to them all.
> Hath swept the marble where her feet
> Gleamed whiter than the mountain sleet,
> Ere from the cloud that gave it birth,
> It fell and caught one stain of earth."

And Professor Carlyle in his translations from the Arabic :—

> " Thro' midnight gloom my Leila stray'd,
> Her ebon locks around her play'd ;
> So dark they wav'd—so black they curl'd,
> Another might o'erspread the world."

Many passages might be produced to show the affinity between Irish and Oriental poetry. They are, however, postponed for some other opportunity, in order here to introduce and preserve a popular Mayo song, composed by a friar of the ancient abbey of Ballyhaunis, in that county, whose name was Costello, and who fell in love with a beautiful girl of that place. Tradition tells, that after pouring forth his soul in these tender stanzas, the love-sick ecclesiastic preserved his vows by tearing himself from the object of his dangerous affection, and departing for a foreign land, where he died. The air is sweet and plaintive.

---

beul-ατh-ȚhaMhȠaIȚ.

Aiȓ ȓhonn Phóiȓτ Zóȓboin.

A Mháiȓe, ȝȓádh, iȓ τú τá'm chȓádh,
Och! τábháiȓ do lámh ȝo blúτh bhámh!
'Ț ȝuȓ buál dámh buádh ná cóiȝe d'ȓháȝháil,
Ȝo bȓáth ná deán mé dhiúlτádh!
A chúil ná n-buál, ȓé mo chúmhádh ȝo buán,
Ȟách bh-ȓuilim leáτ ȓuádhτe á ȝ-cleámhnáȓ,
beidheád ȝo buáiȓc ȓá ȓíoȓ-ȝhȓuáimh,
Má bhídhiȓ bh-ȓád uáim-ȓe á ánnȓácht.

A bhláiτh ná ȝ-cáoȓ, o τháȓláiȝh mé,
Cláoídhτe τȓéiτh le ȝȓeánn duiτ
Τáȓȓ ȓáoí'm dhéiȝhin, á ȓúin mo chléibh,
'Ț τábháiȓ ȝȓádh ȝán chláén ȝán chám dámh.—

Fárcoir ghéur! 'r mé 'n ceann gan chéill!
  'S do chómhairle m'athar mór umhluigheas;
'S gur b'e comhrádh béigheannach dubhairt sé liom
  " Tréig-si béul-áth-rhamhnais."

Acht chug me grádh, do'b chúlfin bán,
  Air chúl an gháirdín póncaire,
Do'b bhéilín cláith, mar chúbhar na tráigha,
  'S do'b dhá ghruadh bheárg mar chaorchon;
Do'b bhéul is binne, ná'n chuach air bile,
  'S na ceileabhar ar éan na n-éunla,
Mo léun 's mo mhilleadh! gan me 's tú chumainn,
  Ag éulóghadh le na chéile.

A ghrádh 's a rúin, a n-gluairseadh liom,
  Go tír na long ar Éirinn?
Ní'l tinneas cinn, na tuirse cróibhe,
  Nach leigheasrraíbhe ann gan amhras;—
'S tú an péulc eóluis, thar mhnáibh na Fóbhla,
  Agus cuingidh agad fein ó'n m-bas me;
Oir gan grása Dé, ní mhairribh mé,
  Air an t-srráid-so bheul-áth-rhamhnais.

The word cuingibh, in the sixth line of the last stanza, should have been written congbhaigh.

Here it may be observed, that the usual term for lyrical composition in Irish is abhrán, which means, literally, *sweet verse*.

This word is compounded of ᴄbh *sweet*, and ꞃᴄn *a verse*. It is sometimes called óꞃbhᴄn, compounded of óꞃ *sound* or *melody*, and bᴄn *a poem;* and óꞃᴄn, from óꞃ, and ꞃᴄn *a verse*. The latter is generally used by the *Gael* of Scotland.

EILEEN A ROON.

Eileen a Roon, *Ellen the secret treasure of my heart*, is one of the most popular of our songs. The present words are the production of a Munster bard, of the seventeenth century, who endeavoured to excel, by profusion of poetic embellishment, the original and sweetly simple song of *Eileen a Roon*, to be found at p. 264. The incident which led to its composition, will appear in a subsequent note. The air is ancient, and one of our finest. Handel, as related by the venerable Charles O'Conor, in his Dissertations on the History of Ireland, (a book which ought to be in the hands of every Irishman,) declared, that he would rather have been the author of *Eileen a Roon*, than of the most exquisite of his musical compositions. This ancient Irish air, which our oldest people familiarly remember from their infancy, has been, some few years ago, introduced to the British public as a Scotch melody, under the name of *Robin Adair*. The grounds for this assumption appear in the correspondence between Robert Burns, and his publisher Thompson, in 1793. The latter in a letter to the bard, wishes him to give " *Robin Adair*," (meaning *Eileen a Roon*,) " a Scottish dress. Peter (Pindar) is furnishing him with an English suit. Robin's air is excellent, though he certainly has an out of the way measure as ever poor parnassian wight was plagued with." Burns in his answer says, " I have met with a musical Highlander, who assures me, that he well remembers his mother singing Gaelic songs to both *Robin Adair* and *Gramachree*," (our *Molly Astore*.) "They certainly have" he adds, "more of the Scotch than Irish taste in them." Here we must differ with the bard. He then continues, "This man comes from the vicinity of Inverness, so it could not be any intercourse with Ireland, that could bring them; except what I shrewdly suspect to be the case, the wandering minstrels, harpers, and pipers, used to go frequently errant through the wilds both of Scotland and Ireland, and so some favorite airs might be common to both." Burns was a poet. In the first part of his letter he was dealing in fiction, in the latter part the truth forced itself on him. On this proof, however, the airs in question were pronounced Scotch. It would seem they were not aware that Robin Adair was an Irishman. He was ancestor of viscount Molesworth; lived at Hollypark, in the county of Wicklow; and early in the last century, was a member of the Irish Parliament. With respect to *Molly a Store*, or as Burns called it, *Gramachree*, as well might it be asserted, that the hill of Howth lay in Perthshire, as that this ancient air was Scotch. Indeed further to notice the assertion would be almost as ridiculous, as seriously to go about proving, that that well known hill was not always "the pride of sweet Dublin harbour," and never wandered to Inverness.

Burns' wish, however, to appropriate these "gems of genius" to his country, is at once evidence of his taste, and of their beauty. The consideration of their ancient names alone, would have been sufficient to show the error of his conclusion. The endearing expressions of love with which our poetry abounds, and the affectionate terms of our colloquial intercourse, are to be found only among the Arabians, and in some degree among the Spaniards. *Eileen a Roon—Gramachree—Molly a Store—Sa Vourneen Deelish—Cean dubh Deelish*, and hundreds of similar phrases, are as familiar to our people in ordinary conversation, as the air which they breathe. Poetic stanzas, full of those tender expressions, are to be met with every where like our shamrock. The following, beginning Ṫiobháin á ṗúin "Johanna my heart's treasure," is taken from among them:—

A Ṫiobháin, á ṗúin ! iṡ tú do ṁáṗbh mé ṗiáṁh :—
A Ṫiobháin, á ṗúin ! iṡ tú do bháin díom mo chiáll :—
A Ṫiobháin, á ṗúin ! iṡ blúiṫ chuáḋáiṡ eábáṗ mé á'ṡ díá,
'Ṡ bh-ṗeáṗṗ ḋúinne bheiṫ ʒán ṗúilibh ná tú ṗheiċṗin á ṗiáṁh !

Iṡ bṗeáʒh é do ṗhnóḋh, 'ṡ tú án t-ṡeóiḋh do cuṁáḋh ʒo ceáṗt,
'Ṡ tú án cáilín óʒ nách poibh óltách, imiṗcheách, leáṁh,
Do ʒhṗuáḋh máṗ án ṗóṡ, 'ṡ do phóʒ máṗ ṗhilleáḋh ná m-beách,
'Ṡ ʒuṗ b'é do cheól ṗéiḋh, ṫóiʒ mé o ṫhinneáṡ, á ṡheáṗc !

PAISTHEEN FION.

Paistheen Fion, pronounced *Fin*, which may be translated either Fair Youth or Maiden; is an ancient and popular Connaught song. The air is sweet, but of a plaintive or melancholy strain; such as can scarcely fail to remind the hearer, that it is " the music of a people who have lost their freedom." By the *Paistheen Fion*, I am inclined to think, was meant, the son of James II. but the allegorical songs of the Irish will be alluded to in another part of this work.

The ingenious translator requests me to observe, that he fears he has not succeeded in transferring all the tenderness of the original word *Suirin*. The disinterested affection, the adhesion of kindred, the endearing diminutiveness expressed by it, are such, as perhaps excel, what even the languages of Italy have been so celebrated for imparting.

The Cur ꞅᴀ, or chorus, has been frequently used by our bards. Carolan introduces it in his " George Brabazon," see p. 70. and it may be found in other places. The term Cur ꞅᴀ, "put under," is used metaphorically. It signifies, a call from the singer to the hearers, to join their voices in raising the song, as mariners, or workmen, unite their strength in lifting burthens. In general, the chorus has but little, and often no connection whatever, with the words. I have known the same chorus in Irish to be employed in the service of several songs. A curious specimen of want of such connection, or rather want of meaning in the chorus, occurs in " a righte merrie and conceited" composition, well known in Galway by the name of *Speic Seoigheach*, or " The humours of Joyce's Country," a mountainous district in the western part of that county: —

ꞅúb í ᴀn ꞅpéıc ꞅeóıgheᴀch 'zᴀ cózbháıl zo h-íncıneᴀch
lóıp nᴀ mnᴀıbh ózᴀ ᴀ'ꞅ nᴀ h-ozᴀnᴀıbh ᴀéıpeᴀchᴀ,

Iꞅ mo líl ló, ᴀbᴀbó.

Cup ꞅᴀ—ᴀ'ꞅ mo pulán, he pulán,
hu pulán, háppı pulán,
Imbo lán, ᴀ'ꞅ mo pulán,
Ǡzuꞅ ᴀmhoch héppın néppın nᴀn.

Cız meᴀꞅ ᴀıp chpᴀnnᴀıbh beıbh cnu 'zuꞅ ꞅubhcpᴀebh ᴀp lᴀp,
ꞅúb mᴀp conznᴀmh beᴀchᴀ bhuıc, ᴀ Chᴀchᴀıl uı Chuıbhzeᴀnáın.

Iꞅ mo líl lo, ᴀbᴀbó.

bhí me lá áepách áip áenách na Cápa 'r me az ól,

Tug me zeán éigin do áen ingín Yhárnáich mhóip,

léig mé coðhla bpeize opm b'rheucháin an m-bláprainn
  b'a póz,

'Y az ionnpáizhe an bhánrhláich, paobáðh mile máide aip
  mo thóin.

Ir mo líl ló, ababó.

The Joyces of Iar-Conaught are literally a race of giants. We are informed from Joseph Ben Gorion, a Jewish author of the sixth century, that the Irish people "are great like giants, men of tall stature and very strong, most skilful in throwing darts, and the stoutest soldiers in war." An old writer adds, " of this' race there is still a family in Conaught, and *one* of them could take *ten* of the valets of the present king of France (Lewis XIV.) on his back, and run a course with a nimble footman. I am apt to believe, that the old Scythian race is as much degenerated in Ireland, as the species of elks and wolf dogs."—*Orig. MS. in the library of the Royal Irish Academy.*

The town of Carra, mentioned in the above ludicrous stanza, is situate near Castlebar, in the county of Mayo. The mart alluded to, was granted to Michael Cormick, of an ancient family of Erris, on 19th May, 1618. The big Englishman, as tradition tells, was one of the Cuffs, ancestors of the late lord Tyrawly, of that county.

As a contrast to the foregoing, I am induced to conclude with a soft little pastoral fragment, called Copmác Óz, composed on the banks of the Lee, in the county of Cork. It is worth preserving for the sweetness of some of the verses:—

Táið na coilm az rugpáðh 'r an ramhpáðh az teácht,

'Y an bláith az bpireáðh tré mhulláichibh na cepann
  amách,

Air chóinn tá'n biolar go tropallach, glúineach, glas,
'S na corcóga ag rilleadh le h-iomad de rhúghadh na m-beach.

Ir iombha topcha a'r mear air an ccoill ro rhuar,
A'r óig-bhean mhaireach, cheart an t-reang-choirp thruairc,
Céud bó bhainne, capall gpoibhe 'gur uan
Choir laoi na m-breac, mo chreach! mé ain bhíbirt uait!

Táid na h'ein ag deanadh guthá agur ceóil,
Táid na laóigh ag geimneadh go tréun chum rochair na m-bó,
Táid na h-éirg ag péubadh corradh air an bh-reór,
A'r me-ri rem a'm aonar a'r Cormac óg!

TRANSLATION.

The doves they are pairing, and summer is near,
Decked in green clustering cresses the streamlets appear;
The blossoms are bursting the tops of the trees,
And the hives are distilling the honey of bees.

With fruits, and with acorns, yon green wood is crown'd,
There damsels, fair damsels, are sauntering around;
Lowing herds, stately steeds, by the trout loving Lee,
Fleecy sheep, graceful fawns, whilst I'm exiled from thee.

The birds there are warbling, there frolic the lambs,
For the hot streaming milk low the calves round their dams;
The fish burst their banks and leap high on the shore,
Whilst I, and young Cormac, our exile deplore.

LITTLE CELIA CONNELLAN.

In this, as in many of our amatory songs, the warmest wishes are expressed for the enjoyment of private meetings with the beloved object, in some shady grove, delightful valley, or sequestered island, where far removed from friends and relatives, they might freely indulge in the unrestrained delight of virtuous intercourse. This is conceived in the purest spirit of romantic love, and without the least taint of any vicious feeling or desire. The unsuspecting confidence which it necessarily implies, is the truest test of its honorable tendency, and the surest safeguard of maiden innocence. This observation is rendered necessary from the present state of society, so very different from that of our ancestors; conclusions might otherwise be drawn from those passages, foreign from the simple meaning of the originals.

"The plumy interloper, in the third stanza of the original, is a 'pheasant,' but we trust the necessity of the rhyme will justify our preference."—T.

Dáopcháin the first Stanza should have been written buáibheápcháin.

The metre of this song is suited to a lively musical strain. It is a composition of the county of Sligo, and an old favorite. The following stanzas in the same metre, from the neighbouring county, Mayo, being the original of the well known, "*Bunch of Rushes*," will, it is hoped, be acceptable to the Irish reader:—

bı η Γ1 η   l u ᴁ c ħ μ ᴁ.

Lá d'áp éıpıʒh me ʒo h-uáıʒneách
A'bul ruár dám' ʒo Conbáe án Chláıp,
Dhí mo ʒhábháıpín lıom ʒo h-uáıbhpeách,
Aʒ uáıllreápc 'r mo ʒhuná ám' láımh :—

Cia charrsidh orm acht rtuadh-bhean
  Ha gruaige geille, finne breadh',
Agus adhbhar binfin buainte aici
  De'n luachair budh gheille blath.

A chailin beag na luachra,
  An léirgá do bheart air lár,
Ho an d-tiocfa liom am uaignear,
  Faoi bhruach na coille ir glaire blath.
Sagairt ni bh-faighidh rgeul air,
  Ha aon neach d'a bh-fuil le faghail,
Go d-tiocfaidh cairt do'n chéirreich,
  A'r beurla do'n lon-dubh bhreadh.

A chailin beag na luachra,
  Glac ruaimhnear a'r fan go réidh,
Ni cail duit a bheith chomh h-uaibhreach,
  Ann uaignear a'r tu leat féin.
Ma rcaip mé do chuid luachra,
  Ir dual go bh-fuil cuid tar héir,
Dainread binfin buan duit,
  A'r ualach mór mar chuille léir.

THE LASS OF FAIR FLOWING TRESSES.

This is one of the numerous sweet little songs to be found in almost every hamlet throughout the *Irish parts* of Ireland. With these ancient ballads, and the delightful old Finian Tales, in poetry and prose, the rural Irish are wont to recreate themselves after the toils of the day, when assembled round their village fire sides, they enjoy the only cessation from suffering, which they know, or expect in this life. To these productions, our gentry, except, perhaps, some few aboriginal families, are almost entirely strangers. From this class of society they have been banished to the cottages of the poor, where they have been preserved, with a sort of religious veneration, as relics of Ireland's better days. " I heard an old Irish air sung," says Trotter, in his Walks through Ireland, " with Irish words, by an Irish woman ; it was mournfully and remarkably melodious, sung very slow, and with astonishing and true pathos; it appealed powerfully to the heart." Nothing can be more correct than this description. It shews of what rich feasts of sentimental poetry and music, political prejudice and religious bigotry have hitherto deprived their infatuated votaries in Ireland.*

---

* Even our national musical instruments, the harp and bagpipe, seem to have been considered as part of the paraphernalia of popery. In one of the first earl of Cork's noted protestant eyries, Bandon, a poor wandering minstrel, has lately been severely beaten, and had his bagpipe broken to pieces. The unlucky wight ventured to play in that town, contrary to an ancient standing rule of the corporation ; and he was thus treated for annoying the orthodox ears of the protestant inhabitants with his native papistical tunes. Were these bigots apprehensive that the charms of Irish music would "sooth their savage breasts?"

¹ LORD MAYO.

This song, or, perhaps more properly speaking, ode to music, which is now for the first time printed, was composed by David Murphy, a poor dependant of Theobald, fourth viscount Mayo, a nobleman who first sat in the Irish house of peers on 14th May, 1661. It was composed in the hall of Castleburke, a baronial mansion, now in ruins, near Castlebar, in the county of Mayo. The music which is well known, and much admired, was the production of Thady Keenan, a harper, with whom the venerable Charles O'Conor was acquainted early in the last century. In Walker's memoirs of the Irish Bards, will be found an interesting account of both bards, from the pen of his anonymous and excellent correspondent.

They have in the west of Ireland a favorite song, often mistaken for this ode, known by the name of Condáe Mhaigheó, "County of Mayo," and sometimes as "The lament of Thomas Flavell," having been composed by a bard of that name, a native of the island of Bophin, on the western coast. It is only remarkable for being combined with one of our sweetest native melodies—the very soul of plaintive Irish music. The words are here given, with a hope, that they may lead to the preservation of the air :—

CONDÁE MHAIGHEÓ.

Is air an loing so pháidí laoinse do ghním-se an dubrón,
Ag ornádh annr an oidhche agur ag fíor-ghul 'r an ló
 Muna m beidh gur dallabh m' intleacht
 A'r me a bh-fad om' mhuíntir,
Dar maireán! is maith a chaointinn-re condáe Mhaigheó.

An uair a mhair mo cháirde budh bhreádh mo chuid óir,
D' ólainn lionn Spáineach i g-comhluadar bán óg,
 Muna m-beith síor-ól na g-cárta
 'S an blígh bheith ro láidir,
Ní a' Sanctepúr d' fágfainn mo chnámha fá'n bh-fód.

Tá gadaidhnidh na h-áite so ag eirígheadh ro mhór
Fo chnocadha á'r fo hair bag gan tráchdt air bhucladha bróg;
 Do mairfeadh damh-sa an iarull
 Dhéanfainn díobh cianach,
Muna m-beith gur chágair dia dham a bheith a
g-ciantaibh fá bhrón.

Do m-beidh Fádruig Lochlainn 'na iarla air iarúil go fóil,
Brian dubh a chliamhain 'na thigheasna air Dhusachmór,
 Aodh dubh Mac Gnada
 'Na choirnéal a g-Cliara,
Is an sin bheidh mo thriall-sa go conbáe Mháigheó.

---

[1] "*By each blessed bell that's there,*"—
Consecrated *bells* were formerly held in great reverence in Ireland, particularly before the tenth century. Cambrensis in his Welch Itinerary, says, " Both the laity and clergy in Ireland, Scotland, and Wales, held in such great veneration portable bells, and staves crooked at the top, and covered with gold, silver, and brass, and similar relics of the saints, that they were much more afraid of swearing falsely by them, than by the gospels, because, from some hidden and miraculous

power, with which they were gifted, and the vengeance of the saint, to whom they were particularly pleasing, their despisers and transgressors are severely punished."—*Hoare's translation of the Itinerary of Giraldus, London* 1805, *p.* 31. Miraculous portable bells were very common, Giraldus speaks of the *Campana fugitiva* of O'Toole, chieftain of Wicklow; and Colgan relates, that whenever Saint Patrick's portable bell tolled, as a preservative against evil spirits and magicians, it was heard from the Giant's Causeway to Cape Clear, from the Hill of Howth to the Western Shores of Conamara, " per totam Hiberniam."—*Colgan. In Triade, p.* 103. Evinus who wrote before the tenth century, says, " Saint Ciaran's portable bell still exists, and is held in high veneration, and carried round to the assemblies of princes, to protect the poor, and to raise contributions for his monastery."—*Vita Antiq. Ciarini in Actis SS. p.* 458. This veneration for bells appears to have been preserved unabated, from the days of Saint Patrick to those of our bard.—*See Doctor O'Conor's Appendix to Cat. Stowe MSS. p.* 30.

It was found difficult to procure a perfect transcript of the present ode. My first copy proved incomplete, and indeed little better than a fragment, but this I did not discover until after Mr. Furlong had versified it. Although his translation of the complete copy is contained in the text, yet I am induced to preserve his previous version of the fragment; and do so as I think, with the suffrage of every reader of taste:—

> No more in sad suspense I'll pine,
>   No longer droop in lingering woe—
> Quick! hand that cup of cheering wine,
>   Let the rich liquor freely flow:
> And long, and loud, my harp shall ring,
> While sheltered here I sit and sing -
>   The praises of Mayo!

Mayo! the flower of chiefs thou art,
  Lord of the free and open heart—
Bold is thy bearing in the strife,
  Where foes before thee sink subdued—
Blest be thy days and long thy life,
  Shield of the friendless multitude.
Spurn not thy minstrel's homage now,
  Branch of the old and stately tree!
Oh! hear his song and mark his vow—
  By every saint or sacred thing
He swears—till life's last hour to cling
  In steadiness to thee—
Tracing thy footsteps faithfully,
Till his dark eye-balls earth shall cover,
And thought and feeling both be over.

---

[1] BROWN THORN.

The *Droigheanan Dunn*, literally Brown Thorn, is one of our most popular ballads, and deservedly so. The words are sweet and simple, and the air is one of those tender plaintive strains which find their way to the innermost folds of the human heart, where they seldom fail to make a lasting impression. The provinces of Munster and Connaught contend for this song; but the latter, where it is known and sung in every hamlet, has, as far as I can ascertain, the best claim. It is a composition of considerable antiquity. John Bernard Trotter, who had been private secretary to the celebrated Charles James Fox, and who made a pedestrian tour through Ireland, says, in a small tract on Irish Music,—" It had been conjectured that the era of *Drionan Don*, was before the introduction of christianity; that it was composed for the celebration of the *Baal Thinne*, or the midsummer fire, in which the thorn was particularly burnt. Be this as it may," he adds, " it is justly celebrated as one of our sweetest melodies ; and, whatever be the era of its composition, is an intrinsic proof that we possessed at the earliest periods, a style as peculiar and excellent in music, as our round towers prove we did in architecture. The origin of both has perished, but the things themselves remain as incontestible memorials."

Some years since, travelling through the plains of the great western county of Mayo, in a poor cabin near Lough Con, the writer accidentally heard a peasant girl sing the *Droigheanan Dunn*, in a strain still remembered with feelings of pleasure. Among other songs which she was prevailed on to sing, was one to the sweet old Irish air, the " Maid in Bedlam," beginning

" *One morning very early, one morning in the spring,*
I heard a maid in Bedlam most mournfully sing."

Struck with the exquisite beauty and simplicity of the stanzas, I transcribed them on the spot, from her dictation, and hope, the same reason may serve as an excuse for introducing them here. — I do not know a sweeter song in any language, and I think it impossible to translate it.

Ἠκch ⱃοιbhín do na h-eiṅíniḃh ḃ'éiṗiʒheán ʒo h-áṗḃ,
'Ꞅ a bhíḃheán a ceileaḃháṗ le na chéile aiṗ aon chṗaoiḃh aṁháin,
Ἠṡí máṗ ṗin ḃamh ꞅéin 'Ꞅ ḃomh chéuḃ mile ʒṗáḃh,
Iꞅ ꞅaḃa o n-a chéile oṗuinn ḃ'eiṗíʒheán ʒach lá.

Iꞅ báine í ionа an lile, iꞅ ḃeiꞅe í 'n an ꞅʒéimh,
Iꞅ binne í 'n an bheiḃhlinn 'Ꞅ iꞅ ꞅoillꞅeíche í 'ná an ʒhꞅéin,

Is feárr ioná sin uile a h-uairleacht 's a méinn,
'S a bhiá thá is na fláithis fuarzáil bom phéin.

An poibh tu air an g-carrais, no an bh-faeaibh tú mo
  ghráoh,
No an bh-faeaibh tu gile no finne no rzéimh na mná,
An bh-faeaibh tu an t-ubhall buoh mhilre 's buoh
  chúmhra bláth,
No an bh-faeaibh tu mo bhailintín no bh-fhuil ri 'z a
  claoioh mar táim?

Bhioh me air an g-carrais a'r chonairc me oo ghráoh,
Chonnairc me gile azur finne azur rzéimh na mná,
Chonairc me an t-ubhall buoh milre 's buoh chúmhra
  bláth,
Azur chonairc me oo bhailintín 'r ní fhuil ri 'z a claoioh
  mar táir.

CASHEL OF MUNSTER, OR CLAR BOG DEAL.

If the foregoing ballad has been conceded to Conaught, the present cannot be denied to Munster, whose right is proved by internal evidence. The words and air are equally sweet and simple, and both are of considerable antiquity.

'Nior o cháith an aóir mé a'r zur liáth mo cheann,

Tho' my locks now look gray and my blood runs chill.

NOTES. 343

This passage may remind the reader of one of Anacreon's Odes, beginning :—

MH με φύγης ὁρῶσα
Τὴν ωολιὰν ἔθειραν.

Our bards appear not only to have been well acquainted with the works of Anacreon, but to have admired, and in many instances, imitated their beauties. One of them sending a book to his mistress, addresses it as follows :—

ỎỈ Ỏ.

A leabhráin, is coibhnn do thriall
A cciinn aindre na g-ciabh g-cam;
Is truagh! gan tu a'm riocht a b-péin,
A's me-ri féin ag dul ann.

A leabhráin, is coibhinn duit
Do thriall, mara a bh-fuil mo ghrádh;
Do chiodhrip ana an fole mara ór,—
Do chiodhrip ann an deád bhán.

Again, on the difficulty of enumerating her charms :—

Dá m-budh dubh an fhairge,
A's talamh bheith 'na pairer bán,
Cleitighe mine, geala,
A's an ála bheith aip a conn ag rnámh;

Dá m-bronnfáidhe dám Epi á'r Sarána,
Ulbá, án Fhráinc 'r á Spáin,
Treighthe O! mo cáilín deir,
Ní thiocfádh liom do sgriobhádh le peánn.

Another bard tells us, that when his mistress was born, a bee came with a shower of honey, which fell on her lips:—

An uáir rugádh án chuilfhionn tháinic beách bín,
Le cioth meálá míne áir á cáér-bheol.

The following fragments, translated by Mr. D'Alton, have been thought worthy of preservation. The first, is evidently an imitation of one of Anacreon's odes, the twenty-second in Mr. Moore's translation; or, perhaps, it bears a closer resemblance to the Epigram of Dionysius, translated in the same fascinating work.

A Dhiá gán mé ám ábháillín,
Nó ám áilneáirín éigin;
Nó ám pór ánn ráin ngáiróin,
Már á ngnáthuíghedán tú ád áonár;
Már rhúil ir go m-bhuáinfeádh bhiom
Geugáirín éigín,
Do bhiádh ágád ád bheár-láimh
No á m-brollách geál do léine.

See the ripe fruit,—oh! were I such,
    That mellow hangs from yonder spray;

NOTES. 345

>To win your eyes, to woo your touch,
> And on your lips to melt away!
>
>Were I a rose, in some fair bower,
> By thee selected from the rest;
>To triumph in thy choice an hour,
> And die—upon thy snowy breast.

Tá rosoch-bhachaill bhuidhe-charda, phiop-dhearn
                              Aip rcaile an oir,
'A'r pizhin-dhearpea, a'r min-ghlaca, ciop-chana
                              Cnaimh 'n a beól,
'Zur zpir-leaca, piob-rhneachda, cioch-chailce
                              Aici, blathnaid óg,
Taeibh-chana min-ghealla, aip li eala
                              Go tracht a bróg.

>Adown her back in curls are roll'd,
>Her yellow hair like beams of gold;
>Her downy hands—her full blue eye,
>Her teeth, like fine set ivory,
> Such is my lovely maid:
>Like kindling flame her blushing cheek,
>Swan-like her majesty of neck;
>Her bosom white as earthless snow,
>Are few of all the charms that glow
> In my beloved Blanaid.

Blanaid was a celebrated Irish beauty of antiquity. For her interesting history, and tragical end, see our Irish Herodotus, Keating.

MOLLY ASTORE.

The air of *Molly Astore*, is one of the most popular in these islands. Burns called it " a heavenly air." Although it has been more fortunate than most of our native strains, in meeting with English words, yet it is confidently hoped, that its original Irish stanzas will be found no way inferior to any of those, with which it has been hitherto associated in English.

General Vallancey, one of the few Englishmen, whose memory ought to be dear to the Irish, was so delighted with the music of *Molly Astore*, that, in his enthusiasm, he very gravely undertook the derivation of the name, and traced it to the most remote antiquity. He tell us, from Diodorus Siculus, that *Bel* or *Baal* was the Jupiter of the east, whose wife, the Juno of the latter, was *Astarte;* and that these were, " the Irish *Beal* and *Astore-th,* the latter pronounced *Astore.*" Mr. Trotter tells us, that the song was composed " at the period of Cormac Mac Con, a century before Christianity." Again, he says, " It is with some probability, supposed to have been addressed to Astoreth, called in Irish, Astore, the Venus of the Phœnicians." Vallancey was perfectly serious, but Trotter could hardly have been so; particularly, as he soon after adds, " It is evidently, however, the production of the purest era of Irish song, as it has the general character of its sweet and touching melody."

English verses have been frequently written to this air. The late George Ogle, member of parliament for Wexford, was author of a pleasing song, beginning, "*As down by Banna's banks I strayed*," whose principal charm lies in the Irish termination of each stanza:—

"*Ah Gramachree ma Colleen oge
Ma Molly Astore*—"

Our celebrated countryman, Sheridan, also wrote to this air, the sweet little song in the Duenna, "*Had I a heart for falsehood framed,*" The sentiments of "*How oft Louisa,*" in the same comedy, are said to have been borrowed from another Irish song, beginning with the following stanza:—

A Anna chaoin ácláide mhin ṫuáipc,
A ṗuin mo chleibh, ná deán m duáipc
Tábháip ṗáoireámh don pheinṗi táoi dom chuáipc,
'Y dá m-budh liomṗá Eipe á'd deiz 'ṫ me án ṫpuáʒh.

"*The Plains of Nair.*"—In the county of Meath there is a lake, which was anciently known by this name. In it was drowned Turgesius, the Danish Tyrant, by Maolseachlan King of Meath, A. D. 844.—*See Annals of Ulster.*

CATHERINE TYRRELL.

Catherine Tyrrell, was a member of the ancient and respectable family of that name, formerly residing at the Pace, (Tyrrell's Pass) in the county of Westmeath. The lake, called in the original "*Erril*" is probably a mistake for "*Ennil*," one of the most extensive and beautiful of the numerous fine lakes in that county.

The fair object of this popular and favorite song has been celebrated in other poetical effusions. Of one of these the following is a fragment:—

'Y τρuαzh zheup zαn me-ρι αzuγ Cαταιlín T'ρíαll,
'Η αρ ρuíbhe no 'n-αρ γεαγαbh, αz zεαταιbh bh'lα'-clíαch
Αn οíbhche bheιτh αzuιnn chomh γαbα γe blíαιn,
Α'γ me γínτε αιρ lεαbα le αιnnγιρ nα z-cιαbh.

Few of our national airs are better known than "*Youghal Harbour*," which bears a strong resemblance to "*Caithlin Tirriall*." The original words of that favorite rustic ballad, have been thought worthy of preservation; with that view they are here inserted:—

eoch αill.

Μαιbιn bómhnαιch α'γ mé αz bul zo h-Eochαιll,
Cαγαbh αn óιz-bheαn oρm 'γ αn τ-γlízh;—
Α zρuαbh αιρ lαγαbh mαρ ρóγ α n-zαιρbín,
'Y bα bhιnne α béιlín 'nα ceólτα γízhe:—
Leαz mé lαmh αιρ α bραzhαιb le γóργα,
Αzuγ b'ιαρρ mé ρóιzín αιρ γτóρ mo chροíbhe,
'Y é búbhαιρτ γí, " γταb α'γ nα γτρóιc mo chloιcín,
'Y níl γιογ mo bhólαιγ αz neαch 'γ αn τ-γαóιzheαl."

Ηíl αchb uαιρ bheαz ó b'γhαιz me-ρι Eochαιll,
Α'γ búbhαιρτ mo γτóρ lιom zαn γιllεαbh αρíγ;—
'Y zuρ cαιlín γcoιchτε me τα αz ρúbhhl αn bhóchαιρ,
Αz ιαρραbh αn eólαιγ zo Ceαραbh-Chóιnn;—

'Η αιmhḋheóin α n-ʒeαllαnn tú ḋe ʒαch uile ṗópt ḋαmh,
Ηí ʒhníḋhim ḋe ḃ' ʒhlóptháιbh αcht cómhpáḋh ḃαoiṫ'
Α'ṫ ḋα ṫeαóilṫeα ḃháιle mé ʒαn ṗiúḋh nα m-ḃpóʒα,
Ṫuαpαṫ cómháιple ʒαn ḋo leαnαmháιn cḣóiḋhche.

Αʒ ṫo mo lάmh ḋhuit nαch ḃh-ṫuιlιm pótςα,
'Ṫ ʒup buαchάιll óʒ me ṫhuʒ ʒeαn ḋo mhnαói;
'Ṫ ḋα n-ʒluαιṫṫeα hom-ṫα αιp ḋ-túṫ ʒo h-Ēóchαll,
Ḋαp leαm, ḋ'αp n-ḋóιch! buḋh leαṫ lóιṫcín óιḋhche :—
Chuιppιnn hiʒh cάul cαp opṫ, α ʒ-ceαṫpṫ 'ṫ α ʒ-cóιp,
Ʒúnαḋh, clócα αʒuṫ cαιpιpιnn,
Ṫιopα ḋpαmαnnα m-bιαḋh ṫíon α'ṫ beóιp αnn,
Α'ṫ báιbín óʒ ḋo ḃheιṫh αʒ ḋiúl ḋo chíoch.

---

¹ COOLIN.

The air of this song is, by many, esteemed the finest in the whole circle of Irish music. It is much older than the words of our text, which have been attributed to Maurice O'Dugan, an Irish bard, who lived near Benburb, in the county of Tyrone, about the year 1641. There are several sweet stanzas in Irish to this charming air, but the present are the best known, and most popular. " Coolin" means, the maiden of fair flowing locks, but the original word is retained in the translation, being now, as it were, naturalized in English. The following is the first stanza of a spirited version of this song, made by our learned and talented countryman, the late Mr. Clinch, in the year 1792 :—

Did you see the long auburn locks of my queen,
As she bounds with dry feet o'er the dew pearled green;
But, oh! if you knew her soft languishing air,
And the virtues that dwell in a bosom so fair.

² "*In Belanagar dwells the bright blooming maid.*"

There are many places of this name in Ireland. One of the most distinguished is Belanagar, in the county of Roscommon, the seat of O'Conor Don, the descendant of the last of the Irish monarchs.

Walker, in his Memoirs, tells us, that when Henry VIII. ordered the mere Irish to be shorn, a song was written by one of their bards in which an Irish virgin is made to give the preference to her dear *Coulin*, (or the *youth* with the flowing locks,) to all strangers, (by which the English were meant,) or those who wore their habits. "Of this song," he adds, " the air alone has reached us, and is universally admired."— For Mr. Moore's beautiful words to this melody, beginning, " Though the last glimpse of Erin," see his Irish Melodies.

The following additional verse occurs in some copies of the original:

A mhúirnín a'r a annracht do mheall mé a d-túr m'óige,

Le'd chluanaidheacht bhinn, mheabhlach 'r zur zheall tú mo phórad,

Má thug mo chroídhe zreann duit, a'r dár liom go m-budh leór rin,

Ir mór táim dul a lionn-dubh 'n uair nach liom tu tráchnóna.

ROISIN DUBH.

Roisin Dubh, *Little Black Rose,* is an allegorical ballad, in which strong political feelings are conveyed, as a personal address from a lover to his fair one. The allegorical meaning has been long since forgotten, and the verses are now remembered, and sung as a plaintive love ditty. It was composed in the reign of Elizabeth of England, to celebrate our Irish hero, *Hugh Ruadh O'Donnell,* of Tyrconnell. By *Roisin Dubh,* supposed to be a beloved female, is meant Ireland. The toils and sufferings of the patriot soldier, are throughout described as the cares and feelings of an anxious lover addressing the object of his affection. The song concludes with a bold declaration of the dreadful struggle which would be made before the country should be surrendered to the embraces of our hero's hated and implacable rival. The air is a good specimen of the characteristic melancholy which pervades Irish music.

"No nation," says General Vallancey, Col. vol. v. p. 363. " is more fond of allegory than the Irish. Their ancient poets were celebrated for their *Meimeadh* or allegorical poems. No other language than the Arabic has a word of this signification, viz. *Mamma,* a verse of occult mysterious meaning."—In the third part of this collection will be found, some fine specimens of this species of Irish composition.

UILE CAN DUBH O.

The song of Sorrow, and well has it been so called, for it is truly a plaint of grief and despair. The words were composed by one of the unfortunate sufferers expelled from Ulster, in the reign of James I. when almost the entire of that province was confiscated, and planted with English and Scotch adventurers. They were addressed by the exile to his mistress, to induce her to accompany him to Conaught, but she seems to have been adverse to his suit. The air is of the most remote antiquity.

In another copy of this song, the first stanza reads as follows:—

Dá d-tiocfá liom-ṡa á peilcionn go tír-Amhlaiḋh,
   Iṡ m' uaileacán dubh Ó!
Bheáṗfáin cṙámh ár bháinne ṡiáigh ḋuit,
   M' uaileacán dubh Ó!
Iṡ go leóṙ bheáṗfáinn áeṙ na long ḋuit aguṡ ṙeolca na m-bád,
A'ṡ fuaim na d-tonn dá m-bualaḋh ár an d-tṙáigh,
A'ṡ bṙáon de'n t-ṡáile ni leigfinn án do chomháir,
   Iṡ guṙ tu m' uaileacán dubh Ó!

Tirawly, mentioned in this stanza, is a barony in the county of Mayo.

CEAN DUBH DILIS.

Lovely maid with the raven locks.—This song is an instance of the superiority of our language for lyrical poetry. Miss Brooke states, that she gave up many a sweet Irish stanza in despair, find herself unequal to the translation, " I wished among others" says she, " to have translated the following lines of a favorite song, *(Cean dubh deelish,)* but it presented ideas of which my pen could draw no resemblance that pleased me." After quoting the first four lines, she adds, ". I need not give any comment upon those lines, the English reader would not understand it, and the Irish reader could not want it, for it is impossible to peruse them without being sensible of their beauty." The tender effect of the repetition of the word *deelish*, lovely or amiable, in the first line, cannot fail to attract the attention of the reader.

The air of the present song presented so many temptations to the taste and nationality of our northern neighbours, that, Robert Burns in a letter to his publisher, boldly assigns it to Scotland. " They have,", says this fine genius, " lately in Ireland published *an Irish air, as they say*, called *Caun du dilish*. The fact is, in a publication of Corri's, a great while ago, you will find the same air called a Highland one, with a Gaelic song set to it. Its name there, I think, is *Oran Gaoil*, and a fine air it is." In opposition to this fact, I may be permitted to adduce another. I have myself, seen and known old people who were acquainted with the air, and words as given in the text, of *Cean Dubh Dilish*, long before Corri's publication, alluded to by Burns, appeared. At that time, however, the literary outposts of Ireland lay undefended. It was customary to appropriate without acknowledgment, and unfashionable even to notice us, except either to censure or condemn.

Repeated aggressions sometimes provoked angry retaliation. An anonymous author, has severely, but justly censured Doctor Burney, the well known English writer on Music. " Doctor Burney," says our author, " has been extensive in his research, and elaborate in his detail of the anecdotes of music, as to dilate his history of them into several thousand quarto pages! Is it from the want of candour, or can it be from the want of information, that he has taken little or no notice of Irish music ? He has been at much pains to ascertain the first song that ever was set in score, and after having, as he thinks, succeeded, he has exhibited the result of his research. Had he no means of knowing to what country the song really belonged. It remains with ourselves to do that justice which others deny, and reclaim for ourselves those gems of genius which enrich other countries with a negligent profusion. It is to our countryman, Dr. Young, the late lamented Bishop of Clonfert, that we are indebted for the restitution of our property in a sweet and touching melody. He proved that this very ancient tune of Burney, is no other than our *Samhre teacht,* or, " Summer is coming." It had been handed down among the traditional melodies of the Irish harpers, rescued at the meeting in Belfast, and secured in the permanent characters of music, in Bunting's Collection; its name imports its origin. The susceptible sensibilities of the Irish, always felt in a high degree those beauties of nature, which the features of their lovely country in happier times presented. This sweet hymn was a tribute of grateful melody, offered up by our ancestors to the opening year, and has been sung from time immemorial by them at the approach of spring. To those who have resided among the peasantry of the Southern and Western parts of Ireland, where the national manners are most unadulterated, this melody is at this day perfectly familiar."

Another of these wandering melodies, is, the well known *Murneen na gruaige baine,* which may be translated, " *My fair or flaxen-haired darling;*" though the latter word conveys but a very inadequate idea of the endearing fondness expressed by our Irish *Murneen.* I am, happily, enabled to preserve the original stanzas of this sweet song, and feel confident that they will not be unacceptable to the Irish reader:—

Muirnín na gruaige báine.

A m-baile na h-inse thiar, a tá mo ghrádh le bliadhain,
Is áilne í 'ná grian an t-samhra;—
'S go bh-fárann mil 'na biadh, air lorg a cos ran t-sliabh,
Dá phucaire an uair, tápéir na samhna:—

Do gheabhainn gan fead mo chiall, dá ngabhainn í a'm
líon

A'r chuirrinn-se an brón-ro dhíom, gan buaidhreadh ;
Air chómhairle rugadh riamh, ní phorrad acht mo
mhian,

'S i Múirnín na gruaige báine !

Ag droichead na h-aibhne móire, chonairceas-ra mo
rtóirach,

Ainnrhir dhear na n-ór-rholt bh-ráinneach ;—
'S go m-ba mhílre go rada aróg, 'ná mil 's ná rúcradh
air bórd,

'S ná deagh-bhlar rógháil ríon Srainneach :—
A bá chíoch choppa, chruinn, bhán, mhilir, chúmhra,
bhreagh,

Mar rhneachta bhiadh dhá chárnadh air rhléibhtibh ;
'S go ngoirearn an chuach gach ám, lár an gheimhreadh
chall,

'S a m-baile m-bídheann mo ghrádh d'á breagadh.

Dá b-ragháinn-se mo rogha, de mhnáibh deara an
domháin,

Agur rágham oprcha roghan rhárra ;—
'S réir mar a deir na leabhair, tha'n chraébh aici ór
a ceionn,

'S táid na céuda rear go dúbhach a ngrádh léi :—

A a 2

'S é ramhail-reo do moladh, léir an g-céud righ Folamh;
'S is aici-ro tá an porc is áilne;—
Pleidhtigh-ri mo dhochar, 'gur ráer mé o bhar obann,
A Mhúirnín na gruaige báine!

EILEEN A ROON.

The air of this sweet and simple ballad has been already noticed. Of the various accounts of the incident which gave rise to the composition, the following is esteemed the most probable.—Carol O'Daly, commonly called *Mac Caomh Insi Cneamha*, brother to Donogh More O'Daly, a man of much consequence in Conaught, was one of the most accomplished gentlemen of his time, and particularly excelled in poetry and music. He paid his addresses to Ellen, the daughter of a chieftain named Kavanagh, a lovely and amiable young lady, who returned his affection, but her friends disapproved of the connexion. O'Daly was obliged to leave the country for some time, and they availed themselves of the opportunity which his absence afforded, of impressing on the mind of Ellen, a belief of his falsehood, and of his having gone to be married to another; after some time they prevailed on her to consent to marry a rival of O'Daly. The day was fixed for the nuptials, but O'Daly returned the evening before. Under the first impression of his feelings, he sought a wild and sequestered spot on the sea shore, and inspired by love, composed the song of *Eileen a Roon*, which remains to this time, an exquisite memorial of his skill and sensibility. Disguised as a harper, he gained access among the crowd that thronged to the wedding. It happened, that he was called upon by Ellen herself to play. It was then, touching his harp with all the pathetic sensibility which the interesting occasion inspired, he infused his own feelings into the song he had composed, and breathed into his "softened strain," the very soul of pensive melody.

In the first stanza he intimates, according to the Irish idiom, that, he would walk with her, that is, that he would be her partner, or only love for life. In the second, that he would entertain her, and afford her every delight. After this, he tenderly asks, will she depart with him, or, in the impressive manner of the original, "Wilt thou stay, or wilt thou come with me, Eileen a Roon." She soon felt the force of this tender appeal, and replied in the affirmative; on which, in an extacy of delight, he bursts forth into his "hundred thousand welcomes." To reward his fidelity and affection, his fair one contrived to "go with him" that very night.

This ballad has been erroneously ascribed to the sixteenth century, for it bears internal evidence of greater antiquity. The first line of the second stanza, "I would spend *a cow* to entertain thee," alone proves that it was composed before coined money was general, or when "living" money was in use. The tribe of O'Daly furnished several bards of celebrity. Donogh More O'Daly, Lord Abbot of Boyle in 1244, was a famous poet, emphatically styled, the Ovid of Ireland, from the sweetly flowing melody of his verse. The publication of his poems, of which there are several remaining, although in general of a religious tendency, would be a considerable and valuable addition to our native literature.

From the concluding stanza of *Eileen a Roon*, was taken the well known motto of Irish hospitality, *Cead mille failte*.

EMON A KNOCK.

Edmond Ryan, better known by the name of *Emon a Knock*, or, *Ned of the Hills*, is said to have been one of those numerous adherents of James the Second, who, on the defeat of that monarch, were outlawed, and had their estates confiscated. After a roving predatory life, pregnant with romantic adventure, our hero was interred in the church of Doon, near Lough Gurr, in the county of Limerick. The song is purely allegorical, Ireland being designated by the beautiful female addressed; but the allegory being now forgotten, the composition is known only as a love effusion, and has been therefore included in the present part of this work.

Although *Emon a Knock* is thus stated to have been a real personage, and even the place of his interment pointed out, yet there is reason to think, that the name is fictitious, and that it was intended to represent, generally, the disappointed followers of the Stuart race. Miss Brooke has translated this as an " Elegiac Song." I do not intend here to make any comparison between her version and that of Mr. Furlong. On their merits the reader will, however, exercise his own judgment, and whatever may be the result, we can never fail to respect the name of our excellent and talented country-woman. The following additional stanza of this song is sometimes sung, particularly in Conaught:—

Goirim thu a rhiup, goirim chú a pūm,
  Goirim chú nói n-uaipe,
Goirim do chúl ta pighte go blúch,
  A'r goirim do chum uaral;

NOTES. 359

Ζοιηιm mo ζhηάbh, m' άnάm άδ' κάη,
Τάιη-η τηά άζuτ Fhuάτζuil,
Α'τ leizheάτ o'n m-bάτ me-η ζάn τηάτ,
Α άιnnτhιη nά n-ζeάζ n-uάτάl.

The air is exquisite, but mournful, "dying in every note." Our distinguished Irish Patriot, Thomas Steele, Esq. whom I have the honor to call my friend, speaking of this melody, says, "It is not excelled by any with which I am acquainted of any country. I think it without an equal: it is a song whose symphonies, to be in unison with its spirit of wild pathos and sweetness, ought to be played on the Æolian harp, and by no other instrument."—*Practical Suggestions, London*, 1828.

In the third stanza, the passage "say must I droop like him—whose star set dark and dim."—seems to allude to James the Second.

IN THIS CALM SHELTERED VILLA.

This is one of the many pleasing ballads to the favorite air of *Coolin*; and the words, like most others to the same charming melody, are inexpressibly sweet and tender. The "Lov'd Maid of Broka," in Bunting's Collection of the Ancient Music of Ireland, versified by Hector Mac Neill, from a literal translation of the Irish, is one of those ballads, though there coupled with a different air. The first stanza sustains the character of the original :—

O lov'd maid of Broka, each fair one excelling!
  The blush on thy cheek shames the apple's soft bloom;
More sweet than the rose-buds that deck thy lov'd dwelling,
  Thy lips shame their beauties, thy breath their perfume.

A copy of this song, which I have lately seen, begins "Iṡ áiṙ án m-bṙóice ṫá án chuilṫhionn," *In Broca dwells the Coolin.* The ingenious Miss Balfour has also given a translation of the "*Maid of Brocah.*" See her poems, printed in Belfast, 1810. No reader of taste will, it is hoped, be displeased with the following extract: —

> Sweet Virgin of Brocah! though humble thy dwelling,
>   Thy manners how gentle, thy beauty how fair;
> Thy form light and graceful, each damsel excelling,
>   What daughter of Erin with thee shall compare?
> Oh vainly to rival thy blushes pretending,
>   The apple her blossoms in clusters may bring;
> Those blushes in nature's soft harmony blending,
>   The radiance of summer, the softness of spring.

From the few beautiful specimens which she has given, it is much to be regretted, that this talented lady had not turned her attention more to the translation of Irish poetry. The field was as ample as the labour was honorable, and she appears to have been eminently qualified to cultivate it with success.

ELEANOR O'KIRWAN.

The fair subject of this old song was a native of Galway, in the West of Ireland, and descended from one of the well-known "fourteen" families of that ancient town. "Comely Nicholas." *Chaoimh Nioclais,* mentioned in the original, is the tutelar saint of the place; and the inhabitants boast that before the reformation there were several grand organs, and chapels in his church there, in all of which divine service was frequently celebrated at the same time, accompanied with a great variety of sacred music.—*See History of Galway.*

This song is remarkable for being the composition of the

famous harper O'Carrol, mentioned by Clyn, the Annalist, as the first musical performer of the fourteenth century. Every effort to recover the music has proved fruitless. I have been assured that it was well known in Galway, in the last century, but it is supposed to have died with an old musical amateur of the name of French, who resided in that town a few years ago; and thus perished, perhaps, the last *known* relic of the genius of O'Carrol.

The following lively stanzas, addressed to a fair namesake of the young lady celebrated by O'Carrol, have been transcribed from the dictation of a gentleman of her native place.

 Air maidin a n-ḋé poimh ġhpéin ʒo moch,
  Do ḋheaspcáṙ an ḃé ḃa néata cpuṫh,
Sneaċta aʒus caop ḃhiḋh aʒ caipmipt 'na pcéimh
  'S a peanʒa-chopp péimh map ġhéiṙ aip phpuiṫ ;—
  'S a chuiple mo chpoiḋhe ! caḋ í an ġhpuaim pin opt ?

Buḋh ḃhinne ʒuṫh caomh a ḃéil le pulṫ
  'Na Oppheup do léiʒ ʒo paon na toipc ;—
Bhiḋh a pamháp-popc péiḋh map chpíoṫal nam-bpaon
  Aip pheamaip ʒhlaip phéip poimh ġhpéin ʒo moch ;—
  'S a chuiple mo chpoiḋhe ! caḋ í an ġhpuaim pin opt ?

The word néata in the second line, though usually so written, should be neamhḋha, compounded of níamh, glow or splendour, and ḋa, for ta, an adjective and participial termination, meaning state, being, or condition.

———

THE HUNTER OF BEARHAVEN.

The youthful heir of O'Sullivan, Dynast of Bearhaven, in Munster, in one of his hunting excursions towards Conaught, accidentally met and became enamoured of, the beautiful object whose perfections are so vividly delineated in these verses. The fair maiden, is said to have been a member of the noble house of O'Conor. She is described by the bard, as, the "beloved of the *Clan Murray*," 'Υ í muιηne cΙᴀnnᴀ Μuιηeᴀò í, under which general appellation were comprehended the aboriginal families of Conaught.

The description of her beauty is quite in the strain and style of Arabian poetry.—Hundreds of swains contend for the fair one—Her clear azure eye leads hearts captive—Her sweet glowing lips resemble the rose—She is a precious stone emitting rays, in which various hues alternately combine—She is the delight of the learned—The charmer of young and old—Fairest of Eve's daughters—Mirror of generosity, conferring rewards on the sons of song, Luchc ceóιL—The darling of the bards—The polar star of *Slieve Guillen*—The white swan of *Loch Glin*, whose side is like the lily—From her fairness a splendour is reflected—Her golden tresses brighten the sun's ray.—They who have particularly studied oriental poetry, may perceive many striking features of resemblance between it and the sentimental song of Ireland. By adequate investigation of this subject, much additional light might be reflected on the early history of the country.

WOUNDED BY CUPID'S BURNING DART.

The fabled deities and poetical machinery of Greece and Rome, were but seldom noticed by our ancient bards. They drew on their own internal national resourses for illustration and imagery. Accordingly, we find, *Connor* the renowned king of Emania, the beauties *Deirdre* and *Blanaid*, the famous *Finian Heroes*, the ærial inhabitants of the hills, *Don, Cliona*, and a numerous host of other real and imaginary beings, constantly referred to as the classic personages of Irish poetry. The goddess *Venus* occurs but once or twice throughout all Carolan's songs; and, in our sentimental effusions to the present, she, and her renowned companions, *Helen, Cupid, Juno*, and *Minerva*, only are mentioned, and that but very sparingly. Modern bards have made more frequent allusion to them, but in doing so, they have incurred the charge of bad taste, and a departure from the simplicity of their predecessors.

The Pagan mythology alluded to, is not suited to the genius of Irish poetry. Many a production, otherwise faultless, has been spoiled by the introduction of scenes and names foreign to the feelings and language of the country. In some of these, the poets, not satisfied that the subjects of their praise should outshine our native heroines, *Blanaid, Deirdre, &c.* make them also bear away the palm from the goddesses *Juno, Pallas, Venus, &c.*—

    Do chug tú bláith ná féad leát

    O bhláchnáid á'r ó Dhéirdre,

    O Iúnó, Phallar águr ó bhénur

    Tá'n t-úbhall 'r á chradobh leát go bráth.

This is a fault which our ancient bards have rarely committed. Even these of modern date stand excused, by the general practice of the poets of other countries in this respect, until a recent period.

In the second line of the first stanza, p. 286, the word ghachaibh, should have been written ghách. See note 4, p. 108.

¹ BLOOMING DEIRDRE.

The incident which gave rise to this ballad, is interesting and curious. About the year 1400, Thomas, the sixth earl of Desmond, after the diversion of hunting, having been benighted between Tralee and Newcastle, in the county of Limerick, took up his lodgings at the Abbey of Feale, (now Abbeyfeale,) in the house of William Mac Cormac, owner of the place; who had a beautiful daughter, whose name, according to Lodge and Leland, who relate the circumstance, was Catherine. With this lady the young nobleman became enamoured, and soon after made her his wife. On this occasion, it is said, the present stanzas were composed, by one of the earl's bards. The fair one is addressed under the name of *Deirdre*, the celebrated Irish heroine of antiquity. In the concluding lines, the powerful and arbitrary chieftain is manifested, for he peremptorily forbids all mankind, even so much as to look at the fair object of his love. The match, however, proved the cause of the earl's ruin. His followers became enraged that he should connect himself with an inferior; and his uncle James, taking advantage of the feeling, drove him from his estate and country, and in 1420, he died of grief in France, where Henry V. King of England, attended his funeral—*See History of Limerick*, vol. II. p. 91.

Mr. Moore has made this story the subject of a sweet song, beginning, " By the Fail's wave benighted."—See Desmond's song, *Irish Melodies*.

² " *Her tutelary power I hail,*
Tho' like a cavern'd hermit, pale,"

When this was composed, there were numerous hermitages in Ireland, and the vestiges of many may still be traced. Smith, in his History of Kerry, gives a drawing and description of one at Galerus, near Limerick, in that county. A small plate of copper in my possession, lately dug up at Ayle in the county of Clare, (the seat of James Mac Namara, Esquire, by whom it has been obligingly communicated,) bears the following inscription, engraven in Irish characters, under the date 1041, all distinctly legible.

ꞏꞏꞏ bᴀinneᴀch neᴀch le bpᴀt,
le pᴀbᴀipín, lebᴀp, nᴀ míᴀr lom,
ꞏꞏꞏ ror le hᴀonpuibe péib
Orolt ᴀn bichpiòhrzh chinn-leich.

Worldling away! the frugal dish—the book
Of holy truths—the beads—the hermit's cloak
Can tempt thee not—the locks that shade his brow,
The power that whitened guards—profane not thou.

This curious piece of antiquity, is supposed to have been affixed to the entrance of one of these penitential retreats. Milton's sonnet, "*When the assault was intended on the City,*" may here occur to the recollection of the reader.

' bocᴀmhlᴀch would be more correct.

' The ᴀbhpᴀn, ceᴀnzᴀl, versicle or combination which sometimes concludes Irish poems, has been already noticed p. 105. Similar terminations have been used by Lopez de Vega, and other Spanish poets. They are also to be found in Arabian authors.

[1] MARY A ROON.

Our highly talented and equally patriotic countryman, Moore, has adapted pleasing words to the air of this song—See his " Irish Melodies," air—*Moll Roone.*

[2] *" Lest the Munster man's flattery "*—

Na mealladh Muimhneach thu, a gradh—" Let not the Munster man deceive thee, my love!" The persuasive powers of some of our southern countrymen have long been proverbial. My worthy friend Mr. Brewer, in his " Beauties of Ireland," informs us, that in the highest part of the castle of Blarney, in the county of Cork, is a stone which is said to have the power of imparting to the person who kisses it, the unenviable privilege, of hazarding, without a blush, that species of romantic assertion which may be termed falsehood.—This statement, is not, however, altogether correct. To the well known " Blarney Stone," there is, no doubt, attributed the virtue of imparting to whoever, at the hazard of his neck, shall venture to kiss it, not the privilege of uttering falsehood, as stated, but an indomitable propensity towards practising the gentle, yet all effective, art of flattery. To praise "in season, and out of season," and against this dangerous quality, our fair female is cautioned in the words of the song.

I cannot avoid observing here, that vulgar stories of this kind, which reflect on the morals or character of a people, should ever be treated with the contempt they deserve. In the despicable pages of the deceived and deceiving " travellers," who libel our country, and the fry of conceited English, or Cockney, " tourists," *et hoc genus omne,* which annually visits our shores, I should not be surprised to meet with such trash; but to find it gravely detailed in the work of so learned and enlightened a writer as Brewer, is, certainly, matter of just regret.

³ "*When on Mullamore's summit* "—

Mulla, or Mullaghmore, near Tuam, in the county of Galway; an ancient residence of the Blake family.

⁴ " *Beside Murneen Bawn* "—

This is another of the many endearing expressions of the Irish, which cannot be transferred to a foreign language. It means, literally, " my fair or resplendant darling, or heart's treasure."

¹ MARY OF MEELICK.

This is one of our finest songs both in sentiment and composition, and the Irish reader will perceive, that the talented translator has executed his task with due attention to the spirit and meaning of the original.

Who the fair female here celebrated was, or when or by whom the verses were composed, I have not been able to determine. From the last line of the third stanza, it may be inferred, that she dwelt at a place called Meelick, and of that name there are two noted places in Conaught; one in Galway county, where there are extensive remains of an ancient castle, the once proud residence of the princely race of O'Madden, of Longford, (of which family, my valued friend, Gregory Ffrench Madden, esq. of Shannon-view, in that county, is now I believe, the acknowledged representative,) and the other in Mayo, where I conjecture our fair one to have resided.

² " *In yon bright distant Isle* "—

We have already seen that it was usual with our bards to wish for retirement, with the objects of their love, in some shady grove, or sequestered island, which often existed only in idea, and I have endeavoured to explain the motives which governed these wishes. In the present instance, the "distant," or rather "western" isle, ᚐᚅ ᚑᚔᚂᚓᚁᚅ ᚈᚆᚔᚐᚏ, mentioned in the original, is, one of those "happy islands," which the inhabitants of the Western coasts of Ireland, think they frequently see emerging from the ocean,* and suppose to be bound by some ancient power of enchantment. The belief in the existence of these *Miranda loca*, seems in former times not to have been confined to the vulgar. In the unpublished History of Ireland, remaining in Manuscript, in the Library of the Royal Irish Academy, Dublin, before referred to, p. 183 of this volume, we are gravely told, that "The *Tuathdedanans* coming in upon the *Fearbolgs*, expelled them into the out islands which lay scattered on the north coasts, and they themselves were served the same measure by the *Clanna Milidhes*, but what became of the remainder of them I cannot learne, unless they doe inhabitt an iland, which lyeth far att sea, on the west of Connaught, and sometimes is perceived by the inhabitants of the *Oules* and *Iris*. It is also said to be sometime seene from Saint Helen Head, being the farthest west point of land beyond the haven of Calbeggs, (Donegall.) Likewise severall seamen have discovered it att sea, as they have sailed on the western coasts of Ireland; one of whom, named Captain Rich, who lives about Dublin, of late years had a view of the land, and was so neere that he discovered a harbour, as he supposed, by the two head lands on either side thereof, but could never make to land, although when he had lost sight thereof in a mist which fell upon him, he held the same course several hours afterward. This I am bold to insert by the way, because I have heard a relation hereof from many credible persons, and particularly from the said Captain Rich, allsoe in many old mapps, (especially

---

* Usher informs us, that they were seen by St. Brendan.—" Ultra quam ad occasum, nulla invenitur habitabilis terra nisi *Miranda loca* quæ vidit S. Brandanus in Oceano."—*Usher, de Hibernia*, p. 813.

mapps of Europe, or mapps of the world,) you shall find it by the name of *O'Brasile*,* under the longitude of 03° 00', and the latitude of 50° 20'. So that it may be, those famous enchanters now inhabitt there, and by their magick skill conceal their iland from forraigners. Yett this is my own conceipt, and would have it taken for no other."—*Orig. MS.*

But the most complete account of this fanciful island, is to be found in a letter from a gentleman in Derry, to his friend in England, printed in London, in the year 1675. The narrative is so curious, and the pamphlet in which it appeared so scarce, that I am induced to lay it entire before the reader. To those possessing strong imaginative powers, it presents an ample field for romantic fiction.

" *O-Brazile, or the Enchanted Island, being a perfect relation of the late Discovery, and wonderful Dis-inchantment of an Island on the North of Ireland, &c.*

" Honoured Cousen,

" I have received yours of the 12th of February, and the printed relation of the certain death of that arch pirate Captain *Cusacke*; of whose death, all our Merchants here in Ireland, are very glad; especially my Cousen *Mathew Calhoon*, from whom, *Cusacke* took the last vessel; which, it seems, brought him to his deserved fatal end. And in requital of your news concerning *Cusacke*, I shall acquaint you with a story no less true; but I believe much more strange and wonderful concerning the discovery of that long-talk't-of island *O-Brazile*, which (I believe) you have often heard of.

" I know there are in the world, many stories and romances, concerning inchanted islands, castles, and towers, &c.

---

* This name may be compounded of ḃṗᴄᴊ, fiction, ᴄoı, an island, and ıle, great.—*Vide O'Brien's Irish Dictionary.*

and that our King's dominions may in nothing be inferiour to any other nation, we have had an inchanted island, upon the North of *Ireland*, long talk't of. And, indeed, when I went first into the Kingdom of Ireland to live, and heard those many stories, which were common in every man's mouth, concerning the island of *O-Brazile*, (as they called it) which multitudes reported often to be seen upon the Coast of *Ulster* in that kingdom; yet I lookt upon it as a perfect romance, and many times laught the reporters to scorn: though many sober and religious persons, wou'd constantly affirm, that in bright days (especially in summer time) they could perfectly see a very large absolute Island; but after long looking at it, it would disappear. And sometimes one friend and neighbor, wou'd one call another to behold it, until there would be a considerable number together; every one of which wou'd not be persuaded but that they perfectly saw it, and some of them have made towards it with boats; but when they have come to the place where they thought it was, they have found nothing. And many old people in the countrey, wou'd tell many old probable stories, how it came first to be inchanted. I confess there were (in those days) two things made me little to wonder:

"1. How it came to be inserted into many of our both ancient and modern maps (as you or any man may find it is) by the name of *O-Brazile*.

"2. The other is, what moved your cousen (that you know, died but within these 4 or 5 years at *Glasslough*) who was a wise man, and a great Scholar, to put himself to the charges and trouble (in the late king's time) to take out a *patent for it, whensoever it should be gained: certainly he, and those that counselled him to it, lookt upon it as some inchanted (if any such thing there be) kingdom or island, that, in time, might be

---

* There is nothing more certain than that a patent was taken out for it in the late king's days.

recovered. And since the happy restoration of his majesty that now reigns, many reports have been, that it hath been disinchanted or taken, yea in the time of the sitting of the last parliament in *Dublin* (in the year 1663) one coming out of *Ulster*, assured the house of Commons (whereof he was a member) that the inchantment was broken, and it gained; but it proved not so, and about two years after, a certain Quaker pretended that he had a revelation from Heaven, that he was the man ordained to take it, with a new ship built by his inspiration, &c. and in order thereunto, he built a vessell, but what became of him, or his enterprize, I never heard; it seems the full time was not then come. I assure you (dear cousen) I was not then so unwilling to believe it as now I am certain of it from very good hands, but whether (in the original) it have been a trick of *Rome*, one of the works and mysteries of *Babylon*, I cannot say, neither dare I dispute, but this I am sure of, that the time, or inchantment (or what you please to call it) is now out and the island fully discovered, or taken, and the manner, briefly thus:

" There is one Captain *John Nisbet*, who lived formerly at *Lisneskey*, in the County of Fermanagh; this man left *Lisneskey* 7 or 8 years since, and came to live at *Killebegs* in the Barony of *Boylagh* and *Bannagh*, in the County of *Dunnegall* in *Ulster*, (a corporation you know right well). This man, Captain Nisbet, since he came to *Killebegs* hath fraught out several vessels to *France* and *Holland*, &c. with such merchandize as that countrey afforded. And in September last he fraught out a vessel of about 70 Tuns, laden with butter, tallow and hides, for *France*, which was to bring back French wines, which vessel being returning, and near the coasts of *Ireland* (as they thought) upon the 2nd of this instant *March* 1674, after a most clear frosty night, in the morning about the time of sun rising, of a sudden, there fell a most terrible thick mist of fog, upon the sea, round about them; which continued the space of about three hours, and then cleared up again, very bright. But when the mist was vanisht, they found themselves upon a certain coast, close by the shore; and of a sudden also, a very high wind, driving them still nearer to the land. When the Master, and the rest with him (who were but 8 persons in all, viz. *James Mac Donnel* the Master, *Alexander Johnson* Skipper, *James Ross*, carpenter, and 5 mariners) saw themselves so near an unknown shore, and cou'd not imagine what place it should be; for though they knew most of the shores of *Ireland* and *Scotland*, yet they cou'd not possibly give any guess where they then were. Finding themselves therefore so near land, and some little rocks not far off them, the master gave orders to sound what water they had; and finding it not 3 fathoms, they thought it was the best course to strike sails and drop an anchor (which accordingly they did) until they might inform themselves where they were. And having cast anchor, they resolved to set 4 of their 8 men ashore, to see if they cou'd learn where they were; and how to get off: which, after they had taken down their boat, they did. The persons that were to goe, were the carpenter *James Ross*, and 3 mariners, who took with them swords and pistols. Presently after landing, they past through a little wood, and within less than an *English* mile, in a most pleasant green valley (wherein were many cattle, horses and sheep feeding) they saw a very strong-like castle appearing, unto which they repaired, and called, thinking to find some that might direct them where they were, and what to do, but after they had long knockt, and saw nor heard any creature (not so much as a dog) answer, they concluded it was some waste place, and therefore left it, and going further up a most pleasant green hill, they saw multitudes of black rabbits, about a mile from the castle: but when they came to the height thereof, look which way they pleased, they cou'd see neither man, woman, child nor house, at last, having ranged 2 or 3 hours about the country, and lighting of none to enquire of, they returned again to their boat, and told their fellows aboard what success they had had; whereupon their fellows calling for the boat, resolved to come ashore also, all but one mariner; which they did, and dividing themselves into two parts, one part took to the right-hand shore, the other to the left; both parties wandering up and down, until 4 of the clock in the afternoon, but neither of them saw any people to enquire of; but much cattle, dear, rabbets, &c. but afar off in the countrey, they saw great woods, into which they dare not venture: so that both parties returned again to their boat. At last the weather being very cold and drawing towards night, finding abundance of old dry wood, in the side of the above named little wood, near unto the shore, they resolved to make a great fire, against a great old oak, that was fallen down with age; and in order thereunto, some brought wood, and some others struck fire; at last, having made a rouzing fire, and sitting warming themselves, discoursing and taking tobacco; of a sudden they heard a most terrible hideous noise, towards that place; especially where they saw the old castle, and almost all over the Island, which did so terrify and amaze them, that they presently left their fire, took their boat, and went all aboard as fast as they cou'd, where they continued in great fear all night, yet neither could nor durst stir out to sea, because when they sounded again, they had not 2 fathoms of water, and the wind directly against them.

"The next morning, as soon as the sun was risen, they saw a very ancient grave gentleman and 10 men following him bare-headed (as if his servants) coming towards the shore where the ship lay, and being come close to the water side, the old gentleman calling to the master (in the old Scotch language) who with the rest stood upon the deck, askt him, from whence they came? whither they were bound, and with what they were laden? the master answered, they came from *France*, were laden with *French* wines, with which they were bound to *Killybegs*, in the Co. of *Dunegall* in *Ireland*, if it pleased God to give them leave, then the old gentleman askt them, how they came thither, and whether they knew where they were?

or how to get forth? the master told him that before the great fog fell upon them yesterday, they thought they were near the Coast of *Ireland* but where they now where, or how to get off, he knew not in the least. Then the grave gentleman told them, if they would please to come ashore again, they should be courteously entertained, told where they were, well rewarded, and guided to their own coast. Then the master askt whether they should have no wrong or harm done to themselves nor vessel if they came ashore? the old man promised they should not, whereupon the master and the rest seeing no arms with them, resolved six of them shou'd come ashore well armed.

" As soon as they were landed, the old gentleman embraced them one by one; telling them, they were the most happy sight that island had seen some hundred of years, that the island was called *O-Brazile;* that his ancestors were sometimes princes of it, telling them also, that he and several other persons of quality by the malicious diabolical art of a great Negromancer, had been tyrannically shut up in the castle they knockt at yesterday, in which several of their progenitors had ended their miserable days; and the whole Island a receptacle of furies, made (to mortals) unservicable, and invisible until now that the cursed time was expired, which (saith he) continued until the last day of the last month, but 3 or 4 days since, being askt why none answered in the castle yesterday, when the mariners knockt so long, he answered, that though the wicked time was expired, and that now the island was visible and any might come upon it, yet he and the rest had neither power to answer any that spoke to them, nor free themselves from imprisonment, until fire was kindled upon the island by some good Christians: being askt, whether it was now absolutely free, and wou'd never be inchanted again? he told them it was now absolutely free, and shou'd never be troubled again, but all the powers of darkness, when they heard that hideous noise were finally departed.

" After which words he led them towards the said castle

(the chief tower, being as it were demolished) where met them, several other grave persons both men and women, who all embraced the master and the rest, giving them many thanks; then the other two were fetcht out of the vessel, and all nobly feasted and richly rewarded, and shewed the glory and riches of the said Island, which they say is above 60 miles in length, and above 30 miles in breath, abounding with horses, cows, sheep, stags, rabbets, but no swine, and all sorts of fowls, and rich mines of silver and gold, but few people, and little or no corn, there have been cities and great towns, but all consumed.

"The men being richly rewarded were conducted to their vessel, and shewed the way out of the harbor, and directed the way to their own coast; and came the next day at night to *Killybegs*, where they acquainted the minister of the town, and many other persons of quality in the countrey, who gave no extraordinary credit to their words at first, until the master and the rest shewed them many of the pieces of gold and silver which were given them there, which were large and of a most ancient stamp; somewhat rusty, yet pure gold, the master also offering immediately to carry any gentleman to the said island, that desired to know the further truth, whereupon some gentlemen of the countrey, within 3 days after sent out another vessel, and the above named *Alexander Johnson*, skipper, and some of the former mariners to guide her, to prove whether it were true or no, who brought them to the said island, where they were nobly entertained, and returned in safety, with several gifts, which were bestowed upon them, as also some farther relation of the nature of the countrey. Since then, several Godly Ministers and others, are gone to visit and discourse them (but at the writing hereof, I heard nothing of their return) who, doubtless, will bring a more perfect relation. Dear Cousen, you need not be afraid to relate this, for I assure you, beside the general discourse of the gentlemen in the country, I had it from Captain *Nisbet* his own mouth, (whose the vessel, &c. was) since which, several gentlemen have sent an express, with the true relation of it, under their hands and seals, to some eminent persons in *Dublin.* Thus not troubling you any farther at present, I rest,

"Your most affectionate
"Cousen and Servant,
"WM. HAMILTON."

Londonderry,
March, 14th, 1674.

"Dear Cousen, I think your young cousen Lesly is still in London, if you can enquire him out, pray shew him this relation; it may be it may concern him, because his father had a patent for it.

"W. H."

³ "*The Cold grave brings repose, let me rest in Kilmain.*"
This line reminds us of a passage quoted by Burns from an old ballad, describing the condition of a poor ruined female. The bard states, that he never met with any thing more truly the language of misery, than the exclamation in the last line.

"O! that the grave it were my lot,
And O! so sound as I should sleep."

END OF VOL. I.

ROBINS AND SONS, PRINTERS, SOUTHWARK.

Lightning Source UK Ltd.
Milton Keynes UK
UKHW02n2009250518
323252UK00005B/50/P